PRO/CON VOLUME 23

POVERTY AND
WEALTH

Published 2005 by Grolier,
an imprint of Scholastic Library Publishing
Old Sherman Turnpike
Danbury, Connecticut 06816

© 2005 The Brown Reference Group plc

Library of Congress Cataloging-in-Publication Data
Pro/con
  p. cm
  Includes bibliographical references and index.
  Contents: v. 19. World Politics – v. 20 Religion and Morality – v. 21. U.S.
Judiciary – v. 22. International Law – v. 23. Poverty and Wealth – v. 24. Work and
the Workplace.
  ISBN 0-7172-5950-1 (set : alk. paper) – ISBN 0-7172-5951–X (vol. 19 : alk. paper) –
ISBN 0-7172-5952-8 (vol. 20 : alk. paper) – ISBN 0-7172-5953-6 (vol. 21 : alk. paper)
– ISBN 0-7172-5954-4 (vol. 22 : alk. paper) – ISBN 0-7172-5955-2 (vol. 23 : alk.
paper) – ISBN 0-7172-5956-0 (vol. 24 : alk. paper)
  1. Social problems. I. Scholastic Publishing Ltd Grolier (Firm)

HN17.5 P756 2002
361.1–dc22

                                                          2001053234

Printed and bound in Singapore

SET ISBN 0-7172-5950-1
VOLUME ISBN 0-7172-5955-2

For The Brown Reference Group plc
Project Editors: Aruna Vasudevan, Claire Chandler
Editors: Fiona Plowman, Chris Marshall, Jonathan Dore
Consultant Editor: Carolyn J. Heinrich, Associate Professor, LaFollette
School of Public Affairs, and Associate Director, Research and Training,
Institute for Research on Poverty, University of Wisconsin, Madison, WI
Designer: Sarah Williams
Picture Research and Permissions: Clare Newman, Susy Forbes
Set Index: Kay Ollerenshaw

Senior Managing Editor: Tim Cooke
Art Director: Dave Goodman
Production Manager: Alastair Gourlay

GENERAL PREFACE

*"All that is necessary for evil to
triumph is for good men to
do nothing."*
—Edmund Burke, 18th-century
English political philosopher

Decisions

Life is full of choices and decisions.
Some are more important than others.
Some affect only your daily life—the
route you take to school, for example,
or what you prefer to eat for supper—
while others are more abstract and
concern questions of right and wrong
rather than practicality. That does not
mean that your choice of presidential
candidate or your views on abortion
are necessarily more important than
your answers to purely personal
questions. But it is likely that those
wider questions are more complex
and subtle and that you therefore will
need to know more information about
the subject before you can try to
answer them. They are also likely to be
questions about which you might have
to justify your views to other people. In
order to do that, you need to be able to
make informed decisions, be able to
analyze every fact at your disposal, and
evaluate them in an unbiased manner.

What Is *Pro/Con*?

Pro/Con is a collection of debates that
presents conflicting views on some of
the more complex and general issues
facing Americans today. By bringing
together extracts from a wide range of
sources—mainstream newspapers and
magazines, books, famous speeches,
legal judgments, religious tracts,
government surveys—the set reflects
current informed attitudes toward
dilemmas that range from the best way
to feed the world's growing population
to gay rights, from the connection
between political freedom and
capitalism to the fate of Napster.

The people whose arguments make
up the set are for the most part
acknowledged experts in their fields,
making the vast differences in their
points of view even more remarkable.
The arguments are presented in the
form of debates for and against various
propositions, such as "Do extradition
treaties violate human rights?" or
"Should companies be allowed to
relocate abroad?" This question format
reflects the way in which ideas often
occur in daily life: in the classroom, on
TV shows, in business meetings, or even
in state or federal politics.

The contents

The subjects of the six volumes of
*Pro/Con 4—World Politics, Religion
and Morality, U.S. Judiciary,
International Law, Poverty and
Wealth*, and *Work and the Workplace*—
are issues on which it is preferable
that people's opinions be based on
information rather than personal bias.

Special boxes throughout *Pro/Con*
comment on the debates as you
are reading them, pointing out
facts, explaining terms, or analyzing
arguments to help you think about
what is being said.

Introductions and summaries also
provide background information that
might help you reach your own
conclusions. There are also tips about
how to structure an argument that
you can apply on an everyday basis to
any debate or conversation, learning
how to present your point of view as
effectively and persuasively as possible.

VOLUME PREFACE
Poverty and Wealth

In 2004 there were just over six billion people in the world. Many live in low-income countries with poor or limited access to vital resources such as food and water. Millions, predominantly women and children, suffer from malnutrition.

A more balanced world

"In a country well-governed poverty is something to be ashamed of. In a country badly governed wealth is something to be ashamed of" (Confucius, 551–479 B.C.).

Economists, sociologists, and politicians are concerned about the fact that most of the planet's wealth lies in the hands of a tiny elite. Many believe that globalization and trade liberalization, both bandied about as ways in which wealth redistribution could occur, are actually exacerbating the divide between the rich and the poor both in and between nations. Among the issues of current concern is how best to redress this imbalance. For example, in the 19th and 20th-centuries wealthy philanthropists donated large sums of money to help alleviate poverty through such projects as building housing, opening soup kitchens, and establishing educational trusts to encourage the poor to stay in school or help them go onto further education. Today, however, some studies indicate that people are less inclined to give to charitable causes, raising the question of whether the wealthy should be forced to help those less fortunate themselves.

Others argue that taxes are the best way to redistribute wealth and fund welfare systems that would provide those in need with adequate health care, for instance. But should people who have worked hard to earn their money be penalized through taxation? And does welfare actually worsen the problem by encouraging a culture of dependency, as some observers argue?

A lack of sympathy

Many governments have been accused of trying to make the poor disappear by introducing legislation to keep them off the streets—through banning panhandling, for example. Critics argue that no one wants to sleep on the streets or beg in order to survive. They claim that if governments and societies provided adequate and sympathetic help to the poor and needy, they would not be forced to beg for money. Many believe we have become desensitized to other people's pain. This also shows in society's treatment of the elderly, they claim. An increasingly aged population dependent on the state for its survival has come under scrutiny. As more elderly people die alone in easily avoidable conditions, commentators are asking if the family unit is shirking its responsibility. They ask if promoting the importance of family would help reduce the burden of the old on the state and lead to a happier elderly population.

These and other important questions are examined in this book. Carefully selected extracts help present the audience with the main issues in each debate in order to help them make informed decisions on key matters.

HOW TO USE THIS BOOK

Each volume of *Pro/Con* is divided into sections, each of which has an introduction that examines its theme. Within each section are a series of debates that present arguments for and against a proposition, such as whether or not the death penalty should be abolished. An introduction to each debate puts it into its wider context, and a summary and key map (see below) highlight the main points of the debate clearly and concisely. Each debate has marginal boxes that focus on particular points, give tips on how to present an argument, or help question the writer's case. The summary page to the debates contains supplementary material to help you do further research.

Boxes and other materials provide additional background information. There are also special spreads on how to improve your debating and writing skills. At the end of each book is a glossary and an index. The glossary provides explanations of key words in the volume. The index covers all 24 books; it will help you find topics throughout this set and previous ones.

background information
Frequent text boxes provide background information on important concepts and key individuals or events.

summary boxes
Summary boxes are useful reminders of both sides of the argument.

further information
Further Reading lists for each debate direct you to related books, articles, and websites so you can do your own research.

other articles in the *Pro/Con* series
This box lists related debates throughout the *Pro/Con* series.

marginal boxes
Margin boxes highlight key points of the argument, give extra information, or help you question the author's meaning.

key map
Key maps provide a graphic representation of the central points of the debate.

CONTENTS

ETHICS AND MORALITY

According to Francois Bourguignon, chief economist at the World Bank (WB), global poverty is falling: In 2004 a WB report found that although 40 percent of the world's population lived in poverty in 1981, this figure had fallen to 21 percent in 2001. The WB's World Development Indicators 2004 also found that around 500 million people in East and South Asia, particularly in China and India, have been lifted out of extreme poverty—when people live on less than $1 a day—in the last 20 years, and in developing nations those living in extreme poverty fell from 1.5 billion to 1.1 billion in the same period. Yet some observers insist that this decline does not mean that poverty is being eradicated: While rapid economic growth in East and South Asia may have lifted many people out of poverty, in regions such as Sub-Saharan Africa the percentage of those living in poverty rose from 41 to 46 percent between 1981 and 2001, and gross domestic product (GDP) decreased by 14 percent. This has led some experts to assert that while the face of poverty may change, the poor—to paraphrase John 12: 8—will always be with us.

Responsibility

If this is the case, what should wealthy people or rich nations do to help ease the burden of poverty? Should governments help the poor through welfare or poor-assistance programs, or should the poor be made to help themselves?

Societal perspectives regarding people's duty to help the poor have changed over time, along with the nature of public efforts to provide assistance. In the past any help given to poor community members was funded by such sources as donations made by the local community, aid provided by the church, from the generosity of philanthropic wealthy members of the community, or as time passed, increasingly by compulsory tax collections. The movement toward publicly funded support for the poor brought forth additional problems, however, including issues of adequate and equal standards for care across localities and equity in resources for care, given that poorer areas were often burdened with a higher proportion of needy residents. In addition, as early as the 1800s, England's Poor Law Reform Bill of 1834 raised concern about the disincentives associated with public assistance. The poor law reform movement argued that although help should not be denied to the poor, they should not be made to feel so comfortable that they would rather accept public aid than work.

More recently, public debate has been peppered with arguments about an emerging "culture of poverty" and concerns that public assistance may perpetuate poverty by encouraging dependent behavior (or a lack of motivation and self-reliance).

The most recent welfare reforms in the United States and other developed (as well as developing) countries have included provisions to promote "personal responsibility." They have often imposed conditions on getting public benefits such as obligated to help those less rich than themselves? Have they earned the right to enjoy their money without feeling guilty? The first two topics in this section look at aspects of wealth: Topic 1 examines if the wealthy have a duty to help the poor; Topic 2 discusses if money brings happiness, or if other factors are equally or more important.

"We have two kinds of morality ... one that we preach but do not practice..., the other that we practice but seldom preach."
—BERTRAND RUSSELL, *SKEPTICAL ESSAYS* (1928)

---

minimum school attendance rates for children and work requirements for adults. But experts have questioned the morality of doing this—for the same reasons that some argue that making aid or loans to developing countries conditional on meeting certain political or economic requirements is wrong.

Too much or too little

A frequently asked question by poverty and wealth students is: How much help is enough? Rebecca Blank, director of the National Poverty Center in the United States, describes varying viewpoints regarding the public social safety net, including one that argues that the moral responsibility is greater where economic and technological capacity is greater. This is consistent with U.S. philanthropist Andrew Carnegie's "Gospel of Wealth" (see pages 22–23) and is akin to the biblical tenet "to whom much has been given, much is expected."

But should people who have worked hard for their money and status feel

Immediate solutions

One vision of the welfare state promoted by advocates argues for a society that universally guarantees a minimum of protection for all citizens in times of old age, disability and ill health, unemployment, and other causes of insufficient income. It suggests that people have an economic right to a basic standard of living. But what happens when this is possible? How do the poor survive if they are unable to feed either themselves or their families and cannot get help from the state or from other sources? Many governments have passed legislation outlawing begging, for example, but is that justifiable if there is no other option? This debate is reviewed in Topic 3.

Some theorists believe that reeducation about the duties of family and community would help reduce poverty. They argue that it is the duty of family in particular to care and provide for vulnerable groups. The last debate looks at whether people have a duty to care for elderly relatives.

Topic 1

DO WEALTHY MEMBERS OF SOCIETY HAVE A DUTY TO HELP THE POOR?

YES

FROM "STICKS AND CARROTS: MUSINGS ABOUT THE WEALTHY AND OURSELVES"
CONSCIOUS CHOICE, JULY 2000
ANA ARIAS

NO

"COERCED CHARITY DESTROYS"
CHICAGO REPORT: A JOURNAL OF POLITICS AND CULTURE, MAY 19, 2004
KYLE SING

INTRODUCTION

In May 2004 the *New York Daily News* reported that out of the world's most developed countries—including France, Germany, Great Britain, and Japan—the United States ranked the most unequal in terms of the distribution of wealth. In Great Britain, for example, the richest 1 percent of the population owns 18 percent of the country's wealth. In the United States, meanwhile, the richest 1 percent owns 33 percent of wealth. In another comparison with the most developed countries the United States is second to last in terms of how easily the poor are able to rise above poverty.

Many observers see the great wealth gap—in the United States and also in many other countries—as being both potentially destabilizing to society and inherently immoral. Most western states have economic and social policies designed to temper some of the discrepancies between rich and poor. As in the United States, for example, many countries have welfare systems that provide the needy with basic facilities and services, such as housing, health care, and education. Many governments have made the redistribution of wealth a political priority. This policy, which some critics relate closely to socialism and other left-wing philosophies, usually operates by taxing rich people's income disproportionately heavily in order to fund programs to help the poor.

Public provision for the poor in the United States remains politically controversial, however. At various stages during the 20th century U.S. administrations have introduced tax breaks primarily for the rich. Some politicians argue that allowing the wealthy to retain more of their money will encourage them to spend it. This cash will then "trickle down" to other levels of the economy and eventually benefit everyone. This is preferable to funding welfare programs, they argue, which encourage dependency in recipients. Others say that the high taxes, the proceeds of which are often used to help the poor, are both a disincentive to the economy's most valuable performers and also a form of theft. Most rich people earn their money fairly, and the state has no right to deprive them of it.

> *"Happiness and moral duty are inseparably connected."*
> —GEORGE WASHINGTON,
> FIRST PRESIDENT (1789–1797)

Another way in which better-off members of society can help the poorer is in the form of charitable donations or philanthropic works. Charity is an important part of many religions, including Christianity, which is by far the most widespread religion in the United States. Virtually all religions place a duty on the rich to help the needy. In the Bible Isiah 58: 10–11 declares, "Feed the hungry! Help those in trouble!" The third of the Five Pillars of Wisdom, meanwhile, which outline the duties of Islam, is that Muslims should donate regularly to charity through the *zakat*, a 2.5 percent charity tax on the middle and upper classes.

The United States has a long history of such private contributions to relieve poverty. Before the welfare system began during the Great Depression of the 1930s, poor relief was funded by individuals, businesses, or charitable foundations. Andrew Carnegie (1835–1919), for example, the steel

baron who was the world's richest man of his day, gave away more than $350 million. Today, wealthy individuals such as media tycoon Ted Turner and TV personality Oprah Winfrey continue the tradition of charitable giving.

In the view of some observers such voluntary contribution has higher moral validity than forced contributions through such methods as taxation. However, charitable donations are also highly variable and often do not meet need: When the Great Depression struck in the 1930s, critics claim that private charity simply could not cope with the scale of the crisis. Some commentators also claim that society has become more selfish and that people are donating far less to charity than they used to. In 2001, for example, donations made in the United States by the top 60 philanthropists totaled $12.1 billion. In 2002 the total had fallen to $4.6 billion. Taxation, they claim, is a good way to make sure that the wealthy support the poor.

Others claim that the wealthy do not have to look after the poor. They believe that it is the American way that individuals should take responsibility and look after both themselves and their families. They see self-reliance as a basic element of the American character and argue that the provision of poor relief encourages certain groups to sponge off hard-working people. In this view poverty is the result of a lack of application or poor but voluntary life choices. This individualist tradition contrasts strongly with the tradition of mutualism, in which neighbors or communities support their less-fortunate neighbors.

The following two articles by Ana Arias and Kyle Sing examine this issue further.

STICKS AND CARROTS: MUSINGS ABOUT THE WEALTHY AND OURSELVES
Ana Arias

Ana Arias is a journalist and publishing consultant.

YES

✓ … Andrew Mott, executive director for the Center for Community Change, in Washington, D.C., feels that the wealthy need to extend a hand in matters of communal change. "The income gap is growing rapidly," he points out, "and young people in poor families are being held back by inferior schools, the virtual elimination of job training programs, and the absence of career opportunities for people who lack a good education, computer, and job skills," says Mott.

"Wealthy people have both a moral duty and a direct self-interest in helping create a society that provides young people with good jobs and bright futures rather than with conditions which push them into lives of crime and violence."

Mott thinks that the wealthy can and should support society in a number of ways. They can provide significant contributions to low-income community organizations and other groups that challenge inadequate policies and conditions. And they can personally address issues of income, jobs, affordable housing, improved schools, and similar areas that especially affect the poor.

Should citizens have the right to challenge laws? Or is it their duty to follow any policies an elected government introduces? Go to Volume 2, Government to look at this issue further.

Do you think Mott's suggestion is too idealistic? Would taxation be more effective?

Responsible investing

"Wealthy people should ensure that their own wealth is invested in companies and organizations that are doing what they can to improve opportunities for low-income people and minorities," says Mott. This, Mott believes, will help establish a society that is stable, just, and productive, and from which all people can benefit.

Dr. Dan Boland brings to the opinion table a background collage of experience as an author, psychologist, adult educator, and theologian. He's an organizational consultant based in Laguna Beach, California, where he works with executives and law firms to assist them in constructing ethical organizational cultures. Boland strongly believes that the wealthy have a moral responsibility to the less fortunate, despite how unpopular it may seem. "By 'less fortunate,' I don't mean those folks who make less than several million yearly. I mean those who are incapable of supporting themselves through no fault of their own," he explains.

"I don't wish to espouse a radical socialist perspective nor do I wish to bolster a welfare state," says Boland. "But there are segments of the American population, such as the so-called Native Americans, whose social, educational, and vocational status is a direct historical result of antithetical political decisions which have resulted in economic enslavement. The not infrequent rush of some Native American tribes to gambling is almost a harsh parable of economic revenge in reverse: the essential toll by which the excessively wealthy can restore social and moral balance is education in its countless forms."

Boland says his beliefs about the role of the wealthy are based on his assessment that no human act is neutral. "As Dr. Jonas Salk wrote years ago, we all share the same planet and breathe the same air. I would add that we all share the same human soul and spirit. We share the same moral space, so what I do—especially if I'm wealthy and therefore possess economic power—definitely affects the quality of your life."

Making a fundamental change

Neil Carlson is director of Communications for the National Committee for Responsible Philanthropy based in Washington, D.C. He also believes the wealthy have a responsibility to society and the environment, "but not as noblesse oblige, which is how the question of philanthropy is often framed," he says. "As Martin Luther King Jr., once remarked, 'Philanthropy is no doubt commendable, but it must not cause the philanthropist to overlook the circumstances of economic injustice that make philanthropy necessary.' The best philanthropy invests in change, not charity, by supporting groups and institutions working for social and economic justice."

Carlson, however, believes that all of us can be responsible —that all people have a part to play in regard to contributing to the less fortunate and as stewards of the environment. And he mentions the surprising fact that low-income individuals generally donate a larger percentage of their income yearly than the wealthy. "Groups like the Funding Exchange help donors locate and fund local grassroots social change organizations," says Carlson. "They're the publishers of *Robin Hood Was Right: A Guide to Giving Your Money for Social Change* [by Chuck Collins, Pam Rogers, and Joan Garner], the best introduction to social change giving around."

Native American reservations have tended to be located on poor-quality land with few natural resources. Establishing casinos, which takes advantage of reservations' sovereign status to bypass state antigambling laws, has been a way in which many have generated income.

Jonas Salk (1914–1995) was a U.S. scientist. In the 1940s Salk developed vaccines against the flu virus and in 1955 created the first vaccine against polio, which has since virtually eradicated the disease worldwide.

"Noblesse oblige" (literally "nobility obligates") refers to the obligations of honorable and responsible behavior associated with high social rank.

See www.fex.org for more details on the Funding Exchange, a "nationwide network of community-based foundations with solid grassroots connections."

13

See www.nng.org and www.nbuf.org for further details on, respectively, the National Network of Grantmakers, an "organization of individuals involved in funding social and economic justice," and the Black United Funds, which supports "Black American opportunity, growth and change."

Peter Singer was born in Melbourne, Australia, in 1946. He has taught at several universities, including Oxford University, England, and Princeton University. Go to http:// people.brandeis. edu/~teuber/ singermag.html to read the text of Singer's article.

Using a story or anecdote can be helpful in keeping an audience interested. It is especially useful when trying to communicate an abstract, moral, or philosophical concept.

Carlson has some specific suggestions. "The National Network of Grantmakers is a great resource for funding social change," he says. "For people with limited resources, workplace fundraising through alternative funds— environmental, community, or Black United Funds—are a great way to leverage resources."

… To illustrate just how thin the lines of right and wrong can actually be, let's take a peek at the views of renowned philosopher Peter Singer, author of *Animal Liberation*, controversial ethicist, donator of a fifth of his salary to famine-relief organizations, and now a Princeton University professor.

Crossing the lines

In "The Singer Solution to World Poverty" published in the September 1999 issue of *The New York Times Magazine*, Singer devoted much of his attention to paraphrasing and analyzing one of the hypothetical examples found in a book by New York University Philosophy Professor Peter Unger, *Living High and Letting Die*. The idea is to stimulate our "intuitions" regarding right or wrong, including the way in which Americans live a good life without providing significant money to folks who are sick, hungry, or on the verge of dying from treatable illnesses.

Highly condensed, the premise goes something like this. Bob is a gentleman who's close to retirement. He owns a highly valuable auto that will afford him a very comfortable living once he sells it, but which he hasn't insured yet. One day he parks his car close to a railway siding and decides to take a walk on the tracks.

Suddenly, he sees a runaway train with no passengers chugging down the tracks. As he looks down the track, he spots a kid who's highly likely to be hit and killed by the runaway train. Bob can't halt the train nor get to the kid in time to warn him. But he does have access to a switch that would change the train's path. The new path would head straight for his car, which would be totaled. The man contemplates the options—and he chooses not to pull on the switch. The kid is killed and Bob gets years of enjoyment from the financial cushion his car has paid for.

While most of us would agree that the man's actions were wrong, Singer points out to readers that they, too, have a chance to save kids' lives by donating to anti-famine organizations. He writes that Unger has figured out that for about a $200 donation, a sickly kid of two would be able to be brought back to health through her sixth year, pulling her through the years most crucial to continued health. Unger has established that by calling Oxfam America (800–693–2687) or Unicef (800–367–5437), readers can pledge money to save the life of a child.

Singer then brings us back to his story: "Now you too, have the information you need to save a child's life. How should you judge yourself if you don't do it?"

And if you did call and make the $200 donation, can you go out with your significant other to celebrate your moral behavior with a fancy meal at a restaurant? Hang on, says Singer, the money you spend for haute cuisine could also help save the life of a child. A month of not dining out could amount to another $200, says Singer. How much of a sacrifice is that compared to saving a kid's life?

Singer contends that in order to really make a sacrifice that's somewhat on a par with Bob had he chosen to sacrifice his car for the child, it would take closer to $200,000 for the majority of folks in middle-level income brackets. Ultimately, he says, "I can see no escape from the conclusion that each one of us with wealth surplus to his or her essential needs should be giving most of it to help people suffering from poverty so dire as to be life-threatening. That's right: I'm saying that you shouldn't buy that new car, take that cruise, redecorate the house, or get that pricy new suit. After all, a thousand-dollar suit could save five children's lives."

Moral prioritizing

Note that this formula puts the wealthy on a different plane. It makes them different from us only in quantity, not quality. Based on research by a not-for-profit research entity that identified that a $50,000 a year household spends approximately $30,000 on "necessities," that household's donation to the poor should be close to $20,000 a year. Adds Singer, those with incomes of $100,000 should be able to write a check for $70,000.

"If it is the case that we ought to do things that, predictably, most of us won't do, then let's face that fact head-on," says Singer. "Then, if we value the life of a child more than going out to fancy restaurants, the next time we dine out we will know that we could have done something better with our money. If that makes living a morally decent life extremely arduous, well, then that is the way things are. If we don't do it, then we should at least know that we are failing to live a morally decent life—not because it is good to wallow in guilt but because knowing where we should be going is the first step toward heading in that direction."

Would it be more effective if government made these contributions on the people's behalf through taxation? Go to http://www.americanprogress.org/site/pp.asp?c=biJRJ8OVF&b=34039 to look at George W. Bush's tax record and its effect on the population. Have the poor benefitted?

Do you think the size of these donations is fair? Should people who work hard for a living be allowed to enjoy the fruits of their labor and choose for themselves how much to donate?

COERCED CHARITY DESTROYS
Kyle Sing

Kyle Sing is a Chicago-based columnist who contributes to several blogs and websites from a libertarian perspective.

NO

This past week as I was driving to the grocery store and as I came off the expressway to a busy intersection, I noticed a homeless man with a sign. I couldn't read what the sign said, but my guess was that it said something to the effect of, "Please give money for food." This was not the first time I had seen a homeless person at this intersection and he didn't seem to behave any differently. As traffic moved along no one offered to give the man any money. I couldn't determine whether this corner had been lucrative for the beggar, but after a couple of minutes the man seemed to be overcome with a look of panic. It was at this point that the man did something I had never seen a bum to do: He knelt down alongside traffic and appeared to be mumbling a prayer. It was at this moment that I realized that if I was considering giving the man any money I surely wasn't going to after he knelt in prayer.

Choosing to be homeless?

One of the phenomena that I never hear discussed, only within a few philosophical circles, is that many homeless folks are in fact quite smart and if they chose to, they could be self-reliant and simply choose not to be. It isn't politically correct to say, but I believe that most people (even if they do not say so publicly) know deep down most bums simply don't have to beg. I have even noticed that Chicago Leftists who proudly wear their "Down with Bush" and "No War for Oil" buttons often ignore the "less fortunate" bums on the street and are hard pressed to give to these "victims."

The truth of the matter is that if a homeless person is smart enough to know how to strategize and use an emotional appeal like crossing himself and kneeling in prayer in hopes of getting money by making someone feel guilty, then he is plenty smart enough to find one of the many taxpayer funded public shelters or private, religious-based help centers that could provide him the resources needed to work himself back to self-sufficiency. But of course, for whatever reason, men like I saw this past week, and others like him, have no desire to be self-reliant. And why should he when so many of you bankroll his moral weakness? It is your prerogative of

A 2002 study in New York (http:/lapha.confex.com/apha/130am/techprogram/paper_45735.htm) found that relationship breakdown, loss of job, and release from prison without a housing placement were major reasons for people becoming homeless. Additional factors were that more than half suffered from some form of mental illness, and a large proportion had alcohol or drug abuse problems.

Do you think the author's assertion that the man had "no desire to be self-reliant" is fair? Do you think anyone could make this kind of judgment based on seeing a man from a car at an intersection?

A homeless man uses a cardboard sign to ask for money from passersby. Research suggests that people who are on low incomes themselves are more likely to give money to the homeless than the wealthy are.

course, but I'm the type of guy who likes to see a return on my investment. Moreover, I understand that if a man is given something for nothing he will not value it as he would if he had to toil and think hard to get it.

This problem of the homeless brings me to a greater question. Is it right providing help to people who have no intention of taking initiative to become independent and self-reliant? All I have to do is look at the housing projects of Chicago or the bum-littered streets of San Francisco and it is clear to me that if you feed laziness you condone it and those expecting help for nothing become larger and larger parasites. Do it enough and they will overrun your city, like in San Francisco. I doubt that Chicago or New York City would adopt such liberal policies (I hope) due to the fact that bums are bad for business, that is tourism, so it seems that so far capitalism is holding is some places. But one never knows where the political winds blow. Apparently, catering to the Leftist vote has been lucrative for politicians wanting to stay in power in San Fran, much to the dismay of a minority of hard-working, tax-paying citizens.

Politicians are as bad

Politicians in our Windy City play on emotional appeals just as the bums do, only their aim is to get votes and to justify squandering taxpayer dollars some of which goes to social services many of which are all for naught as I said. Whether individual or political there is a rampant emotional blackmail occurring in our culture based entirely on making people feel guilty for their own earned success be it monetary or intellectual. Moreover, as I said before many of us know this but are afraid to say it for fear of being called "insensitive" or God forbid "selfish." But I ask you which is worse? Saying that the Emperor has no clothes or accepting unearned guilt and encouraging the culture's imitation morality and ethics that takes from those who earn and gives it to those who do not. Deep down we know that allowing either bums on the street or politicians in office to load unearned guilt onto our shoulders, insisting that we are responsible for the lives of others is wrong. For the sake of ourselves and our right to enjoy the fruits of our hard work, we have to stop being afraid and stand up for ourselves. In this world, you are responsible only for yourself (in addition to any of your offspring) and no one may make any demands of you. Nobody is entitled to your time, talent and certainly not your earned money or achievements. If you choose to share that which is yours, it is of your own accord, but to be coerced by

---

Does the author's description of "the bum-littered streets of San Francisco" add or detract from his argument? By carefully choosing words or phrases, you can strengthen or weaken your debate.

Go to http://www.dof.ca. gov/html/fs_data/ stat-abs/sec_D.htm to find statistics for taxpayers in San Francisco. Are they a minority? How do the figures compare to the rest of California?

Do you agree that wanting to help people in need only comes about through being made to feel guilty?

If we are only responsible for ourselves, does this make the idea of society or community redundant?

force or be blackmailed emotionally by unearned guilt is wrong and baseless. Sometimes I feel that we Americans, especially those of us who are individualists, have forgotten part of freedom of speech is to speak in spite of it not being popular. We're in the right, and ought to be as vocal for our true just cause, like the imitation rebels of the Left who work tirelessly denigrating your achievement, talent and hard work. Stop allowing yourself to be held hostage by a code of ethics that subjugates you and your life desires for the "common good."

The author's argument assumes that differences in wealth are entirely due to merit and hard work. Do you agree? What other factors might come into play?

It's all about you

Americans must understand that charity loses all virtue when it is either coerced by government, or emotionally extorted by an individual. When the concept of "helping others" is not governed by the ethic of the individual's rights to one's own life and to the product of one's ability to do as one chooses, then virtue, morality and life lose all meaning. Remember to take care of number one and say it proud because your life is all about you. Let the man on the side of the road and the politician on the stump beg all they want, but don't give in, because when they win you lose.

The author ends on a strong statement. Do you think it is convincing? What effect would it have on society if everyone just considered their own interests?

Summary

Ana Arias writes about a number of NGO professionals and philosophers who argue that the wealthy have a responsibility to meet societal needs. The reasoning behind this conclusion varies: Andrew Mott believes the wealthy have a duty—based on morality and self-interest—to help provide the young with good jobs rather than pushing them into crime and violence. Dan Boland's position, exemplified by the case of Native Americans, is based on the belief that no human act is neutral, while Neil Carlson argues that everyone has a duty to work toward economic and social justice. The article concludes by quoting the views of philosopher Peter Singer, who believes that while many people can do more, the wealthy can do more than most if they take seriously the moral challenge of donating their surplus wealth to antifamine organizations.

Kyle Sing's article, which centers around the issue of America's homeless, provides a contrasting view: that the poor have the ability to be self-reliant but choose not to be. If the homeless have the intelligence to use tactics that make people feel guilty enough to give, then they should be able find the help centers that will provide them with the resources necessary to become self-sufficient. The article also refers to broader issues of welfare provision in the United States and suggests that giving people something for nothing merely "bankroll[s] ... moral weakness" and "feeds laziness." In particular, Sing criticizes the "emotional blackmail" employed by the poor and by government to coerce people to share their hard-earned wealth. He says people are only responsible for themselves and their offspring—not for anyone else.

FURTHER INFORMATION:

Books:

O'Flaherty, Brendan, *Making Room: The Economics of Homelessness,* Cambridge, MA: Harvard University Press, 1998.

Shipler, David K., *The Working Poor: Invisible in America*. New York: Knopf, 2004.

Unger, Peter, *Living High and Letting Die: Our Illusion of Innocence*. New York: Oxford University Press, 1996.

Useful websites:

http://www.hud.gov/homeless/index.cfm
U.S. Department of Housing page on homelessness.

www.oxfamamerica.org
Oxfam uses donations save the sick and starving.

http://www.pbs.org/wgbh/amex/carnegie/
PBS resource page on industrialist and philanthropist Andrew Carnegie.

The following debates in the Pro/Con series may also be of interest:

In this volume:

Topic 3 Is begging wrong?

Topic 7 Are income taxes an effective way of redistributing wealth?

Topic 13 Should rich nations compensate countries whose economic resources they have exploited?

DO WEALTHY MEMBERS OF SOCIETY HAVE A DUTY TO HELP THE POOR?

YES: The existence of free or subsidized education, health care, social security, and so on, acts for the good of society as a whole; the rich should pay proportionately more for such public services

YES: Helping to provide the poor with opportunities to get a good education and lucrative, fulfilling employment benefits wealthy people by creating a society with less crime and violence

WEALTH REDISTRIBUTION
Should government seek to promote equality through taxation?

SELF-INTEREST
Is it in the interests of the rich to help the poor?

NO: High taxation acts as a disincentive for the wealthy to work, save, and invest; this causes greater poverty and hardship in the long term

NO: Giving people something for nothing encourages laziness and moral weakness; more and more people refuse to be self-reliant and leech off those who work hard

DO WEALTHY MEMBERS OF SOCIETY HAVE A DUTY TO HELP THE POOR?

KEY POINTS

YES: It is possible for a person to lead a truly moral life only by donating his or her surplus wealth to society's most needy individuals

YES: Many rich people have helped change the lives of the poor through large donations of money and by establishing such things as educational trusts

MORALITY AND JUSTICE
Is it morally "right" and "just" for the rich to help the poor?

CHARITY
Do the rich contribute enough in charity?

NO: Arguments about justice and morality are emotional blackmail; they seek to inflict unearned guilt and coerce hard-earned money from the wealthy

NO: Research has shown that charitable donations have declined, but the need for vital services has increased

ANDREW CARNEGIE AND THE "GOSPEL OF WEALTH"

"Surplus wealth is a sacred trust, which its possessor is bound to administer in his lifetime for the good of the community."
—ANDREW CARNEGIE (1835–1919)

When American industrialist and philanthropist Andrew Carnegie retired in 1901 at the age of 66, he was the world's richest man. Instead of using his money to try to buy happiness, Carnegie donated his fortune to good causes. He believed in the "Gospel of Wealth"—that the wealthy were morally obligated to give back to others. Millions have benefitted from Carnegie's generosity in the United States and many other countries. This article examines Carnegie's life and legacy.

The American dream: From rags to riches

Carnegie's life is the American dream come true. Born in 1835 in Dunfermline, Scotland, into an extremely poor family, Carnegie and his parents emigrated to the United States and settled in Allegheny, Pennsylvania. Carnegie's father was a weaver and political activist who instilled in Carnegie from a young age the importance of political and economic equality.

When he was 13, Carnegie went to work as a bobbin boy in a cotton mill. In 1849 he got a job at a local telegraph company and later went to work for Western Union, where he came to the attention of Thomas A. Scott, the superintendent of the Pennsylvania Railroad. While working at the railroad, he made his first investment, helped by Scott, in the Adams Express Company. By 1865 he had enough money to establish his own business enterprises, which included iron works, steamers on the Great Lakes, oil, and the railroad. He also organized the Carnegie Steel Company, which launched the steel industry in Pittsburgh. Carnegie's company went from strength to strength, and at the age of 66 he sold his business to the New York banker J. P. Morgan for $480 million.

The "Gospel of Wealth"

Carnegie believed strongly that the rich should help the poor. As his fortune increased, he donated increasingly more money to charitable causes. Although there were other wealthy philanthropists helping the poor at the time, Carnegie was perhaps the first person to openly state that the rich had a moral obligation to give away their fortunes before they died, rather than hoard them. In 1889 he put his views down in the essay "The Gospel of Wealth." Carnegie stated that the wealthy should live moderately; he said that beyond providing for the needs of their own families, they should use their remaining fortunes to help the community at large, especially those in need.

Carnegie's legacy

After his retirement Carnegie disposed of his fortune through personal gifts and through the establishment of various trusts. Later he created seven philanthropic and educational organizations in the United States, including the Carnegie Corporation of New York (see below), and several others in Europe. In 1902 he founded the Carnegie Institution to fund scientific research and donated $10 million to establish a pension fund for teachers.

One of Carnegie's lifelong interests was the creation of free public libraries. Carnegie loved to read: As a boy he had benefitted from the generosity of a philanthropist, James Anderson, who had an extensive private library. Anderson allowed any working boy to read his books for free. Influenced and impressed by Anderson's generosity, Carnegie spent over $56 million of his fortune building about 2,509 free public libraries throughout the English-speaking world.

By the time of his death in 1919 Carnegie had given away over $350 million, around 90 percent of his fortune. His contribution to the improvement of humankind has been greatly praised.

CARNEGIE CORPORATION OF NEW YORK

In 1911 Carnegie established the Carnegie Corporation of New York to promote "the advancement and diffusion of knowledge and understanding." He originally donated $135 million (equivalent to $1.8 billion in 2003). Under the terms of his will grants are used to benefit U.S. citizens or to help countries that are (or have been) members of the British Commonwealth, with an emphasis on African Commonwealth countries. The corporation works in four main areas: education, international peace and security, international development, and the promotion of democracy.

• **Education:** This focuses on improving literacy and promoting reading, urban school reform, and education reform for teachers. Carnegie was instrumental in helping establish the public library system in the United States.

• **International peace and security:** Carnegie also believed in world peace. He established the Carnegie Endowment for International Peace and funded the building of the Hague Palace of Peace, the Netherlands, which houses the UN's World Court. In 1983 the International Peace and Security program was established to identify and prevent the greatest dangers to world peace.

• **International development:** Africa has been a major focus since 1925, and the corporation has worked to facilitate access to education in order to promote development and to help the region participate fully in the global economy. With this in mind, in 1999 the International Development Program was established. It aims to strengthen African universities, promote women's education, and revitalize selected African universities.

• **Promotion of U.S. democracy:** This program works to increase civic participation in the United States, particularly among young people and immigrants—those most vulnerable in society.

Topic 2
CAN MONEY BUY HAPPINESS?

YES
FROM "MATERIALISM, POVERTY, AND THE ROOT OF EVIL"
WWW.UNQUIETMIND.COM, JUNE 17, 2000
THE MYSTIC

NO
FROM "CAN MONEY BUY HAPPINESS?
UC BERKELEY RESEARCHERS FIND SURPRISING ANSWERS"
UC BERKELEY NEWS, JUNE 16, 2003
CAROL HYMAN

INTRODUCTION

Everyone wants to be happy. Most people also believe that they know what happiness is. However, happiness is a difficult concept to define, and in practice people have widely different ideas of its constituent parts. To some it may lie in loving relationships; to others it may stem from the satisfaction of physical or professional achievement, or in the attainment of social status. Many people believe that happiness is more likely to be derived from inner contentment or personal realization, such as that achieved through religious devotion, for example.

According to some definitions, happiness is achievable in almost any physical circumstances, even those of discomfort and hardship. Many ideas of happiness, however, are based on freedom from want: People cannot be happy if they are short of such things as water, food, or shelter. These requirements can only be met when people have enough money to afford them. Some observers therefore argue

that money is prerequisite to happiness. While many commentators agree that this is true, others insist that this idea is different from saying that money can "buy" happiness. The latter, they say, relates happiness to materialism and the idea that material possessions can bring happiness. There is little evidence for this, they claim. For example, Barbara Hutton (1912-1979), heiress to the Woolworth fortune, was one of America's wealthiest women, but she had a very unhappy life. Hutton had seven failed marriages and became estranged from her only son. Similarly, although actor Marilyn Monroe and singer Kurt Cobain, from the rock band Nirvana, could afford anything they wanted, they both ended up with alcohol and drug problems. Monroe and Cobain are just two of many celebrities who wound up taking their own lives.

On the other hand, celebrity magazines and TV shows—such as *Lifestyles of the Rich and Famous*—seem to reinforce the popular perception that wealthy people are more contented than the poor. This kind of program allows the audience a glimpse into a world that seems perfect—luxurious, highly privileged, and one in which the protagonists always appear to be happy and smiling.

Some commentators argue that this has helped strengthen the idea that there must be a link between money and happiness. Certain individuals may perceive that their lives would be better and they would be happier if they could only afford a longer holiday, a bigger house, a more comfortable car, or more fashionable clothes, for example. But to people with little or no income having enough money to pay the rent or to eat can create great happiness.

> "A feast is made for laughter, and wine maketh merry; but money answereth all things."
> —ECCLESIASTES 10:19

In recent years research into what makes people happy has grown. For example, in the United States—one of the world's wealthiest nations, in which Americans enjoy high average incomes and have immense advantages in terms of quality of life compared to many of the world's poor—only 10 to 15 percent of Americans claim to be happy. This has led some researchers to wonder why, if money really can buy happiness, more people in the United States are not happy.

Many religions, however, have long stressed that happiness and material wealth are separate. Christian teaching, for example, tends to view poverty as a more spiritually pure and rewarding state than wealth, which it associates with indulgence and laziness. A recent Gallup poll concluded that spiritually committed people were twice as likely to say that they were very happy. Similarly, studies show that people following a religion are less prone to depression and are more resilient during crises. Other observers have also noted higher ratings of "life satisfaction" among those who habitually perform altruistic acts, such as giving to charity.

Health is another factor mentioned in happiness surveys. Some experts contend that health has a positive or negative influence on happiness. They claim that since the poor are more susceptible to certain diseases and are more likely to fall ill, they have a greater chance of being unhappy. Others claim that most people take good health for granted, and that it is the sick who often have the most positive attitudes.

University of Pennsylvania psychologist Martin E.P. Seligman has found that the happiest people share certain characteristics. They spend the least time alone, they judge themselves by their own achievements, and they invest time and resources in their own personal growth. Seligman argues that everyone has a set point for happiness. That is why some people do not get depressed even in extreme circumstances such as the death of a partner, while others with more material wealth find even seemingly small events difficult to deal with.

The following articles examine this issue further.

MATERIALISM, POVERTY, AND THE ROOT OF EVIL
The Mystic

The Mystic is a founder of a website called www.unquietmind.com, which features articles on topical subjects.

✔ Consider materialism, not in the philosophical sense— "the theory that physical matter is the only reality" or "the theory ... that physical well-being and worldly possessions constitute the greatest good ..."—but in the common, informal sense, i.e., excessive regard for money and what it will buy.

Thinking about money: A matter of context

There are many people who spend a great amount of time and energy thinking about money. Day in and day out, practically their only concern is how to acquire more wealth and what goods and services they'll buy when they get it. They can't seem to find time to enjoy the worthwhile aspects of life that make it worthwhile, like well-balanced people enjoy: romance, poetry, a good book, a sunset, spirituality ... whatever clicks your lock. It seems so sad, sometimes.

The author makes the point that perspectives change as humans get older. Does this have to do with experience and education? What other factors might come into play?

It's interesting how one's perspective changes over the years. When I was a little kid, the world was made up of the "rich" and the rest of us. The "rich" were people who owned a car that was newer than the ten-year-old Rambler my father drove. (If they were exceedingly wealthy, they owned two cars.) They lived in houses where every kid had his or her own bedroom. To the "rich", a vacation meant going somewhere other than to stay with distant relatives, for two whole weeks at a time, and they didn't travel cramped together with suitcases in a car, neither. We knew that all the "rich" thought about was making money, spending money and what they could buy with it and paying good money to eat in restaurants all the time instead of staying at home to eat like us decent folk. The "rich" were materialists; two words that were practically synonymous in my juvenile vocabulary.

Do you think these are western standards by which to judge wealth? Might a poor person in a developing country crave water security, for example, rather than electricity?

Then I grew up, went away, and spent some time in other parts of the world. I met people, some of whom were so bastardly dirt poor that their idea of "rich" meant having electricity, a working refrigerator and food in it too. I have been inclined to agree with them ever since.

COMMENTARY: Oprah Winfrey

Oprah Winfrey (1954–) is one of the most famous media personalities in the world. She is also one of the richest; she appears in *Forbes* magazine's list of wealthiest entertainers year after year. A billionaire, Winfrey donates a large percentage of her fortune to charity—more than most people earn in a year. Commentators believe that Winfrey draws enormous life satisfaction from her career, her money, and her philanthropic acts. She is an example, they claim, of someone who uses her fortune to maximize her own happiness and to enhance that of other people.

Background

Winfrey grew up in poverty in a small town in Mississippi. She spent her early childhood with her paternal grandmother, who taught Winfrey how to read and instilled in her strong Christian values. When Winfrey was six years old, she went to live with her mother, who exposed the child to very different experiences: During this time Winfrey was sexually abused. She later said that reading became her only escape from the horror through which she lived. At 14 Winfrey's life changed; she was sent to live with her father in Tennessee. A strict disciplinarian with high moral standards, he pushed Winfrey to do well in school. Under her father's guidance she won a full scholarship to Tennessee State University.

By the time she was in her sophomore year, her media career was well underway—she became the first African American and the first woman to anchor a newscast in Nashville. In 1976 she moved to Baltimore, where she initially worked as a reporter and coanchor for a television station. Eight years later Winfrey was invited to Illinois to host a show, soon renamed "The Oprah Winfrey Show." Winfrey quickly became a household name, and her success enabled her to amass her fortune.

Helping others help themselves

Supporters insist that wealth has not changed Winfrey. She remains an intrinsically caring and giving woman. Her show, which began by tackling often sensitive and controversial issues—including domestic violence, child abuse, and alcoholism—continues to allow the average person to have a voice on issues that many people still believe should be swept under the rug. A strong advocate of greater and more far-reaching children's rights, Winfrey has talked openly about her own abuse as a child. Some say that has made it easier for others to discuss their own traumatic experiences. She championed the 1993 National Child Protection Act, which helped create a national database of convicted child abusers in the United States. Winfrey also founded the Angel Network in 1997; it has helped pay for hundreds of disadvantaged youths to go to college. Winfrey's supporters say that she has helped thousands of Americans.

Do you think it is true that the poor spend more time thinking about money? Go to your local newstand, and leaf through some popular magazines. Do you think our society is overloaded with images equating money with happiness?

Somewhere along the way, I discarded my childhood ideas about materialism too. I have known people at various levels of wealth and poverty. Maybe it's just a strange coincidence, but it seems to me that the true materialists I've known—people who were greatly concerned with money and what they could buy with it—happened to be the people who had little or none of it.

A matter of necessity

Every person I've ever met who consistently thought about money did so out of a painful mixture of responsibility and necessity. They had to be materialistic; there were babies to feed, rent to be paid, and barely (or not) enough money to cover it all, let alone take care of unexpected emergencies.

Do you think being poor makes people more practical?

Even though I have found it impossible to completely rid myself of the thought processes I acquired in youth, in many ways, having known poverty first-hand has been useful. I learned skills out of necessity that I probably wouldn't have bothered to learn otherwise. When your car is broke down out in the sticks, far from a phone and a tow truck, it's nice to know how to make that simple repair that will allow you to limp to a garage or auto parts store.

Another myth I believed as a child and later outgrew was the idea—common among many traditional religionists—that poverty is somehow compatible with sainthood. There may be some incredibly good people who choose to live in poverty. I've known the occasional hobo-like person who had nothing and seemed happy enough, but they also had no responsibilities and didn't mind living off the kindness of strangers or on the dole. (One that I met claimed to have founded the Jesuits.)

However, many people don't have the luxury to choose to be poor [irony intended]; they just are. Many "poor" people (that's as relative as is "rich") that I have met were not only materialistic (again, out of necessity), they were also incredibly jealous of those who had more. That's the reality behind the "rich people aren't happy" theory. That theory is crap! Considering the third-world countries I have visited, I'm both rich (since I know I will eat tomorrow and probably the next day) and happier than most of the impoverished people I met overseas.

Do you think Americans are used to comparing themselves to people overseas, or are they mainly interested in other Americans?

Given what some people have to do to make ends meet—cheat, steal, borrow money they know they can't pay back, sell their bodies—money isn't the root of evil. If evil were a plant with a single root, that root would be poverty.

That's not to say that "poor" people are bad because they are poor (or vice versa). The root of poverty is usually nourished by social conditions and government-enabled limitations that keep certain people—whole societies, in some cases—poor, regardless of how intelligent, motivated and pure of heart they might be.

Poverty often leads to society's common illnesses, such as exploitation, substance abuse, child abuse, domestic violence and—ultimately—war.

> Is this argument valid? Why should poor people be more likely to use drugs or commit child abuse than rich people?

> *A ragged urchin, aimless and alone,*
>   *Loitered about that vacancy, a bird*
> *Flew up to safety from his well-aimed stone:*
>   *That girls are raped, that two boys knife a third,*
>   *Were axioms to him, who'd never heard*
> *Of any world where promises were kept,*
> *Or one could weep because another wept.*
> —From "The Shield of Achilles" by W.H.Auden.

Jesus of Nazareth said, "The poor will always be with us." I happen to agree with him on this point. Short of selective breeding of the entire race, there will always be a certain number of people who are unskilled, unintelligent, unmotivated or unlucky. There will always be the necessity of charity (or government subsidy, which has almost entirely replaced it).

> Should it be a function of government to eliminate poverty, even among these groups of people? Or is this an unrealistic aim?

It will also always be necessary for decent people to fight the injustices that lead to poverty. The next time some pious apologist for government oppression and the status quo feeds you the line that poverty is good for the soul, remember that when everybody's standard of living starts to increase, materialism will begin to decrease....

CAN MONEY BUY HAPPINESS?...
Carol Hyman

Carol Hyman writes for the UC (University of California) Berkeley News online, where this article appeared in 2003.

NO

Few would disagree that, to a certain extent, money brings happiness. But according to researchers at University of California, Berkeley, once enough is earned to meet basic needs, money in relation to happiness is a very personal equation.

In fact, employees who are primarily motivated by the love of their work become less happy the more money they make.

Go to http://bdp.lmi.net/ article.cfm? archiveDate= 06-24-03&storyID =16868 to read more on this topic.

Malka and Chatman's study

Psychology PhD candidate Ariel Malka and Haas School of Business professor Jennifer Chatman posed the question: Does the effect that money has on happiness differ between individuals? Specifically, depending upon work values, does one's level of income impact his or her feelings about life?

Malka and Chatman's findings are published in the June issue of the *Personality and Social Psychology Bulletin*.

They conducted a study using a sample of 124 UC Berkeley MBA graduates who participated in an MBA Assessment Project conducted by UC Berkeley's Institute of Personality and Social Research.

Between 1986 and 1991, those participants completed initial surveys while still in graduate school assessing, among other things, work values. In 1995, four to nine years after completing the surveys, participants completed another survey to measure several psychological and work-related variables, including measures, at the time, of their well-being, job satisfaction and annual income.

The researchers' findings lend strong support for the idea that the way money impacts happiness does indeed depend on the individual.

Do you think people living in developed nations are more likely to place a greater value on the importance of money than people in poor nations? Why?

"First of all," said Malka, "we found that income had a positive relationship with both well-being and job satisfaction for individuals high in extrinsic orientation. That is, if money is what you value, then money, indeed, will make you happy."

"However," he continued, "we found a more surprising pattern regarding intrinsic orientation. Specifically, for those high in intrinsic orientation, money actually had a negative

Billionaire megastar Michael Jackson has led a controversial life. Many observers believe that Jackson's fortune and success have blighted rather than enhanced his life.

effect on well-being. In other words, among those who had a relatively strong tendency to value work because they enjoyed it or it fulfilled them, those making more money were actually less happy than those making relatively little money."

Are people in poor societies more likely to believe that being "rich is better"?

"In a capitalistic society, people generally believe that—all other things being equal—being rich is better," Chatman added. "But that is not what we found."

The researchers offered two potential explanations for their findings.

"Earning a lot of money might, to some extent, be a marker of having chosen a job based on what it pays, neglecting factors such as how fulfilling it is," Malka said. "We suspect that neglecting these intrinsic factors would be harmful to a person's happiness. Conceivably, this detrimental effect is especially strong for those who have strong intrinsic work values in the first place."

The researchers' other explanation seemed to them less intuitive, but grounded in previous research. "Perhaps making a lot of money in your job can actually cause you to question why you are working at the particular job you have, even if you chose the job for intrinsic reasons," Malka said. "There's a substantial psychological literature showing that receiving monetary rewards for doing a fun task can make the task seem less enjoyable. This past research suggests that your sense of how fulfilling and personally rewarding you find a task is very fragile, and money can shake this delicate sense of enjoyment."

Do you think pop stars or movie stars find being paid large sums of money reduces their enjoyment in their jobs? Do you think that money might bring them greater freedom to do what they want both personally and professionally?

"Individuals have a fundamental psychological need to feel as though their actions are freely chosen," the authors wrote. "In other words, we all need to feel that we are not just doing the work for the money, and intrinsically motivated individuals need to feel this even more so," Chatman added.

While the researchers believe their research has relevance in the real world, they cautioned that sweeping generalizations from their findings should not be made.

"This research was conducted with a relatively high-income sample—mostly white individuals who attended a top-tier MBA program," Malka said. "We would not expect income to have a negative relationship with well-being for any type of person, regardless of their values, within a lower income sample."

If this is the case, would wealth redistribution through taxes, for example, help make people happier?

Past research, he explained, has shown that the effect of income on well-being is actually quite strong among those who make less money … differences in income translate into differences in how well basic needs are met.

"However, further up the income ladder, at the levels where basic needs are satisfied, the effect of income on well-being diminishes," he continued. "It is at these higher income levels that we expect higher order psychological needs—such as those represented by intrinsic orientation— to have implications for how income affects happiness."

The researchers believe their study contains important lessons.

Managers, for example, should not let the extrinsic rewards they give employees, such as raises, better offices or bonuses, be used "to displace or undermine the natural intrinsic rewards people get for doing the work itself," said Chatman.

The research also raises questions individuals should ask themselves when they investigate career paths.

"When prioritizing life goals, people should think carefully about which outcomes will have the strongest effect on their well-being and allocate their efforts accordingly," Malka said. "Also, people should be aware of how organizing their lives around making money can have implications for their other values. For example, will having lots of money impact your well-being enough to justify you spending 12 hours a day, every workday, doing something you hate?"

Does this argument seem valid? Why should the rich be less satisfied?

See Volume 24, Work and the Workplace, Topic 12 Is there a culture of overwork in the United States?

Summary

Can money buy happiness? The authors of the preceding articles examine some of the themes raised by this question.

In the first the writer calling himself or herself the Mystic examines the idea of materialism. The Mystic claims that most of the people who spend their time thinking about money and materialism are actually the people who do not have monetary wealth. The writer claims that perspectives on what being rich means change as people get older. The Mystic argues that it was only as an adult that the realization came that many of the things he or she had believed in as a child were myths, including the idea that that poverty is compatible with sainthood. The writer states that people do not choose to be poor, and that many people are jealous of those with wealth. The Mystic also asserts that most people in developed nations are both richer and happier than those in poor nations.

Journalist Carol Hyman, on the other hand, reports on a 2003 University of California, Berkeley, study that looks at whether the effect that money has on happiness differs between individuals. Hyman states that while few would disagree that money brings security, the study found that once enough is earned to meet basic needs, money in relation to happiness is a very personal matter. Researchers Ariel Malka and Jennifer Chatman found that money has a negative effect on well-being, especially among people actually enjoying their work for reasons of personal fulfillment. Chatman claims, "In a capitalist society, people generally believe that—all other things being equal—being rich is better, but that's not what we found."

FURTHER INFORMATION:

Books:

Chatsky, Jean, *You Don't Have to Be Rich: Comfort, Happiness, and Financial Security on Your Own Terms*. New York: Viking Books, 2003.

Useful websites:

http://www.arfamilies.org/family_life/human_development/what_makes_people_happy.asp
Article on what makes people happy. Cites some recent studies.
www.jeanchatsky.com
Financial expert Jean Chatsky's site, with articles and links to related sites.
http://www.usatoday.com/news/health/2002-12-08-happy-main_x.htm
Article examining the claim that psychologists now know what makes people happy.

The following debates in the Pro/Con series may also be of interest:

In this volume:

Part 1: Ethics and morality, pages 8-9

Andrew Carnegie and the "Gospel of Wealth," pages 22–23

The Big Issue, pages 48–49

CAN MONEY BUY HAPPINESS?

YES: It is a fact that people who have little or nothing are less happy than the well-off and more envious of the rich

YES: People are naturally competitive and seek to improve their lot; the more they achieve, the more they earn, and the happier they become

MATERIALISM
Is happiness directly proportional to income?

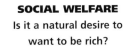

SOCIAL WELFARE
Is it a natural desire to want to be rich?

NO: Happiness is a matter of temperament; a person who does not want an expensive car will not be made happier by owning a Cadillac

NO: Materialism is fueled by the media. They have created the myth that materialism and happiness are related.

CAN MONEY BUY HAPPINESS?
KEY POINTS

YES: People who have money are usually successful at one or more things. They have the satisfaction of knowing that their talent has earned them the opportunity to do or be whatever they want.

YES: Money can buy a place to live and provide food and water security, among other things. Anxiety about how to acquire such things often makes people feel insecure.

LIFE SATISFACTION
Does money buy life satisfaction?

SECURITY
Does money buy security?

NO: There are many examples of celebrities—including Michael Jackson—who seem to have everything but are still unhappy

NO: People with money are often more insecure about losing their wealth or having their homes broken into, among other things

Topic 3
IS BEGGING WRONG?

YES
"BEGGING FOR A DOWNTOWN BEGGING BAN"
CREATIVE LOAFING ATLANTA, SEPTEMBER 4, 2003
RICHARD SHUMATE

NO
"COURT ORDERS SAN FRANCISCO TO PAY LEGAL FEES IN BEGGING CASE"
ACLU PRESS RELEASE, JULY 11, 1997
AMERICAN CIVIL LIBERTIES UNION

INTRODUCTION

Beggars, or panhandlers, are a common sight in many of the world's urban centers. They ask passersby for money; they do not perform music or render any other service in return. Today panhandlers are often associated with alcoholics or narcotics users who want to fund their habit.

Begging itself, however, has a long history as a means of redistributing wealth in cultures with no other welfare or charity. In such societies it was an acceptable way in which the rich supported the poor. Begging also has a long connection with numerous religions that equate poverty with holiness. For example, in Christianity mendicant, or begging, orders of monks and nuns emerged during the Middle Ages in Europe. They depended for their subsistence on alms, or charity, from the communities among whom they lived. In some Buddhist countries today monks still receive alms from citizens. They believe that begging teaches humility and compassion.

In other countries, however, governments and city authorities have targeted begging as an undesirable social problem and have introduced legislation to prevent it. This is partly because of its perceived connection with drug and alcohol abuse, and partly from concerns that it is antisocial behavior that can leave citizens feeling intimidated. In New York City, for example, although panhandling itself is legal, it is illegal on the transit system and anywhere when it is accompanied by threats or intimidation. As part of the "zero-tolerance" policing policy—which argues that cracking down on minor misdemeanors prevents more serious illegal activity—panhandlers are regularly moved on or prosecuted.

Critics of begging argue not only that it is antisocial but also that it is unnecessary. There is welfare that guarantees no one needs to beg in order to have enough money to survive, and there are hostels to provide shelter for the homeless. In the view of such critics many beggars panhandle not out of need but out of laziness. They do not want to work for money, but they expect those who do to support them. Such arguments are bolstered by often sensational media reports about panhandlers—that there are gangs of professional beggars, for example, who live comfortable home lives, or that they are illegal immigrants who exploit their children to gain the sympathy of passersby.

> *"Never stand begging for that which you have the power to earn."*
> —MIGUEL DE CERVANTES
> (1547–1616), SPANISH WRITER

Other people are uneasy about the crackdown on panhandling. They see begging as an option that is only taken up by those who are truly desperate. In the United States and other developed countries there are often people who for reasons such as mental or physical disability, alcohol or narcotics abuse, or homelessness have fallen through the welfare safety net. In countries without welfare, meanwhile, begging is the last resort for society's most vulnerable members. Not only is begging necessary, some people say, but there is also a moral obligation on other members of society to make donations to the needy. In the United States such a view echoes the way in which Americans have traditionally helped each other during crises such as the Great Depression of the 1930s. At a time when there was little in the way of organized poor relief, the Depression

era became characterized by the well-known appeal "Buddy, can you spare a dime?"

Even people who are not essentially opposed to panhandlers sometimes argue that while begging is not wrong, it is an inefficient way to redistribute wealth. They argue that if someone wants to help the poor, he or she should not give money to individual panhandlers but to charities that will ensure that it is used effectively.

With the widespread creation of welfare systems in the second half of the 20th century governments have treated begging as less of a social necessity and more of a social problem. New Delhi, India, for example, has an ordinance that seeks to control begging by fining motorists who hold up traffic to give money to beggars and street vendors. Several U.S. states and cities have outlawed panhandling. These measures, while often supported by local communities, alarm humanitarian organizations, civil rights groups, and churches. They protest that beggars should not be criminalized for being poor. In 1996 Jerry Mazer, a panhandler, sued the government of Kansas City, Missouri, in a bid to overturn a 1956 antibegging regulation. Mazer argued that the law violated his constitutional right to free speech; he received a $3,000 settlement from the city.

Other governments are working with organizations such as the World Bank to promote programs to reduce the numbers of beggars, especially children, on the streets. Some Brazilian cities, for example, have opened centers to encourage children to stay in school and train for a profession, thus breaking the cycle of poverty.

The following articles debate this issue further.

BEGGING FOR A DOWNTOWN BEGGING BAN
RICHARD SHUMATE

Richard Shumate is a columnist for Creative Loafing Atlanta, a weekly newspaper covering news, culture, contemporary music, and the arts. This article was published in September 2003.

YES

✓ We should all be stunned, chagrined and downright mortified by Atlanta City Councilman H. Lamar Willis' proposal to ban begging downtown.

Not because of what Willis has set out to do. That's way overdue and just plain common sense (which is, I'll admit, a description one rarely gets to use in referring to the Atlanta City Council). Rather, what should shock and trouble us is that his proposal has ignited such controversy.

Misguided compassion

We've come a long way, baby—down a very wrong road of misguided and misdirected compassion. Why in the world would anybody with a lick of common sense object to this proposal? Why would anyone who cares about the quality of life in Atlanta, or the city's economic future, think it is desirable to have unkempt vagrants panhandling on street corners?

Rather than answering such questions, critics of Willis' approach instead change the subject. They warn, in ominous tones, that the ban could be challenged in court on free speech grounds.

"Quixotic" means idealistic but impractical. It is derived from the name of the eponymous hero of Miguel de Cervantes' novel Don Quixote de la Mancha (1605, 1615).

Since when has the city of Atlanta been shy about plunging into quixotic legal adventures in pursuit of social policy? Granted, many of those fights have not been worth fighting. This one is. I say we give William Rehnquist and today's Supremes the opportunity to weigh in on the constitutional right to beg and see if they come down on the side of common sense.

William Rehnquist (1924–) has been chief justice of the Supreme Court since 1986.

And while we're at it, let's cut through the politically correct crap we've used to cocoon the issue of "homelessness." First of all, we ought to dispense with the word "homeless," which is meant to convey the image of people who, all of a sudden and through no fault of their own, find themselves out on the streets. They must not be stigmatized, lest their self-esteem suffer.

Bullshit. Many, if not most, of these people are out on the streets because of their own bad life choices, primarily drug

COMMENTARY: Cyberbegging

Most people associate panhandling with images of the needy with their hands outstretched, asking for money for food or drink. Many people often feel threatened or irritated by continuously being asked for money by beggars sitting beside ATMs or outside restaurants. Today, however, commentators claim there is a completely new begging phenomenon. People of all ages, from all walks of life—from single mothers and people with large credit card debts to students paying off loans and people wanting cosmetic surgery—are using technology to make their pleas for financial help reach a wide audience. Observers have labeled this "cyberbegging"—that is, using the Internet to beg for money. Cyberbegging has become a popular and potentially highly lucrative way of raising funds. But for some people it is a matter of huge concern.

Cyber-celebrity

Cyberbegging received a lot of attention in the United States after New Yorker Karyn Bosnak set up a website, SaveKayrn.com, asking for small donations to clear more than $20,000 in debts she had run up by shopping. Within a few months the site received over two million hits, and Bosnak's debt was paid off. She has now written a book about her experience. Bosnak and others who have allegedly had similar success—including people who have raised money for fertility programs or have cleared study loans—have generated much debate on the ethics of cyberbegging. However, some critics are skeptical about how successful these sites can be.

A clever innovation or a moral decline?

Others applaud cyberbeggars for their initiative, arguing that the novelty value of their sites is why many people donate funds to them. The more entertaining the story, the more likely that people will give money. But some observers believe that people who donate to sites like Bosnak's do it only once and never again.

Opponents of cyberbegging include charities and civil rights groups. They question the ethics of cyberbeggars. They claim that the majority of truly needy people do not have Internet access. Most live on the street, and they certainly do not have home pages through which they can beg for cash or PayPal accounts through which to receive funds. Some commentators also believe that cyberbegging is indicative of society's moral degradation. That people can beg for donations toward luxuries such as breast implants or nose jobs makes a mockery, they argue, of the millions who struggle to live below the poverty line.

Cyberbegging has fueled support for antibegging legislation to outlaw these sites. However, it is difficult to regulate the Internet, and such laws may be adjudged to infringe on the individual's freedom of expression.

What choices do you think homeless people can make to change their situation? Is it simply a matter of deciding to get a job? What difficulties might they encounter?

Shumate refers to the work of the American Civil Liberties Union (ACLU), which has campaigned to clear hospitals for the mentally ill of all involuntarily committed patients except those thought to be an immediate danger to themselves or others. See pages 42–45 for the ACLU's viewpoint in this debate.

Commentators point out that the homeless are often victims of violence and intimidation themselves. The National Coalition for the Homeless reported that in the years 1999– 2003 nearly 300 hate crimes, including 130 murders, were committed against homeless people. Go to http://www. nationalhomeless. org/hatecrimes/ index.html for details.

and alcohol abuse, and they are making a conscious decision to remain dazed and destitute. Yes, people are born into poverty or have it thrust upon them by misfortune. But staying there is a choice—one we should neither enable nor encourage by mollycoddling them.

A more appropriate term for these folks is "vagrant," defined as an idle person without visible means of support. Yes, this carries a stigma. But some stigma might be a welcome tonic to motivate change.

Institutionalizing the problem?

OK, OK, I can already hear some of you out there picking up poison pens to inform me that a substantial portion of those living on the streets are not drunks or addicts but mentally ill people who can't, or won't, take care of themselves.

True enough. But these people are out on the streets today (rather than in institutions where they wouldn't be a danger to themselves or a nuisance to the public) thanks to legal challenges brought by the same merry band of liberal do-gooders who now want to enshrine "homelessness" as a right.

If somebody is too mentally ill to take care of himself, what truly helps them more: confining them to a mental institution, where they're at least warm, fed and medicated, or letting them roam free to eat out of Dumpsters, sleep on park benches and scream at pedestrians? The first choice is compassion; the second, merely a mirage.

It is absurd that people who live, work or visit downtown must put up with the unpleasantries of rampant vagrancy because of someone else's misguided political agenda. Here's an idea—let the chickens go home to roost and turn every ACLU office in the country into a homeless shelter.

If Willis' proposal passes, Atlanta is likely to rise higher on a list of the 20 "meanest" cities recently put out by the National Coalition for the Homeless. (We're fifth, with a bullet.) The group's criteria for "mean" includes not only restrictions on begging, but also laws banning defecation in public and bathing in public waters.

Funny, my copy of the Constitution seems to be missing the section where pooping on a city street is enshrined as a right. If this is "mean," let us have more of it. And don't dare suggest that we're somehow lacking in compassion if we insist on basic rules of civilized behavior.

Our compassion should rest with the downtown resident who has scrimped and saved to buy a nice home—but is now afraid to invite guests over at night because of the gauntlet of derelicts outside, whacked out on God knows what.

Our compassion should rest with the struggling business owner putting in long hours and trying to build a future—who sees his customers intimidated and chased away by vagrants demanding money. Our compassion should rest with the conventioneer who comes to Atlanta to enjoy himself—and vows never to return after being accosted by a wild-eyed, un-medicated schizophrenic.

But compassion should not be used as an excuse to help people maintain a pathological lifestyle eating at the fabric of our city. That's not compassion; it's delusion. Banning panhandling would help all of us—including the homeless—by discouraging the pathology.

Is it reason enough to ban begging because beggars frighten people?

"Pathological" in this context means something abnormal.

In your opinion would a ban be an effective way to eliminate begging? Do you think it be difficult to enforce? Go to http://news.bbc.co.uk/1/hi/england/manchester/3169359.stm to read an account of how the city of Manchester in England has dealt with persistent beggars.

COURT ORDERS SAN FRANCISCO TO PAY LEGAL FEES IN BEGGING CASE
American Civil Liberties Union

This text is a press release from the American Civil Liberties Union (ACLU) of Northern California dating from July 1997.

NO

SAN FRANCISCO—In the final installment of an eight-year legal battle that resulted in a landmark decision that the First Amendment protects the right of poor people to request funds, US District Judge William Orrick has ordered the City to pay $323,785.56 in fees and costs in *Blair v. Shanahan*.

Begging a protected expression

"This fee award underscores the significance of Judge Orrick's important 1992 decision that peaceful begging is protected expression," said Thomas McInerney, of Thelen, Marrin, Johnson & Bridges, a cooperating attorney for the ACLU who handled the case on a pro bono basis. Michael Hallerud of Thelen, Marrin and Margaret Crosby of the ACLU of Northern California also represent the plaintiff in the case.

"Pro bono," short for pro bono publico—*Latin for "for the public good"*—refers to legal work donated for free by lawyers to help people or organizations with limited funds.

"This decision should put cities on notice that violating the rights of the poor is not only wrong, but carries a price," McInerney added.

The case was originally filed in 1989 on behalf of Celestus Blair who was arrested five times for peacefully asking people for money in downtown San Francisco. He was charged with violating California Penal Code Section 647 (c), which makes it a misdemeanor to approach others on public sidewalks "for the purpose of begging or soliciting alms."

An unconstitutional prohibition

In 1991, Judge Orrick declared the state law prohibition against begging unconstitutional and the appellate court rejected the city's appeal. On remand, Judge Orrick granted a motion to vacate his opinion on procedural grounds. However, that ruling did not eliminate the opinion as an influential precedent.

To "vacate an opinion" means to set aside or annul a judgment.

In the final stage of the lawsuit, the City argued primarily that Blair had achieved only modest success and should not receive substantial compensation for attorneys' fees. Judge Orrick rejected that contention.

COMMENTARY: Brazil's children

In recent years many human rights and child-protection organizations have highlighted the numbers of children living on the world's streets. This is a particular problem in Brazil, where some 12 million children live a desperate existence in cities such as Rio de Janeiro and São Paulo. In 1993 world attention became focused on Brazil's *abandonados*—"abandoned ones"—when it was revealed that eight children had been killed in Rio by a vigilante group including soldiers and policemen. After that came many more reports of Brazil's feral children allegedly being hunted down by death squads hired by shopkeepers and law-enforcement officers who were tired of dealing with them. The plight of these children, who are subject to abuse and exploitation on a daily basis, has led many to argue that the international community and the Brazilian government have a duty to ensure that they are given an alternative to begging, prostitution, or street crime. In this way the government and international agencies will, critics believe, offer these children a future and also provide the Brazilian economy with a larger pool of skilled and educated labor.

Giving children an option

In the last 20 years, however, industrialization and changes in the Brazilian rural economy due to deforestation have led to increased numbers of poor people moving to urban areas. Families often arrive in cities with no prospect of finding employment. Children are frequently sent to work or are abandoned on the streets, forced to earn their living from begging or from casual labor such as selling goods or shining shoes. Some, however, resort to crime or prostitution in order to survive. Organizations like the World Bank believe that it is important to encourage these children to attend school and get a decent education.

Working for change

In 1991 the state of Ceará established a program aimed at helping street children. Fifteen municipalities built centers that were open only to children who were prepared to enroll in or reenter school. Staffed by volunteers, the centers hosted sporting and cultural activities, and provided skills and vocational training such as computing, car mechanics, and cooking. The World Bank supported the program by funding the public works necessary to build the centers.

Other Brazilian cities are also attempting to help *abandonados*. Porto Alegre has established "open schools" to encourage former and current street children to attend classes. Belém and São Paulo have committed resources to keep children off the streets, such as hostels and substance-abuse programs. While supporters claim this is a great step forward, critics argue that Brazil still has a long way to go in tackling this huge problem.

A Brazilian boy, one of the thousands of the country's abandonados—"*abandoned ones*"—
sleeps under a blanket on a beach in Rio de Janeiro.

The court concluded that the civil rights suit had accomplished its purpose of protecting the constitutional right to beg. The 1991 *Blair* opinion ruled that begging informs the community about "the way our society treats its poor and disenfranchised" and can change "the way the listener sees his or her relationship with and obligations to the poor."

The decision also ruled that the government could not constitutionally distinguish between the fundraising appeals of organized charities and of destitute individuals on the public street. Courts throughout the country invalidating laws prohibiting begging have cited Judge Orrick's *Blair* decision.

In addition, Judge Orrick wrote in the June 16, 1997 decision, the 1991 *Blair* opinion halted San Francisco's enforcement of the state law and prompted the City to enact a new ordinance regulating begging "more consistent with the First Amendment." Finally, the court ruled that Blair's success in securing a damage award for his arrests (approximately $4,800) and expungement of his arrest record was not trivial.

The opinion of Judge Orrick and the ACLU is that begging has a political message. Do you find this argument persuasive?

In 1992 San Francisco adopted a municipal ordinance barring "aggressive" panhandling. Several other U.S. cities have similar bans.

Berkeley case

Last month, the City of Berkeley agreed to pay the ACLU $110,000 as part of settlement in a case challenging its law restricting the right to request funds. The City substantially modified the law following a district court opinion striking down major portions of the ordinance (*Berkeley Community Health Project v. City of Berkeley*).

"Judge Orrick's 1991 decision emphasizes the importance of the rights of free expression which were denied to Blair, and as a result of the order, these rights are now protected for all persons in California.

It is ironic that this City, whose namesake is St. Francis, would deprive the poor of their right to seek alms," McInerney said.

Francis of Assisi (about 1181–1226), patron saint of animals and the environment, founded the Francisan order of friars. He gave up his material possessions to devote himself to caring for the poor and the sick. In the 1770s the Spanish dedicated a mission to him on the site that is now San Francisco.

Summary

The question of whether begging is right or wrong leads to much debate. In the first of the preceding articles journalist Richard Shumate examines Councilman H. Lamar Willis's proposal to ban begging in downtown Atlanta. Shumate claims that people should be shocked not by the suggestion itself but by the reaction to it. He claims that compassion toward panhandlers is misguided. Many of those people living on the streets deserve their situation because of the bad choices they have made in life, Shumate says, and it is their choice to remain there. He criticizes "liberal do-gooders" such as the American Civil Liberties Union (ACLU) for seeking to enshrine a right to homelessness, which has resulted in mentally ill people being on the streets instead of living safely in institutions. Shumate concludes that compassion should be reserved for Atlanta residents and businesses that have to put up with threatening behavior from beggars. A ban would benefit all, he says.

 In the second article the Northern California branch of the ACLU defends the right of people to beg in its report of the case *Blair v. Shanahan*. The case was originally filed in 1989 on behalf of Celestus Blair, a man arrested five times in downtown San Francisco for peacefully asking people for money. He was charged with violating the California law that made it illegal to ask money from people "for the purpose of begging or soliciting alms," but the judge ruled that the law was unconstitutional. Citing another case involving the city of Berkeley, the ACLU applauds the fact that the right to free expression has been protected in California.

FURTHER INFORMATION:

Books:

Hermer, Joe, *Policing Compassion: Begging, Law, and Power in Public Spaces*. Oxford, England: Hart Publishing, 2004.

Mayers, Marjorie, *Street Kids and Streetscapes: Panhandling, Politics, and Prophecies*. New York: Peter Lang, 2001.

Useful websites:

http://www.boulderweekly.com/archive/011603/coverstory.html
Issue of the *Boulder Weekly* devoted to begging.
http://www.city-journal.org/dev/html/4_2_the_aclu.html
Critical examination of the ACLU's fight for the rights of beggars.
http://www.csmonitor.com/2002/0930/p01s05-wosc.html
Article about how a new traffic law is affecting beggars in New Delhi, India.

www.nationalhomeless.org
Site for the National Coalition for the Homeless.

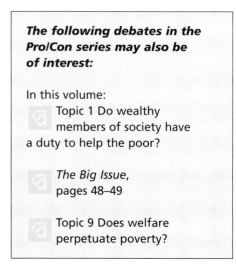

The following debates in the Pro/Con series may also be of interest:

In this volume:
 Topic 1 Do wealthy members of society have a duty to help the poor?

 The Big Issue, pages 48–49

 Topic 9 Does welfare perpetuate poverty?

IS BEGGING WRONG?

YES: People should have more dignity. Everyone should earn what they need to survive.

YES: The gap between rich and poor has widened since globalization began to take effect, and there are simply more people on the streets

MORALITY
Is begging immoral?

RICH–POOR DIVIDE
Is begging a natural byproduct of globalization?

NO: The vulnerable, old, young, and infirm are often unable to earn a living. Begging may be their only option aside from a life of crime.

NO: Historically beggars have always existed. Panhandling is not a new phenomenon.

IS BEGGING WRONG?

KEY POINTS

YES: Governments such as Brazil's are working with the World Bank to invest in education programs to provide beggars with the opportunity to train for a profession

YES: Begging leads to street crime, drugs, and other social ills. It is unpleasant for people to be subjected to panhandlers hectoring them for money.

EDUCATION
Could governments stop begging through increased investment in education for the poor?

LAW
Should begging be made illegal?

NO: It is not that simple. Other factors, such as housing, access to food and water, and employment, are also important.

NO: A ban on peaceful begging violates an individual's right to freedom of expression, protected by the First Amendment

THE BIG ISSUE

*"It's an awful success, being as it is
the product of a social
crisis that won't go away."*

—JOHN BIRD, EDITOR-IN-CHIEF OF *THE BIG ISSUE*, COMMENTING ON
THE MAGAZINE'S SUCCESS (*THE NEW STATESMAN*, 1996)

The Big Issue, a magazine sold by homeless people, has become a global publishing phenomenon. Established in London, England, in 1991 by Gordon Roddick, of Body Shop International, and John Bird, *The Big Issue* was originally a monthly publication; in 1993 it became a weekly. The magazine has won several editorial awards, but more importantly it has given millions of people in more than 27 different countries the opportunity to reach beyond poverty.

Inspiration: New York's *Street News*

Gordon Roddick, husband of Anita Roddick, founder of the international company the Body Shop, came across *Street News,* the New York newspaper sold by the homeless, while on a business trip. Roddick recalls that a vendor told him that selling the newspaper gave him the opportunity to be part of "the throbbing race of life and not a bit of garbage sitting on a corner waiting for someone's indulgence." On his return to England Roddick asked old friend John Bird to help him set up a similar venture in London. On September 9, 1991, the first magazines hit London's streets, sold by a group of 30 homeless people.

Empowering the homeless

From the beginning *The Big Issue* was run on business principles, and this, many people believe, may be what lies at the very heart of its success. As John Bird said, "Everybody's always banging on about giving people things. But if you are a giver then you create takers, if you create takers then you create dependency."

In order to qualify as vendors, people must prove that they are homeless or are threatened with the prospect of homelessness. Vendors are treated as retailers rather than employees and are responsible for their earnings—from declaring them to a welfare or social security office to dealing with tax. *The Big Issue* trains potential vendors on how to pitch the magazine to the public, and sellers are expected to sign a code of conduct in which they agree not to beg, swear, drink alcohol, or harass the public while selling the magazine. They can also only sell the magazine when they are wearing an official badge. Vendors are usually given 10 copies of the magazine to sell in the first instance, after which they buy copies of the magazine up front at a wholesale rate, usually at between 40 and 50 percent of the cover price. They keep the difference as profit.

Success and awards

The Big Issue's success happened quickly. In December 1992 it published a supplement on Manchester, in northern England, and soon created an independent edition, *The Big Issue in the North*. *The Big Issue in Scotland* first appeared in 1993. These magazines were later joined by two other regional editions—*The Big Issue South West* and *The Big Issue Cymru* (Wales). By 1993 *The Big Issue* had become a weekly magazine and was already winning praise for its content: John Bird received Magazine Editor's Editor of the Year award that year. Other accolades followed, and a series of scoops helped cement the magazine's success.

The Big Issue began to expand beyond its British origins. In 1994 it established the International Network of Street Papers (INSP), an association of about 50 street papers in 27 countries around the world. The INSP's guiding principle is that all profits should be plowed back into social support for the homeless. *The Big Issue* also has international editions published in Australia, South Africa, and Namibia.

In 1995 *The Big Issue* established a charity—*The Big Issue* Foundation—which works to empower homeless people by raising their self-esteem and encouraging independence. The foundation provides all vendors with an individual action plan and assists them in pursuing education, training, and permanent employment.

Although the benefits of *The Big Issue* have been praised and admired around the world, the fact that it is a businesslike operation has also brought criticism. The British newspaper *The Sun*, for example, claimed that *The Big Issue* vendors were earning £1,000 ($1,800) a week. Bird responded to the allegation by saying that vendors would have to work from 6:00 A.M. to 6:00 P.M. and to sell a paper every 39 seconds to earn such a sum. Some vendors have also accused the magazine of exploiting them. Many others claim, however, that selling *The Big Issue* motivates them to do other things. *The Big Issue in the North* boasts, for example, that it helps one vendor to get a job every seven days.

Burgeon Creative Ideas

In 1999 John Bird extended the fight against homelessness into cyberspace. Along with partners Gordon Roddick and Tony Cook, from the left-wing political magazine *Red Pepper*, he established Burgeon Creative Ideas (BCI). BCI plows 20 percent of its profits after investment into *The Big Issue* and acts as an "incubator" for new media sites. It has launched Get Ethical, a shopping site that promotes ethical consumerism; ABCtales, a storytelling website and literary magazine; and *Big Issue* Lists, a collection of checklists to help people deal with situations such as buying a house and applying for a job.

BIG ISSUE WEBSITES

www.ABCtales.com—a literary storytelling site
www.bigissue.co.uk—the magazine's UK site, with links to international sites
www.bigissuelists.co.uk—a collection of useful checklists, some free
www.getethical.com—an online source of ethical products

Topic 4

SHOULD PEOPLE HAVE TO LOOK AFTER THEIR ELDERLY RELATIVES?

YES

"WE HAVE NATIONALIZED THE ELDERLY, AS WE ARE TOO BUSY TO CARE FOR THEM"
THE INDEPENDENT, FEBRUARY 21, 2003
JOHANN HARI

NO

"IN RURAL COMMUNITIES, ELDERLY HELPING THEMSELVES AND LOOKING
TO NETWORKS OF VOLUNTEERS"
FOSTER'S HEALTH BEAT, APRIL 2004
CURT WOODWARD

INTRODUCTION

Census projections estimate that as many as one in five Americans will be aged 65 or over by 2050. Other developed countries face similarly aging populations. As more people live to advanced old age, more are also likely to face chronic, debilitating illnesses and to require long-term care. Increasingly, observers claim, younger generations will face a dilemma: Who will look after old people as they age and become dependent on others?

The chances of becoming dependent increase with age. While only about 1 percent of Americans age 65 to 74 years live in a nursing home, nearly 25 percent of those age 85 or older do. Around half of those age 85 or older who are not in residential care require help with daily activities such as preparing meals. As more people in the West live longer, so increasing numbers of their relatives must care for them or arrange for others to do so.

In developed countries there has been a shift away from family care of the elderly toward a reliance on institutions such as nursing homes and sheltered accommodation, and on the employment of nurses and other formal carers. A key factor in this trend is the breakdown of extended families as more people get divorced or move away from home towns for education, work, or retirement. Many families have little space to accommodate an aged relative. For others there is no one at home during the day to look after an elderly relative, and it is seldom feasible financially for a family to sacrifice income from paid employment in order for a working-age adult to stay at home.

Some commentators argue that it is therefore a practical reality of modern life that professional caregivers, the government, and private or nonprofit institutions must be involved in care of the elderly. Were people to be forced to look after aged relatives, they say, women—who currently provide between two-thirds and three-quarters of all care to elderly and disabled family members—in particular would be forced out of their jobs, and poor and single-parent families would face further hardship.

Observers suggest that one possible solution would be for pension programs to be made compulsory. Advocates argue that people should be obliged to plan and provide for their old age so as not to be a financial burden on their families and the government.

> *"Old people have a duty to die and get out of the way."*
> —RICHARD LAMM,
> GOVERNOR OF COLORADO
> (1975–1987)

At the extreme of this argument are critics such as Richard Lamm, former governor of Colorado, and the philosopher John Hardwig, who have controversially suggested that old people have a duty to die. Their reasoning is that western society has no good financial plan for long-term care of the elderly. They argue that rather than requiring family members to alter their own lives and goals to care for an aged relative, the elderly person should arrange to die. Lamm and others have proposed limiting health-care resources for old people.

Others see such arguments as a symptom of an increasingly selfish, individualistic society. In developing countries, where traditions of respect

and duty toward senior citizens remain intact, people view western attitudes and treatment of the aged as near-barbaric. Parents often care and provide for their children well into adulthood, yet when the balance of responsibility begins to swing the other way, children are not there for parents.

For many people, therefore, the obligation toward the elderly is not based on charity so much as justice: A person's past contributions both to his or her family and to society deserve something in return. For others the obligation is a moral one or one based on religious teaching. The Bible, for example, advises readers to "Honor your Mother and your Father" (Exodus 20), and "Listen to your father who begot you, and do not despise your mother when she is old" (Proverbs 23).

Finally, there is the issue of the quality of care that nursing homes provide. A study prepared by the House Committee on Government Reform found that nearly one-third of the 17,000 nursing homes in the United States were cited for instances of abuse between January 1999 and January 2001. Other factors, such as the use of inappropriate medication and the ratio of staff to patients, lead some people to argue that old people would receive a better level of care from their families.

However, some commentators point out that such attitudes may overlook the feelings of many elderly people themselves, who are horrified by the possibility that they could become a burden to their children. Where at all possible many seniors choose to remain in their own homes and communities, with family, friends, volunteers, or paid carers providing assistance if necessary.

The articles that follow discuss some of the arguments in this debate.

WE HAVE NATIONALIZED THE ELDERLY, AS WE ARE TOO BUSY TO CARE FOR THEM
Johann Hari

Johann Hari is a journalist and playwright. This article first appeared in the British newspaper The Independent on February 21, 2003.

YES

Across the Arab world, people are fond of recounting a popular horror story about the West. A few years ago, I overheard a middle-aged man in a Syrian souq tell his children: "When Westerners get old and can't look after themselves, their families send them off to live in big buildings. They visit them once a week, if that, and let nurses do the rest. Sometimes, they forget them all together, and old people die alone and crying for their families."

He could have added—if he had read a survey released this week—that we drug them into catatonia if they begin to rebel against their abandonment. The journal *Age and Ageing* has found that almost a quarter of people in nursing homes are being given powerful psychiatric medicines—and of those, a chilling 80 per cent were prescribed either for the wrong reason, without proper monitoring of the effects, or without any thought as to whether the patient's condition still required it. This is even more scandalous than many front-page child-abuse shocks because it is much more widespread and systematised. Yet it was reported, if at all, only on the inside pages of our newspapers.

Why do you think the press gives more coverage to child abuse than to abuse of the elderly?

Different standards of care

A friend of mine has recently switched from working in an old people's home (and by no means a bad one) to working with children who have cerebral palsy. She was startled by the difference in standards of care. "When I started working with the elderly, I was given three days' training—two of which consisted just of watching the other care workers doing their job. That was it," she explains.

"But before I could do anything with the kids I work with now, I had a week of detailed training courses, and I'll be on probation—where I'm very carefully monitored—for another 26 weeks," she continued. "It's only when I got the training in my new job that I realised how unprepared I was before. I didn't know really basic things about how to lift people

The movie actor Kirk Douglas surrounded by his sons (from left to right) Michael, Joel, Eric, and Peter. As America's population ages, many families face the dilemma of deciding what is the best care for their elderly relatives.

without harming them or causing them distress. Why are the elderly worth so much less than disabled kids?" The truth is that old people aren't sexy. We don't like to think about all that sagging flesh and those failing bladders; much easier to sympathise with doe-eyed children.

A problem of numbers

Numbers, numbers, numbers—if politicians bothered to make up soundbites about care of the elderly, this would be it. The number of care workers is not nearly high enough. Disabled children have, at most, a child-to-care-worker ratio of two to one. It is a sign of how little we care about the old that, as Polly Toynbee's new book *Hard Work: Life in Low-Pay Britain* explains, nobody even bothers to compile national statistics about the ratio of care workers to the elderly. It seems anecdotally to be around six to one. Quality care is impossible in this situation; instead, we end up with factory-

In the United States the National Citizens' Coalition for Nursing Home Reform (NCCNHR) recommends a minimum of one direct caregiver to five residents. In 2000 it estimated that 91 percent of U.S. nursing homes fell short of this standard of care.

farming of the old. They are fed, washed and clothed, but there is no time to treat them as individuals.

The mass drugging stems from the numbers problem. If you have no time to talk to a distressed old person, it's much easier to give them a pill. New Labour took several steps forward last year when they introduced much higher care regulations, mandating, for example, that all old people are entitled to a room and toilet of their own. Yet, dismayingly, the Government retracted many of these commitments this week—and the numbers problem festers on.

"New Labour" refers to the Labour government that came to power in the United Kingdom in 1997.

Even the best nursing homes are depressing

Yet even if we had extremely high-quality, well-funded homes (a distant dream), we would still have high numbers of old people on drugs, especially anti-depressants, because of a simple fact: being left in even the best care home in the world is appallingly depressing.

A "state home" is a nursing home that is funded by the government.

Nobody could deserve it less than the generation now left in this situation. My grandmother, who is in an excellent state home, is of an age group who have shown a level of altruism and self-sacrifice that beggars belief. Four years ago, my grandmother was on her way to post some money to my sister, a broke single mum. As she crossed the road, some fool driving at 70mph smacked into her, and she was thrown into the air and hit the road at the other side of the car. When the paramedics arrived, as she lay bleeding into the road, the first thing she said was, "Excuse me, but would you mind putting this envelope into the post-box? My granddaughter's really desperate for the money." Six months later, she was back on her feet and back to health.

An appropriate personal anecdote is often a useful way to make a point.

How do we repay people like her? My grandmother would hobble across deserts for me if I was in trouble; yet I am too selfish to look after her now she is old and in need of help. I called her yesterday, and she cried, saying simply, "You won't ever forget about me, will you?"

Our growing individualism, where we value our own space and freedom from constraint above all else, claims the old as victims. We cannot be bothered to look after the people who brought us up. The collapse of extended families, who in cultures such as India's look after the elderly as automatically as they look after their children, has had some liberating effects. Yet it reaches its dark apotheosis in care homes. Their conditions should shame us into reintegrating the elderly into our everyday lives. Or, as the population greys, will we simply build more and more homes until a third of the population ends up in one?

The word "apotheosis" means a glorified thing or ideal. What do you think "dark apotheosis" means in this context?

Shifting care back to the extended family

The real alternative to the ongoing misery of care homes is radical. We must shift care of the elderly from depersonalised care homes back on to the extended family. In Britain today we have nationalised our old people, handing them over to the Government so we can get on with our terribly busy lives. But the Government does not care for the old any better than it provides for children in care; governments should not be in the business of looking after people directly through institutions, because it always ends in disaster.

At the moment, we hand £279 a week on average to a care home for each elderly person. Wouldn't it be far better spent not by the state but by families caring for their own relatives? My family and I would look after my gran, I suspect, far better than nurses who don't know her—so hand us the money to make it possible and we'll do the job, with the help of a hired nurse. This would reverse the existing ratios: not six elderly people per carer, but rather four or five carers (who happen to be family members) per elderly person. The numbers problem is solved in a flash, for all but the most incapacitated elderly. Those old people without families could be "adopted". This would transform the system without spending an extra penny.

Such a shift would require, of course, a massive cultural change. It requires sacrifice, a word which is deeply out of fashion; but looking after an old person with £14,000-worth of support a year is pretty negligible compared to the sacrifices that their generation made for us. Bringing in these changes now would only be enlightened self-interest anyway: we too will end up in homes if we don't change the system now. My grandmother wants to age and die with her great grand-children playing at her feet. Don't you?

In the United States and some other western countries, including Australia and Canada, between 94 and 95 percent of people aged over 65 live in their own homes or with family.

£279 was about $500 at 2003 exchange rates. Use the Internet to find out what the average cost is in the United States.

Do you think there would be sufficient families willing to "adopt" elderly people, as Hari argues? Is it reasonable to expect families to look after elderly relatives if they are given sufficient financial help, or are there other reasons they might be reluctant to do so?

IN RURAL COMMUNITIES, ELDERLY HELPING THEMSELVES AND LOOKING TO NETWORKS OF VOLUNTEERS
Curt Woodward

Curt Woodward is an Associated Press writer. This article was first published in April 2004.

NO

Despite the challenges the elderly face in rural towns across America, there is no overlooking the value of neighbor helping neighbor.

Seniors are relying more on each other to keep living at home and they're getting help to tap into a wide range of programs for the day-to-day assistance they need to avoid moving to a nursing home.

Helping out the elderly

In Robinson [North Dakota], that includes taking turns as a chauffeur to get friends to the senior center for meals or gathering them for a bus trip to Bismarck, about an hour away, for a doctor's appointment.

"We've had people that have had cancer and the whole town offers to drive them around," said Mary Lou Hanson, the center's manager. "It's a pretty close-knit community."

In Traverse County, Minn., a clutch of rural farm communities where more than a quarter of the 4,100 or so residents are older than 65, a "phone mate" program pairs the elderly or disabled to check on each other at a prescribed time each day. Volunteers also home-deliver meals or drive older people to see a medical specialist.

There is often a tradition of people helping each other in rural communities. Do you think such a system would work as well in urban areas?

More community safety nets will be needed

Across the country, the need for such community safety nets is expected to climb significantly in coming years. By 2050, Census figures show 5 percent of the country will be 85 or older, compared with 1.5 percent now.

North Dakota has the distinction of having the country's highest proportion of residents age 85 and older, and that population is growing. By 2020, state officials predict the number may jump to more than 24,000, nearly 4 percent of the population.

Robinson, a community of about 70, sits amid miles of farmland in central North Dakota.

Many residents, like 93-year-old widow Emilia Randall, wouldn't live anywhere else. She has lived in Robinson since 1968, when she moved off of the family farm.

"I call this God's country," she said. "The great wide open spaces—it's beautiful."

But to stay here, Randall and her friends need help, particularly if they no longer have a spouse.

More than 30,000 women in North Dakota are widows. In Kidder County, where Randall lives, about 42 percent of the people over 65 have outlived their husband or wife.

The average life expectancy of women in the United States is 79.9 years; for men it is 74.24 years. Why do you think this difference exists?

A low-income, eight-unit apartment building owned by 82-year-old Elsie Whitman is home to her and four other single ladies who look after each other, get together for regular card games and move in a pack from home to the senior center for meals.

Without that community of neighbors to rely on, "they'd have to be in nursing homes," Hanson said.

Even Randall drives other seniors to errands at the grocery store, the post office, around town or even to the mall or movie theater in Bismarck, although recent eye surgery left her temporarily grounded.

Market value of unpaid help is enormous

Networks of family and friends lend so much unpaid help to the elderly or disabled that losing their services "would break the Medicaid and Medicare system very quickly," said Cherry Schmidt, a regional administrator for the state's aging services program.

The National Family Caregivers Association offers support and information to family caregivers of the ill, disabled, and elderly. Go to www.nfcacares.org for more details.

A recent study by the National Family Caregivers Association said more than 27 million people—usually family members—act as caregivers for others. The group said the market value of those unpaid services is about $257 billion each year.

In rural areas, where the population often is older, residents sometimes find themselves separated from relatives living in the city. That presents an extra challenge for caregivers.

Why do you think the population is often older in rural areas?

"A great many people who are caregivers are people who might need the services of a caregiver themselves," said Andrew Zovko, a director at the caregivers association. "Certainly, an elderly person caring for another elderly person is a common situation."

And it's a situation that presents its own problems.

"Our volunteers are getting older and more frail," said Evie Rinke, an aging programs coordinator for Traverse County, Minn. "When it's ice and snow we wonder, 'Oh my, should we even send them out?'"

Retired couples dance at Port St. Lucie, Florida. Keeping active and being involved in the community helps many older people continue to live in their own homes as long as possible.

With elderly people and younger children making up a large portion of the county's population, "it doesn't leave a whole lot of us in that middle area to provide a lot of care for the elderly," Rinke said.

State funding for elderly lags behind

Pat Randall, Emilia's daughter-in-law and the director of Senior Services for Emmons and Kidder counties in North Dakota, said volunteers at the three senior centers in her territory logged more than 1,030 hours in January and February alone. She said the federal Older Americans Act, which has paid for buses and meal programs, has been a lifesaver, though state funding has lagged behind.

"It's like our state legislators are having a hard time understanding that we need to increase the funding to match the needs of the people," Randall said. "If there's more elderly and there's less money, what are you going to do?"

State officials say a relatively new federal program gives them some flexibility in offering help to those who are taking care of an elderly or disabled person at home. The National Family Caregiver Support Program allows states to tailor assistance to the particular needs of caregivers, said Judy Tschider, a regional coordinator.

In one case, a woman needed driving lessons because her husband, who had always handled the transportation, was in poor health and under her care.

"That can help her in taking care of him as well," Tschider said.

It also helps both of them stay in their community as long as possible. That's a familiar refrain for those who work with seniors, Randall said.

As she ate lunch with a group of ladies at the senior center in Tuttle, 78-year-old Rachel Wolff recalled that a doctor was puzzled by her decision to move to the small town when she decided to leave the family farm.

"He said, 'How come you moved to Tuttle? Why didn't you move to Bismarck?'" Wolff remembered.

Seventy-seven-year-old Anita Wagner answered for her: "You feel more at home here."

Go to the Administration on Aging website at http://www.aoa.gov/about/legbudg/oaa/legbudg_oaa.asp to find out more about the Older Americans Act Amendments of of 2000.

Visit http://www.aoa.gov/prof/aoaprog/caregiver/overview/exec_summary.asp to find out more about this program.

Summary

In the first article Johann Hari criticizes attitudes to caring for old people in the West, where people often arrange for their elderly relatives to live in nursing homes. Drawing on the situation in the United Kingdom, Hari quotes some alarming statistics and anecdotal evidence about the quality of care in such institutions and the frequent and inappropriate use of psychiatric drugs. In his view elderly people are victims of the collapse of extended families and "growing individualism." The answer, Hari says, lies with a shift of care back to families. He argues that the government should redirect the money it spends on each elderly person in a nursing home back to the family to be spent on that person's care. Care within the family would then be financially feasible, of a higher quality, and would enable senior citizens to live at home surrounded by people they know and love.

Curt Woodward presents a different viewpoint with his piece on rural communities in the United States. He describes how, even in the absence of family, people in small towns establish a support network via a community of neighbors who transport the less able to medical appointments and social centers, and provide telephone services to check up on one another. Family members are still the main caregivers, but there are also many friends and volunteers to help people continue to live in their own homes and communities as they age. Woodward recognizes that in a population of mainly young children and the elderly there are not many people of working age to act as carers. The way forward, he contends, is to offer more government assistance to these mutual networks of friends and neighbors.

FURTHER INFORMATION:

Books:

Angel, Ronald J., and Jacqueline L. Angel, *Who Will Care for Us? Aging and Long-Term Care in Multicultural America*. New York: New York University Press, 1997.
Conner, Karen A., *Continuing to Care: Older Americans and Their Families*. New York: Falmer Press, 2000.

Useful websites:

http://aging.senate.gov
U.S. Senate Special Committee on Aging.
www.aoa.gov
Administration on Aging, part of the Health and Human Services Department, has articles on aging-related issues and links to other relevant sites.
www.globalaging.org
Global Action on Aging has articles on aging-related issues from around the world.

The following debates in the Pro/Con series may also be of interest:

In this volume:
Topic 1 Do wealthy members of society have a duty to help the poor?

In *Family and Society*:
Topic 12 Should the elderly pay for their own health care?

In *Work and the Workplace*:
Topic 6 Should there be a mandatory retirement age?

SHOULD PEOPLE HAVE TO LOOK AFTER THEIR ELDERLY RELATIVES?

YES: People prefer to age and eventually to die surrounded by family members

YES: People who have devoted so much of their lives to their families should expect some sacrifice in return

CHOICE
Do the elderly actually want to be cared for by family?

DUTY TO CARE
Do families have a duty to look after their elderly relatives?

NO: Given the choice, most people prefer to remain in their own homes and communities in mutually supportive networks of friends and neighbors

NO: Senior citizens should not expect their families to give up careers and life goals simply to look after them. Their lives are almost over; younger members of the family should have the chance to lead their own lives.

SHOULD PEOPLE HAVE TO LOOK AFTER THEIR ELDERLY RELATIVES?

KEY POINTS

YES: Children moving away can free up space in the family home. Nurses and outside carers can be employed to assist with medical care.

YES: If governments redirect the money already spent on care for the elderly back to families, care within the home would become feasible for all concerned

PRACTICALITY
Is it practical to force people to care for their relatives?

NO: People's homes may not be large enough to accommodate elderly relatives. Some illnesses and conditions require a high level of expert, around-the-clock care.

NO: It is not practical or reasonable to expect people, mainly women, to forego paid employment and fulfilling careers to look after the elderly

PART 2
SOCIAL AND ECONOMIC ISSUES

The 2000 Nobel laureate in economics James Heckman and fellow economist Alan Krueger have drawn attention to growing income disparities in the United States. They acknowledge that although income differentials provide incentives for individuals to work hard, if the differences in rewards do not relate to productivity, they may be harmful to society and contribute to the inefficient use of resources.

Minority groups

Among the most significant contributing factors to inequality, particularly in nations like the United States, critics claim, are discrimination and social injustices committed against minority groups, particularly women and blacks. The statistics presented in Topic 5, which looks at whether race and inequality are related, suggest that in 2002 African Americans earned less than two-thirds of the average white person's income. Similarly the female average income in 2000 was less than three-fourths of the median income of a man; Topic 6 discusses whether women are more likely to be poor than men.

Although there are without doubt greater opportunities for minority groups today, some of the barriers that historically have stood in the way of their economic advancement still exist,

including inadequate access to education and problems in occupational advancement: The poor quality of inner-city, predominantly minority-attended schools, inadequate access to affordable childcare for single parents, and banking and credit constraints, among other factors, have contributed to economic inequality among these groups. Some of these issues are discussed in Topics 5 and 6.

The role of taxation

Among the issues raised when discussing inequality is how to best achieve more equitable redistribution of resources. The effectiveness of taxation—on income or on goods and services—in doing this is often debated.

According to the Luxembourg Income Study, more people in the United States suffer from extreme relative poverty than in other high-income countries. Some economists believe that further aggravating this trend has been the declining distributional effectiveness of the U.S. tax system since 1980. The percentage increase in inequality was greater for posttax, posttransfer income than for pretax, pretransfer income over the last two decades. In other words, according to some experts, tax and welfare policies have exacerbated rather than helped reduce income inequality. The reduction in total cash public assistance and the relative decline in assistance going to the nonelderly poor are also important factors contributing to this situation.

Topics 7 and 8 consider the role of the tax system in income redistribution and promoting equality. A growing concentration of income among a tiny percentage of people, many experts

and more women and children in particular are living below the poverty line, cash assistance, food stamps, and public housing are among the most effective ways of helping the poor to have a basic standard of living; they also give these people a chance to break the cycle of poverty. Topic 9 discusses some of these issues in its analysis of whether welfare perpetuates poverty.

""Look at what's in your hand instead of complaining about what you don't have.... See what you have and work with it."
—MORGAN FREEMAN, AFRICAN AMERICAN ACTOR

---

argue, diminishes opportunities for the advancement and well-being of the less wealthy. Income redistribution through a progressive tax system is one way to redress any imbalances. Social insurance programs—including retirement (social security) payments and health-care insurance for the elderly, and unemployment insurance, workers' compensation and disability insurance for the nonelderly—are often financed through taxes on earnings.

Many people are resistant to the idea of progressive income taxation, however, arguing that high-earners are being penalized for working hard. They believe that welfare promotes a "something for nothing" attitude among the poor. Such critics claim that income-assistance programs foster dependency, and once someone receives welfare, he or she is unlikely to want to seek paid employment. Advocates counter that this thinking is wrong primarily since this is not the reasoning behind low-income assistance programs. As the divide between rich and poor increases,

Comparative problems

Some experts believe that many of today's social and economic problems stem from income inequality. Sociologists have highlighted some of these areas as being ill health due to bad diet or malnutrition, increased rates of truancy from school, higher levels of juvenile delinquency and teenage crime, decreased job security among low-wage workers, and an increase in stress-related ailments and mental illness.

Observers argue that many of these issues are usually associated with developed societies. For the more than one billion people globally who live on less than $1 a day, the problems faced are far more fundamental. Many do not have adequate water security, for example—a fact made even more difficult by the high incidence of water supplies controlled by transnational corporations. TNCs often charge water rates that the poor cannot afford; many believe that such resources should be free. Topic 10 examines this issue.

Topic 5

IS INCOME INEQUALITY RELATED TO RACE?

YES

"PROSPERITY CAN'T CLOSE METRO AREA INCOME GAP"
THE DETROIT NEWS, SEPTEMBER 10, 2002
BRAD HEATH

NO

FROM "CONTEXT, PLEASE"
NATIONAL REVIEW ONLINE, MAY 18, 2004
J.A. FOSTER-BEY

INTRODUCTION

In any debate on income inequality the issue of race is almost always raised as an influential factor. While some observers claim that ethnic minorities are discriminated against in the workplace, earning far less than their white counterparts for doing the same jobs—if they get the jobs at all—others insist that protective legislation and affirmative action policies (which give minority groups preferential treatment in education and the workplace) have resulted in improved employment opportunities and income levels in general. Others see factors such as gender as being far more relevant to any income inequality discussion.

In the United States some commentators claim there has been a significant improvement in the lives of minority groups since the 1960s, when legislation, such as the 1963 Equal Pay Act and 1964 Civil Rights Act, was introduced to help counter prevailing inequalities in society. Many assert that research shows that in health, education, and housing, among other areas, the situation for ethnic minorities has also improved: They now have more opportunities than ever before. Some experts, including economists, counter that improvement is not the same as equality, however.

In 2002 the Census Bureau published a report on income in the United States. It concluded that real median (average) household money income had declined by 1.1 percent between 2001 and 2002 to a level of $42,409 from $42,900. It also found that in 2002 African Americans earned on average $29,177 compared to the $44,964 earned by the average white person (including Hispanics); whites (excluding Hispanics) averaged $46,900. This data shows that race does have an influence on income, observers say.

Critics argue that income disparity is not confined to low-paid and unskilled employment. In 2002 the U.S. Office of

Professional Management noted that Native Americans in professional positions earned over $12,000 less than the national annual average. Similarly, the National Asian Pacific American Legal Consortium claims that white college graduates earn 11 percent more than their Asian peers.

Critics claim that it is easy to manipulate statistics to prove a point. Some state that income levels inevitably vary according to region, and that while in some places whites earn more than other racial groups, in other areas the situation is reversed. Research shows, for example, that in Washington, D.C., which has a 60 to 40 percent black to white population, black income rose by 8 percent between 1989 and 1999, whereas white income rose by 13 percent. In Portland, Oregon, however, the income of the 6.6 percent black population increased by 29.7 per cent, compared to the 16.4 percent rise experienced by the white population. Factors such as education, types of local industry, and gender makeup also come into play in income–race studies.

> ## "Education helps all workers."
>
> —AMY HANAUER, POLICY MATTERS, OHIO (NONPROFIT POLICY RESEARCH INSTITUTE)

In 2004, for example, journalist Jennifer Hicks published an article in which she asserted that men earn between 23 to 54 percent more than women. She claimed that even among physicians and surgeons (the highest earners) the median wage for a man was $140,000, compared to $88,000 for a woman. This suggests that even educated women have not achieved income parity.

The Bureau of Labor Statistics, meanwhile, supports the idea that income is influenced by education. High-school dropouts are around twice as likely to have an income below the poverty line than graduates, for example. Data also shows that people who drop out of school before getting a high-school diploma are far more likely to be of African American or Hispanic origin. Some people blame this on high immigration levels and the fact that large numbers of students have little or no English. The education system is not accommodating them properly, and these students are far more likely to drop out of school. Another explanation is that many single-parent families come from ethnic groups and are on or below the poverty line. They tend to be dependent on the earning power of their children, who quit school to get jobs: Census figures show that Hispanic high-school dropouts tend to be from poor families, for example.

Affirmative action was introduced to improve racial inequality. Supporters claim that it has helped improve the situation for many, but critics, both from white and ethnic minority backgrounds, argue that such preferential treatment increases racial intolerance. Others simply say that it is unnecessary: A 2001 survey found that around 40 to 60 percent of whites believed that economic parity between races had been achieved, and that most blacks earned at least as much as most whites.

Brad Heath and J.A. Foster-Bey further examine whether income inequality is related to race.

PROSPERITY CAN'T CLOSE METRO AREA INCOME GAP
Brad Heath

Brad Heath is a journalist for The Detroit News. This article appeared in the edition published on September 10, 2002.

YES

✓ A decade of prosperity swept unevenly through Metro Detroit, lifting the fortunes of blacks and other minorities, but still leaving them far behind their white neighbors, U.S. Census figures show.

That change was among the most dramatic symptoms of an income shift that brought an economic surge to some depressed corners of southeast Michigan and sent others reeling. Throughout the Metro area, black households in 1999 made 60 cents for every dollar of income in white households.

That's a marked improvement over 1989, when incomes in black households were scarcely half of what they were in white households. And it came as poverty rates among area minorities plummeted and education levels soared.

But the chasm that separates white and black in Metro Detroit remains vast. Blacks are four times more likely than whites to live in poverty and half as likely to have a college education, census figures show. Black households had a median income of $32,151 in 1999. Among whites, it was $53,920.

Given that more than 25 percent of America's population classifies itself as a race other than white, is enough being done to make sure that income disparities between races are ironed out?

"It's clear the color line in Detroit continues to be a very powerful factor," said John Logan, head of the Lewis Mumford Center in Albany, NY, which studies segregation. "But it's nice to see improvement. At least there are some signs that something is going right."

The findings are among the latest results of the 2000 U.S. Census and are based on the long form questionnaire sent to one of every six American households. The results are the most detailed glimpse in a decade of how we live and they illustrate clearly how the 1990s' economic boom was better for some Metro Detroiters than for others.

For instance:
• The gap between rich and poor widened slightly in Metro Detroit and throughout Michigan. That means the contrasts between the area's dying city neighborhoods and its wealthy suburbs are as stark as ever.

- While the incomes of people in many inner-city neighborhoods grew 25 percent or more, many suburban neighborhoods ended up less well off than they were in 1989, based on inflation-adjusted income growth.
- Women, whose incomes have long lagged behind those of men, made headway during the 1990s. In 1999, female workers made 67 cents for each dollar earned by a man, compared to 63 cents in 1989. That's because, statewide, men's earnings fell slightly while women's grew more than 7 percent.

Too much disparity?

But the most striking disparities remain those between black and white.

Terrence Fields understands. In the past decade, he went from putting together seats for Chevrolet trucks to being a supervisor for Canadian Pacific Railway. For him, it was a step in the right direction—a bigger paycheck without the volatility of the auto industry. But he'd still like to do better.

Do you think that the American dream still exists? Is it getting harder for poor people to move beyond poverty?

> *"Life is definitely improving," said Fields, 35, of Detroit. "I can definitely say I'm better off today than I used to be."*

Income for black households far outpaced income growth among whites in Livingston, Macomb and Wayne counties. The change was most evident in such places as Southgate and Bloomfield Township, overwhelmingly white communities where household income grew at least six times faster among blacks than it did among whites. In Oakland County, income for black households grew less than 2 percent, compared to more than 11 percent among whites. Income among Hispanics has grown, but not as rapidly.

Nationwide, progress in closing the economic divide separating white and black has been slow. And in at least 36 metropolitan areas throughout the United States, it actually grew wider during the 1990s, census figures show. The U.S. Census Bureau is releasing results of its survey a few states at a time, so a full nationwide comparison is not yet possible.

Is total equality really achievable in an ethnically diverse society? Or is inequality a natural phenomenon?

"There's no question the gap's still big, but any progress is good," said Kurt Metzger, research director for the Center for Urban Studies at Wayne State University.

Education levels rise

The upswing in minority income accompanied a big increase in education levels for black and Hispanic Metro Detroiters.

A 2004 article published in the British newspaper The Guardian stated that although the children of immigrants tended to be better educated than their white peers, they did not necessarily get the jobs they deserved and were often paid less than parity. Is this an argument for the continuance of affirmative action?

In Wayne County, for instance, the number of blacks with a high school degree jumped nearly 20 percent. The number with a bachelor's degree is up 25 percent.

A better education almost always adds up to better job opportunities—and more money—experts say.

Kevin Davis was among those who cashed in. The 30-year-old from Detroit has a degree from Morehouse College in Atlanta, and now makes almost $40,000 a year working for lawyers and lobbyists at General Motors. That puts him well ahead of many of the city's black households, whose median income is less than $30,000.

But living in the city means he doesn't have to look far to see the gaps that remain. "You can see there's not a lot of income coming into the city," he said.

Growth in cities

Much of the growth came in city neighborhoods that are still a long way from escaping poverty's stranglehold. In 1999, at the end of a decade marked by a strong economy and plentiful jobs, one of every four blacks in Metro Detroit still lived in poverty, compared to about 6 percent of whites. While poverty rates fell across the board in the 1990s, the sharpest decline was among blacks, the census shows.

In Detroit, the poverty rate among blacks dropped from 35 percent to about 26 percent, while remaining largely unchanged among whites and Hispanics.

Meanwhile, some suburbs suffered. In Farmington Hills, incomes scarcely budged during the 1990s—among whites and Asians they actually fell. And the change was more abrupt in other cities. In parts of Sterling Heights, Riverview, Dearborn and elsewhere, inflation-adjusted household incomes fell by a fifth or more.

Go to www.google.com, and search for statistics on other western nations with ethnically diverse populations, such as Great Britain and France. Are the situations for ethnic minorities similar?

"Things are not as easy as they were 10 years ago," said Robert Taipala, a 40-year-old Farmington Hills computer programmer. "You need two incomes to have the money one person used to make."

The case of Detroit

Is the relationship of black to white earnings as important as that of poor to rich?

Detroit is the only big city in the United States where blacks make more than whites, census figures show. In booming San Francisco, for example, blacks make less than half of what whites make. But that doesn't mean blacks in the Motor City are more affluent than elsewhere—it means the city's white households have incomes far lower than whites in other big cities.

But there's also evidence that some wealthy and middle-class blacks are doing what many white families did decades ago: packing up and heading for suburbia. Now, even in some affluent neighborhoods in West Bloomfield, Farmington Hills and Plymouth Township, black households are making more than whites.

Barbara Diggs is among those who left. Eight years ago, she took her two kids and moved to Southgate to escape city life. The more than $45,000 she makes as a Detroit community policing director puts her well ahead of most white residents of Southgate, but it wasn't money that lured her away from Detroit. "I miss the atmosphere of the city, but (Southgate) is a lot safer, a lot more orderly," she said.

Whatever progress they show, the Census Bureau's findings are still troubling, said Detroit Urban League President N. Charles Anderson. "I don't know anything fancy to say about it except that it points out the unfairness and discriminatory practices that still exist in our society," he said.

"Obviously it's good news that we're closing the gap. But it's bad news that we haven't closed it more."

Go to www.census.gov and find out if Ms. Diggs's income is above or below the median income for the United States.

The author ends by making a strong point—that things may have progressed but not far enough. A pithy or strong statement is a good way to end an argument or article.

CONTEXT, PLEASE
J.A. Foster-Bey

J.A. Foster-Bey was formerly a senior researcher and director of the Program on Regional Economic Opportunity at the Urban Institute. This article appeared in the National Review Online in 2004.

The National Urban League (NUL) is the oldest and and largest community-based organization "empowering African Americans to enter the economic and social mainstream." Go to www.nurl.org for more information.

When you construct a case against something else, breaking it up into easy-to-follow points should help your audience follow your reasoning. Is the author successful here?

NO

In a recent *Washington Times* column, Clarence Page expressed surprise that the National Urban League's 2004 edition of "The State of Black America: The Complexity of Black Progress" reported that over 40 percent of blacks surveyed for the report believed that there had been little or no improvement in the economic and social mobility of blacks since the passage of the 1964 Civil Rights Act. Such a conclusion seems difficult to square with the facts. However, reading the report provides some basis for understanding why so many black Americans believe so little has changed in 40 years....

For the first time the Urban League has attempted to capture the full picture of black economic, social, and political progress in one indicator: The Equality Index. According to the Equality Index, in 2004 African Americans' economic and social status is only 73 percent of white Americans', a figure that would certainly seem to support the conclusion among many blacks, and others, that little.... The problem is that the report has a number of flaws.

Problems with evidence

First, attempting to capture every aspect of black life compared to whites' in a single indicator is—to say the least—ambitious. Social reformers, researchers, scholars, and policymakers have always been interested in finding indicators that can provide a quantitative measure of success in the area of social change similar to the role that the profit margin plays in the private sector. The difficulty with this approach is that in order to achieve the simplicity and elegance inherent in a single indicator, one has to reduce the complexity and nuance of a multidimensional world into a single number. Even in the business world, profit indicators do not provide a full picture of a business's operation and long-term success. In fact, because profitability is actually the culmination of a number of factors related to business operation, any good manager spends a considerable amount of time analyzing a number of indicators in addition....

Second, the report attempts to talk about black progress, but instead tends to focus on a single snapshot in time. This unfortunately is a very common practice. If you want to show that poverty is deepening, or jobs are declining, or that blacks have made little progress, you focus on a single point in time rather than progress over time. Despite the questionable nature of using a single index to capture the full range of factors related to the progress of blacks compared to whites, the Equality Index might have some limited utility if it were measured over the 40 years since the Civil Rights Act of 1964 was passed. Instead the index simply examines one year. The 73 percent Equality Index score certainly seems to underscore blacks' lack of progress. However, would we draw the same conclusions if we knew that the Index was 35 percent in 1964? This type of progress would suggest that not only had blacks enjoyed absolute improvements in their status but that over the last 40 years they have progressed faster than whites.

Go to http://usinfo.state.gov/usa/infousa/laws/majorlaw/civilr19.htm to read the text of this act.

Does the author's argument make sense given that the world has changed greatly in the 40 years since the Civil Rights Act was passed? All citizens are considered equal under U.S. and international law. If this is not happening in reality, are new laws necessary to enforce equality?

Third, these types of multifactor indicators are very sensitive to how much weight is given to each factor. The actual value of the Equality Index could be easily improved (or made worse) by changing the importance (i.e., the weight) given to each of the factors that compose the index. For example, the Equality Index gives economic factors an importance of 30 percent. That is, the value of economic factors is multiplied by 30 percent and added to the other factors that compose the index. On the other hand, education, health, social justice, and civic engagement are given the weights of 25 percent, 25 percent, 10 percent, and 10 percent respectively. What would happen if we changed the weights assigned to each of these factors? By varying the importance of these factors in the index it is possible to increase the value of the Equality Index to 80 percent or reduce it to 67 percent. This suggests that the index may not tell us the actual gap between blacks and whites; instead, what it may actually reflect is the subjective values of the index's creators.

Fourth, the greatest potential flaw in the report's Equality Index, and in the report as a whole, is that it treats race as the only relevant dimension for judging social progress. In this report, differences in education, family status, gender, work history, and residential location have little if any bearing on the analysis. For example, blacks on average tend to have higher unemployment rates and lower earnings than whites. This finding could easily tend to lead one to believe that racial discrimination in the labor market remains an on-going problem. And, while it may be true that there continues to be some level of racial discrimination that affects blacks' labor-market status, comparing racial differences in average unemployment and earnings is misleading.

For example, it is well documented that workers with less than a high school education experience higher rates of unemployment and lower earnings compared to those with at least a high-school education. By 1999, the percentage of blacks 25 years and over without a high-school education was 28 percent compared to 16 percent for whites, while the proportion of blacks and whites with a college degree was 20 percent and 33 percent respectively. This means that in order to determine the true differences between blacks and whites it is critical to control for the differences in education between the two groups. Using data from the 2000 census, I calculated what the black–white earnings gap would be after controlling for education. It appears that roughly $4,600 in the black–white earnings gap can be explained by the differences in educational attainment. Put another way, if blacks and whites had the same level of educational attainment then $4,600 in the annual earnings gap between the two groups would disappear.

In addition to educational differences, there are other factors that also contribute to the racial-earnings gap. For instance, single female-headed households with children tend to have lower incomes than two-parent households. Because blacks have a disproportionately high number of such households, this also tends to depress racial earnings and labor-market participation vis-à-vis whites. Moreover, these factors not only influence labor-market earnings, but also affect a range of other social and economic indicators, such as employment rates, home ownership, wealth creation, and interaction with the criminal-justice system.

Interpretation

What does all this mean? ... What it does suggest ... is that if one is interested in understanding the actual progress and status of blacks—or for that matter any other group—it is critical to do the following:

* First, examine group progress over time. Even if the Urban League's Equality Index was a perfect measure of racial status, progress can only be determined by assessing the measure over time. As any parent knows, it is hard to appreciate the growth and development of a child by simply looking at the last picture you took at the most recent birthday party. In order to determine if things are changing you need to review a series of pictures over time.

Would the author's argument be more convincing if he or she explained his or her process?

Many people believe women are still treated as inferior to men. Go to Volume 1, Individual and Society, Topic 3 Are women still the second sex?

Using visual imagery can help focus your audience's attention. Is this a good comparison?

• Second, control for differences in education and other factors that tend to have an independent influence on social and economic status. …

• Third, use groupings that transcend race and ethnicity. For example, when blacks and whites are grouped according to educational attainment, are there differences in economic and social status between blacks and whites within educational groupings? Given that it is reasonable to expect those with similar levels of educational attainment to have similar social and economic experiences, if black college graduates were to earn less than white college graduates then we may have uncovered a real racial difference. This does not mean that racism is the only explanation, but it does suggest that there is a racial difference that ought to be examined more closely.

Go to http://www.nation master.com/ graph-T/eco_pop_ bel_med_inc, and look up income levels for the United States and for a predominantly nonwhite nation such as South Africa. Does the white population earn more than the median in each case?

Legacy of racism?

Many well-meaning observers will say that it is the historical legacy of racism that is responsible for low levels of educational achievement and problems such as female-headed households. Indeed, some of these observers will even go so far as to assert that it is not just the legacy of historic racism, but on-going racial discrimination that continues to plague African Americans. Even if these observers are correct, they would be hard pressed to demonstrate empirically that there have been no substantive improvements in the economic and social status of blacks in the United States over the last 40 years. Moreover, it would still be better and would lead to more effective policymaking to determine the extent of racial differences after properly controlling for factors such as education and family makeup. For example, given that we know that education is critical to economic success, and if children from low-income families are at a higher risk of not finishing school, or finishing with below average skills, policies aimed at improving school performance such as No Child Left Behind, or school choice, are likely to be the most effective strategies for reducing racial differences.

For more information on this see Volume 16, Education, Topic 1 Can the No Child Left Behind Act work?

The challenge for blacks—and for the nation—is to distinguish between the real progress made in black economic and social status over the last 40 years, while also recognizing those arenas where improvements still need to be made. A more balanced report would attempt to do this. Most of all, a balanced report would attempt to treat blacks as a socially and economically diverse group, and move beyond using race as the primary factor in explaining differences.…

Summary

The relationship between race and income inequality is a complicated one. In the preceding articles Brad Heath and J.A. Foster-Bey look at the issue.

Brad Heath, in the first article, claims that although U.S. Census 2000 figures seem to indicate improvements in income and educational achievements for African Americans living in Metro Detroit, Michigan, there is still inequality between white and black income. He states that blacks are four times more likely than whites to live in poverty and half as likely to have a college education, census figures show. He also argues that black households had a lower median income of $32,151 than whites, who earned $53,920 in 1999. He also quotes people who claim that the situation has improved and that more blacks are staying in education, among other things, although most conclude that there is still a long way to go before equality is achieved.

J.A. Foster-Bey, in the second article, examines the situation for African Americans as described in the National Urban League's "Equality Index" of 2004. He is critical of this report for several reasons. He believes that it is far too ambitious. Foster-Bey provides a point-by-point analysis of where the report is flawed. He suggests that a survey of data since 1964 might reveal more realistically how far African Americans have progressed in comparison to whites. In addition, he argues that the way that data is weighted is subjective. He accuses the report of neglecting nonracial factors such as education and social grouping. The author concludes by calling for a more balanced report that may reveal more about the many causes of inequality and that may also treat blacks as a socially and economically diverse group.

FURTHER INFORMATION:

Books:

Arrow, Kenneth, Samuel Bowles, and Steven Durlauf (eds.), *Meritocracy and Economic Inequality*. Princeton, NJ: Princeton University Press, 1999.

Useful websites:

http://www.guardian.co.uk/racism/Story/0,2763,596856,00.html
Article in the British newspaper *The Guardian* on how the children of immigrants are better educated but tend to have higher unemployment levels or lower incomes for similar jobs.

www.inequality.org
Looks at poverty and inequality and provides links to other sites.

http://www.wsws.org/articles/2001/jul2001/us-j13.shtml
Examines a 2001 Pew Study on inequality.

The following debates in the Pro/Con series may also be of interest:

In this volume:

Part 2: Social and economic issues, pages 62–63

Topic 6 Are women more likely to be poor?

In *Individual and Society:*

Topic 6 Should affirmative action continue?

IS INCOME INEQUALITY RELATED TO RACE?

YES: *Census data shows that people from African American and Hispanic backgrounds are more likely to drop out of school than white students*

YES: *Rising income levels have not closed the gap between black and white earnings*

PROGRESS
Is income inequality between races still a long way off?

EDUCATION
Does education disadvantage minorities?

NO: *Statistics indicate that the situation for many racial groups has improved drastically since the 1960s*

NO: *Immigrant parents tend to make their children work harder and stay in education longer. The children tend to be better educated and high achievers.*

IS INCOME INEQUALITY RELATED TO RACE?

KEY POINTS

YES: *Affirmative action has helped many ethnic minorities enter previously restricted and better-paid industries*

YES: *Ingrained prejudice prevents ethnic minorities entering or rising within certain professions. Research shows that even where such people have managed to get jobs, they are often paid less.*

AFFIRMATIVE ACTION
Has affirmative action improved the incomes of ethnic minority groups?

PREJUDICE
Do employers discriminate against ethnic minorities?

NO: *Evidence shows that affirmative action policies have increased resentment toward ethnic minorities and have not helped raise incomes*

NO: *Laws such as the Equal Pay Act and Civil Rights Act help prevent discrimination and support minorities*

Topic 6
ARE WOMEN MORE LIKELY TO BE POOR?

YES
"WOMEN IN POVERTY"
THE IRAQ JOURNALISM PROJECT, DEPARTMENT OF COMMUNICATION,
UNIVERSITY OF WASHINGTON, MAY 27, 2003
MARILYN HARTLAUER

NO
FROM "SHE WORKS, HE DOESN'T"
NEWSWEEK, MAY 12, 2003
PEG TYRE AND DANIEL MCGINN

INTRODUCTION

In 1980 the United Nations (UN) concluded that women make up about half of the world's population, do two-thirds of the world's work, earn one-tenth of the world's income, and own one-hundredth of the world's property. Today many people argue that women continue to bear an unequal share of the burden of poverty: Some reports indicate that 70 percent of the world's poorest people are women, the majority of whom live in developing nations.

Many commentators, however, believe that women's prospects are gradually improving. While statistics suggest that women are still more likely than men to be poor, the number of people in the world living in poverty has fallen since the 1990s. Moreover, some experts question the high ratio of poor women. They argue that reliable statistical evidence of gender bias in poverty is lacking. They point out, for example, that studies only occasionally rely on household surveys, which are the best method of gauging poverty levels.

Others, however, say that if anything, the gap between the numbers of men and women living in poverty is growing wider. This phenomenon is known as the "feminization of poverty." Women worldwide earn on average just over half of what men earn. This inequality is not limited to the developing world. In 2004 the Institute for Women's Policy Research reported that women who worked full time in the United States earned 77 cents for every $1 earned by their male counterparts. Some 60 percent of American women who work are employed in 10 female-dominated occupations such as sales, clerical, and service jobs, which are usually among the lowest-paid jobs.

Women not only often receive less pay than men, but they also have less choice in the kind of work available to them. Single mothers, for example, frequently have to work part time in order to manage childcare. The UN Development Fund for Women (UNIFEM) Biennial Report for 2000 showed that in the United States there were 141 women for every 100 men living below the poverty line, and that many of them were single parents. In addition many women are unable to earn any wage because they care full time for children or elderly relatives.

"The inevitable consequence of poverty is dependence."
—SAMUEL JOHNSON (1709–1784), ENGLISH WRITER AND CRITIC

In developing nations the situation of women is often compounded by repressive social conditions. Many studies indicate that educated women are likely to earn more and have better health, yet in sub-Saharan Africa, for example, girls are about 80 percent less likely to receive an education than boys. Although elementary schooling is compulsory in most countries, girls in rural areas in particular are discouraged from attending classes and are often forced to leave school to work on family farms. Furthermore, in many countries women's inheritance and property rights are not guaranteed. As a result, commentators argue, women are more likely to be forced to take low-paid service jobs with long hours, no security, and few rights.

Nonetheless, some observers maintain that with support from agencies such as UNIFEM, women in both developing and developed countries can be freed from poverty. The UN Fourth World Conference on Women, held in Beijing, China, in 1995, identified the eradication of women's poverty as an area of concern for the international community, and around the turn of this century national governments began to focus their poverty-reduction policies on addressing the needs of women. China, for example, claimed that women accounted for 60 percent of the total number of citizens who benefitted from its poverty-eradication program in the late 1990s.

Most experts agree that providing women with access to economic and educational opportunities is crucial. The UN Development Program reports that today millions of women around the world are assisted by small loans to help them invest in local enterprises. For example, in Trinidad and Tobago, in the Caribbean, the Small Business Development Company has distributed 65 percent of its loans to women.

Commentators also point to positive trends emerging in the United States. American women are now gaining more college degrees and business qualifications than men. Although the gender wage gap is closing by only small increments each year, a University of Maryland report in 2003 suggested that in almost a third of U.S. households with a working wife, the woman earns more money than her husband. According to some estimates, women now occupy almost half the country's high-paying executive, administrative, and managerial positions. Some observers have labeled these women "alpha earners." They attribute this trend to the growing acceptance of "househusbands" and to the large number of layoffs affecting male workers from the technology, finance, and media industries in recent years.

The following two articles address these issues in greater depth.

WOMEN IN POVERTY
Marilyn Hartlauer

Marilyn Hartlauer teaches in the Iraq Journalism Project, a reporting course focusing on the U.S. war with Iraq, at the University of Washington.

YES

✔ In 1994, then Texas Governor Ann Richards was soundly criticized for urging an audience of young girls to become self-reliant and to abandon the myth that "they could count on Prince Charming to take care of them."

Republicans branded Richards as "anti-family" then promptly defeated her in the 1994 election behind Republican candidate George W. Bush

It didn't take longer than one decade for studies on women and poverty to indicate Richards was right on target.

Ann W. Richards (1933–) was the Democratic governor of Texas 1991–1995. She oversaw an upturn in the state's economy and was known for her unprecedented appointments of women and minorities to important positions.

Poverty is women's biggest problem

At the 2000 International Women's Day forum held in Tasmania, Australia, Council of Social Services director Lis De Vries said that poverty was the biggest issue facing females in the 21st century.

Ms. Vries called on women to band together and face the uncomfortable reality.

And the reality is, worldwide, women represent one half of the planet's population, but account for the 70 percent of the 1.3 billion people who live below the poverty threshold, Benedicte Manier said regarding a 1995 United Nations research report.

Single mothers

Not only are women over-represented in lower-paid, casual, seasonal and part-time jobs, but according to the report, 68 percent of those living in poverty worldwide are headed by single mothers, which represents one-third of all families. Some women are pushed into single-parent households through divorce, non-marital child-bearing or marital separation.

"A snapshot of the battle of the sexes has revealed that women who become the main breadwinners are more likely to live in poverty than their male counterparts," a January 2001 Scottish Household Survey indicated.

The survey also shows that families in which women are breadwinners, that is the source of household income, were the most likely to be dependent on state benefits for survival.

The Scottish Household Survey is a regular biennial study based on data collected from more than 15,000 households in Scotland. The most recently published survey is from 2001.

Burmese women refugees sewing in a sweatshop in Thailand. Women workers often have to work in poor conditions and with few health, maternity, and union rights.

"We talk about the feminization of the work force and the empowerment of women, but I think this survey shows that many women in employment are just stumbling along and barely managing," Barbara Little, a Glasgow University sociologist said of the Scottish survey.

Lower pay

Experts blame the high number of women and children living in poverty to many factors, including the fact that of the 848 million working women in the world, incomes are generally 30–40 percent less than that of men. For example, in the United States, women working full-time earn 76 cents for every dollar men earned in 2000, according to a recent report from the AFL-CIO and the Institute of Women's Policy Research. Working U.S. women earn a median income of $24,973, while the median income for men is $33,674 according to the 2000 U.S. Census Bureau.

Arguments justifying higher pay for men who have families to support are outdated, said Dianne Bruce of the YMCA [Young Men's Christian Association], who works with

Even though women are earning wages, that does not mean they are managing to live adequately. The phrase "feminization of poverty" refers to the phenomenon of the increasing gap between men and women living in poverty. Go to http://www.un.org/ womenwatch/daw/ followup/session/ presskit/fs1.htm for a United Nations fact sheet about this issue.

The American Federation of Labor–Congress of Industrial Organizations (AFL–CIO) is a grouping of labor unions that represents more than 13 million U.S. working men and women. Go to www.aflcio.org to visit the website.

teenage mothers trying to support their children and women trying to establish independence from abusive partners.

"These women need higher pay because they have families to support," Bruce said.

"The truth is, one quarter of all working women are paid poverty level wages," said AFL-CIO president Lane Kirkland at a convention of bakery, confectionery and tobacco workers in Las Vegas July 1994.

"Today, economically disadvantaged women have little choice but to accept work, when they can find it, from the expanding sector of employers who have concocted every conceivable method of keeping wages down and workers powerless."

Closing the gender wage gap

The National Committee on Pay Equity (NCPE) organizes the observance of Equal Pay Day each year to raise awareness about unfair wages for women and ethnic minorities in the United States. Go to http://www.pay-equity.org/day.html for details.

In August 2001, at a three day event marking "Pay Equity Day," in Worcester, Massachusetts, James P. McGovern, a U.S. Representative said at the discussions on proposed legislation aimed at eliminating the nation's gender wage gap that "if we can lift the wages of working women in this country to where they should be, we can lift women out of poverty."

However, many do not understand that equality does not just mean improving the circumstances of women, Leung Lai-chung, a university professor and former chair of the Association for the Advancement of Feminism, said at the 1995 United Nations Conference on Women in Beijing.

"We need to get rid of gender bias in all policies and enhance public awareness of women's rights under existing laws," Lai-chung said.

Do you agree that many societies across the globe are still a "man's world"? What about your own society?

Women face an uphill struggle to promote economic equality in societies that are still very much a man's world, Linda Yeung said at the 1995 Conference on Women in Beijing.

The poorest of the poor

Women are the poorest of the poor, and poverty of women is one of the central indicators of inequality, Shelagh Day, co-author of a study entitled *Poverty and the Equality Deficit*, said at a session of the Human Rights as Global Security conference in April 2002.

Would it help the argument to explain the term "structural discrimination against women"? Can you think of any examples?

"It is not an accident women are poorer than men," Day said. "It's a manifestation of long-standing, structural discrimination against women."

Day points to the facts that being single, a mother and unattached are significant indicators of poverty.

The oppression of women flourishes today despite efforts by the United Nations to pave the way for women's equity. Poor women are sexually commodified and subordinated in their daily interactions with men, Day said. "They accept it because it's a way to survive … and they have no political voice."

What do you think Day means by saying that poor women are "sexually commodified"? Do you agree with her?

War and women

"Sometimes national, ethnic, and religious problems and historical hostilities trigger dozens of regional wars and armed conflicts, whose major victims are women," said Sunila Abeyesekera, director of Inform, a human rights organization regarding military conflicts in Iraq.

War and conflict push women into decision making positions in their families and communities, in particular into the role of head of household and breadwinner to support their children, Abeyesekera said. "War and poverty not only affect women, but whole families."

In October 2000, thousands of protesters converged in Brussels, Belgium as part of an international "World March of Women" to draw attention to women's problems around the world.

The idea for the World March of Women came from the Women's March against Poverty, which took place in Quebec, Canada, in 1995, when 850 women marched for 10 days to win nine demands relating to economic justice.

"When you hear of social exclusion, unemployment, low wages, it's always the women who are the first affected," Belgium's Vice Premier Laurette Onkelinx said at the event.

The Brussels demonstration was one of the more than 4,000 events organized around the world under the World March of Women banner since the movement began in March 2000 outside the U.N. Headquarters in Geneva.

Experts agree that more arduous work is to be done if we are to fully achieve the general goal of equity for women around the world.

Full-time working women still make up two-thirds of those working at minimum wage. The "path to poverty," as Governor Richards points out begins the day women start working at low wage, no benefit jobs.

As Richards put it, "When Mama works, she's usually not an architect or a lawyer."

Statistics suggest that more U.S. women are getting college degrees than men. Do you think this will change the careers women pursue? Will some women continue to put their families before their careers?

Richards said there are some obvious solutions. First, equal pay for equal work. Second, better enforcement of anti-sex bias laws. And third, women in particular, should become educated on personal finances.

Richards wants young women to get the message that while marriage and motherhood are worthy goals, they must grow up educated, savvy about money and capable of supporting themselves.

What do your female classmates think about Richards's message to young women?

SHE WORKS, HE DOESN'T
Peg Tyre and Daniel McGinn

Peg Tyre and Daniel McGinn are journalists who write for the weekly magazine Newsweek. This article was published in May 2003.

NO

Since the beginning of time, anthropologists believe, women have been programmed to seek a mate who can provide for a family—whether that means dragging the mastodon [extinct mammals] back to the cave or making the payments on the Volvo. So when Laurie Earp walked down the aisle, she joined hands with a man most brides would consider a good catch: a lawyer.

"By marrying a lawyer," she says, "I thought he'd be able to bring in money." Freed from the need to earn a big paycheck, Laurie imagined herself in a part-time job, one that allowed her to spend long afternoons with their children.

For a time the Earps realized that vision. Jonathan earned a six-figure salary as a lawyer at [internet music company] Napster, while Laurie worked leisurely hours as a fund-raising consultant. But last May Jonathan was laid off; he still can't find work. So, reluctantly, Laurie has become the breadwinner....

Downsized dads

"White collar" refers to professional or clerical workers whose job at one time called for a dress code often typified by the wearing of a shirt and tie. The phrase dates from the 1920s.

Like several million American families, the Earps are experiencing the quiet, often painful transformation that takes place when Dad comes home with a severance package. The unemployment rate hit 6 percent last month, and while that's low by historical standards, some economists say it underestimates the difficulties facing laid-off workers— especially white-collar men who've been victimized by corporate downsizings. Despite Alan Greenspan's predictions of rosier times on the horizon, some experts talk of a growing problem of "underemployment" that goes beyond the nation's 8.8 million jobless....

MBA is the abbreviation for Master of Business Administration, the highest qualification in business studies.

The good news, at least for the 1.7 million unemployed men who are married, is that their wives are better equipped than any generation in history to pick up the financial slack. Women are currently earning more college degrees and M.B.A.s than men. In 1983, women made up 34 percent of high-paying "executive, administrative and managerial" occupations; in 2001 they were nearly half of that category. They've also weathered the recession better than men, because traditionally female industries like health care and education have suffered less than male-dominated businesses like manufacturing. Although the average woman's wage still trails a man's (78 cents to the dollar), enough women are breaking into better-paying professions that in 30.7 percent of married households with a working wife, the wife's earnings exceeded the husband's in 2001. Many of these women were born and bred for the office; they wouldn't want it any other way.

Within these homes, some of the husbands have voluntarily dialed back their careers (or quit work entirely) to care for kids and live off their wives' income. Some experts use a new phrase to describe high-income female providers: Alpha Earners. For some families, this shift works wonderfully; for others (especially those forced into it by layoffs), it creates tensions. Regardless, it's a trend we'd better get used to. Like runners passing the baton in a track event, many 21st-century couples will take turns being the primary breadwinner and the domestic god or goddess as their careers ebb and flow....

How many alpha earners?

Most experts believe the number of families converting to the "Mr. Mom" lifestyle remains quite small. According to the Bureau of Labor Statistics, just 5.6 percent of married couples feature a wife who works and a husband who doesn't. But that information is misleading: most of those nonworking husbands are retired, disabled or full-time students, not househusbands who care for the kids. On the other hand, many of the men who have put their careers on the back burner to watch the kids still have part-time or entrepreneurial gigs of some sort, so they don't show up in that number. So to better understand the Alpha Earner phenomenon, some researchers focus instead on those households where the wife outearns the husband. They're crunching the data to eliminate men who are retirees or students, and to seek families where the wife's career appears dominant (by finding, say, households where the wife earns 60 percent or more of the family income). Until the 1990s these numbers were tiny. But University of Maryland demographer Suzanne Bianchi recently began analyzing new 2001 data. Her initial results suggest that 11 percent of marriages feature an Alpha Earner wife.... [I]n the *Newsweek* Poll, 54 percent of Americans said they "personally know a couple where the woman is clearly the major wage earner and the man's career is secondary."

The shift is showing up more frequently in pop culture, too. *Friends* fans spent much of this season watching Monica

The phrase "alpha earner" plays on the description "alpha male," which refers to the socially dominant animal in a group. Do you think labels like this are helpful in such debates?

What are the advantages of men and women taking turns in being the primary breadwinner? Are there any disadvantages?

Do you think changes in who the major breadwinner is will affect how people assess their potential spouses?

Do you think that popular culture accurately reflects the true position of women in U.S. society today? Is the authors' use of pop culture references useful to their argument?

support her unemployed husband, Chandler…. Eddie Murphy hits theaters this week in *Daddy Day Care*, in which he plays a laid-off dad whose wife becomes the primary breadwinner. In bookstores, Alpha Earners are at the heart of Allison Pearson's novel *I Don't Know How She Does It* and *The Bitch in the House*, a collection of feminist essays. "There are few things that make a man less attractive to women than financial instability," writes one contributor. "We can deal with men in therapy, we can deal with men crying, but I don't think gender equality will ever reach the point where we can deal with men broke."…

Deciding who works

Many … couples have simply decided that no matter how much lip service companies pay to "family friendly" policies, it's simply not possible to integrate two fast-track careers and kids without huge sacrifices. So they do a cold-eyed calculation, measuring the size and upside potential of each parent's paycheck, and opting to keep whoever's is larger. For the highest-achieving women, the trend is striking. Last fall *Fortune* reported that more than one third of its "50 Most Powerful Women in Business" have a stay-at-home man (it dubbed them "trophy husbands"). But this trend reaches women far below the executive-vice-president rank….

Ms. Magazine *was founded in 1972 by Gloria Steinem (1934–) and other feminist activists. Its title came from the then-current controversy over how to address women correctly. "Ms." is still preferred by many women since it gives no indication of marital status.*

Feminists see the emerging era—when it's no longer the default choice that the kids will be watched by Mom, the nanny or a day-care center—as a necessary evolution. "The first half [of the feminist vision] was to liberate women from domestic servitude," says Suzanne Levine, a founding editor of *Ms. Magazine*…. "The second half was to integrate the men back into the family." But while many dads now help with 3 A.M. feedings, it hasn't led to wholesale acceptance of wives as breadwinners. In the *Newsweek* Poll, 41 percent of Americans agreed that "it is much better for everyone involved if the man is the achiever outside the home and the woman takes care of the home and family." … While those attitudes may fester, the data suggest women's economic power will only grow. And as you plot out those trend lines [over] a few decades, it's easy to imagine more dramatic implications. For example, conventional wisdom is that once a man earns a certain income, whether his wife works becomes optional. Does that mean work will become equally optional for men whose wives bring home big paychecks?… [I]t appears so: in the *Newsweek* Poll, 34 percent of men said that … if the wife landed a big pay raise, the husband would consider not working or reducing his hours.

Why do you think people's attitudes often take much longer to change than their circumstances?

Redefining "good catch"

Here's a related twist: we know many women consider a man's earning potential when choosing spouses…. But as women's earnings rise, are more men paying attention to women's earning potential when they choose a mate? Yes, says University of Wisconsin economist Maria Cancian, who believes high-earning women are starting to be seen by men as a "good catch." As for high-powered women, Cancian wonders if their view may be changing, too. "Are we now in a situation where very career-oriented women might look for husbands that are less career oriented" and better equipped to nurture the kids full time?…

> Do you think it is a positive thing that the traditional working roles of men and women are changing? See Volume 1, Individual and Society, Topic 3 Are women still the second sex?

Future career changes

For many couples, switching in and out of roles may become a routine part of life. Counselors say that 21st-century careers will involve more jumps between industries and more time out of work for retraining or as a result of downsizing. Ted and Jenny Cater, 40 and 43, already have that routine down pat. In 1999 Ted, a salesman, relocated to San Francisco with his company. When his employer went bankrupt, Jenny, who works in marketing, immediately received a call about a $100,000-a-year job in Atlanta. So they moved her career to the front burner; Ted stayed home with daughter Megan. Then two months ago Jenny was laid off. They're expecting a baby next month, but by July they'll both be job hunting. "Whoever wins the best position wins a ticket back to coffee breaks…" Jenny says. "Not that we don't want to stay at home with the kids, but we are both geared for working."

Some younger couples are talking about these issues long before kids or joblessness enters their lives. Jennifer McCaskill is a 33-year-old Washington, D.C., lawyer; Ryan Schock, 28, is an accountant. As they look ahead to their September wedding, they're already talking about who might care for their future children. "Quite honestly, I don't want to stay at home," McCaskill says. "I won't make partner if I'm not working full time—and my earnings potential is higher." Schock's response: he'd love to be a full-time father. "He has a lot more patience than I do," McCaskill says. "I think he would be a better parent for our kids." With his master's degree and experience, Schock doesn't think a few years off would kill his career. "She would lose more than I would," Schock says. As more Alpha Earners roam the earth, that kind of outlook may be worth a premium. Forget doctors or lawyers. For a certain kind of woman, a laid-back guy like Ryan Schock may become the ultimate good catch.

> Do you think that whichever parent earns more should work regardless of which one is better suited to caring for the children?

Summary

In the first article academic Marilyn Hartlauer refers to comments made by former Texas Governor Ann Richards in 1994, when she was criticized for urging young American women to be financially self-sufficient. Hartlauer argues that Richards has since been proved right: Today poverty is the biggest issue preventing women's equality. Hartlauer summarizes the findings of a number of women's conferences and studies, including the 2000 International Women's Day Forum and the 1995 United Nations Conference on Women. She focuses her argument on working women in the developed world, particularly in the United States. Some experts believe that American women need higher pay than men since they are often supporting families as single parents. Hartlauer cites other commentators who urge action to remove policies and laws leading to gender bias and a gender-based wage gap.

In the second article journalists Peg Tyre and Daniel McGinn highlight a new phenomenon in which high-earning, or "alpha-earner," women work while their partners stay at home. Tyre and McGinn describe several cases in which conventional roles have been reversed, and the woman is the sole breadwinner. The authors relate this trend to other factors, such as the downsizing of large companies, which has led to many men being laid off. They point out that because women are now better educated, they are more likely to have jobs that can compensate for losses in family income. Experts admit that the number of alpha earners appears to be very small—partly because of the way statistics are measured—but suggest that around 11 percent of marriages contain higher-earning women.

FURTHER INFORMATION:

Books:

Albelda, Randy, and Chris Tilly, *Glass Ceilings and Bottomless Pits: Women's Work, Women's Poverty*. Cambridge, MA: South End Press, 1997.

Useful websites:

http://www.heritage.org/Research/Welfare/wm187.cfm
Heritage Foundation report on hardship and poverty.
www.marchemondiale.org
World March of Women site.
http://Observer.guardian.co.uk/print/0,3858,4671480-102275,00.html
British newspaper article on America's alpha earners.
www.unifem.org
Site for the United Nations Development Fund for Women, which works for gender equality.

The following debates in the Pro/Con series may also be of interest:

In this volume:

Topic 4 Should people have to look after their elderly relatives?

Topic 5 Is income inequality related to race?

Topic 9 Does welfare perpetuate poverty?

Part 3: International development

ARE WOMEN MORE LIKELY TO BE POOR?

YES: In many societies, especially in the developing world, women do not have equal access to education. Educated women are likely to earn more than uneducated ones.

YES: Women are often the main caregivers for children and the elderly or are the single head of a household. This limits their work opportunities.

EDUCATION
Are women poor through lack of education?

FAMILY
Are women poor because they are more likely to have family to support?

NO: Statistics show that more women are gaining degrees and professional qualifications, particularly in developed countries

NO: Governments are trying to help women with family commitments work, and employers are becoming more flexible over jobshares and part-time work

ARE WOMEN MORE LIKELY TO BE POOR?

KEY POINTS

YES: Globally, women work for roughly half the money earned by men. They are also less likely to inherit land or own property.

YES: Women from minority ethnic groups are doubly disadvantaged since many studies indicate that ethnic minorities earn less than their white counterparts for doing the same work

INEQUALITY
Are women treated less fairly than men?

RACE
Is race a factor in women's poverty?

NO: Equality of opportunity is law in many countries, and affirmative action policies are helping reduce discrimination

NO: White women also suffer from gender inequality and poverty. However, women are better protected by laws and policies in the developed world.

Topic 7

ARE INCOME TAXES AN EFFECTIVE WAY OF REDISTRIBUTING WEALTH?

YES
"TAX FACTS AND FAIR SHARES"
WWW.NOTNEWS.ORG, MAY 2001
DAVE THOMER

NO
FROM "LET'S ABOLISH THE INCOME TAX"
YOUR MONEY OR YOUR LIFE: WHY WE MUST ABOLISH THE INCOME TAX
SHELDON RICHMAN

INTRODUCTION

A tax is a compulsory charge imposed by a government on citizens. The main purpose of taxation is to finance government expenditure, including public services. Governments can also use taxation to promote social goals such as full employment. A more controversial use of taxation is to lessen inequalities in society through the redistribution of wealth. Governments can try to achieve this either by offering tax credits (reductions in tax owed) to poorer people or by using tax revenue to make welfare and social security payments to people who are unable to support themselves.

Direct taxes levied on individual and business incomes are the largest source of government revenue in developed countries, including the United States. The federal government collected about $1 trillion in personal income taxes and $211 billion in corporate income taxes in 2002. Most states and some local governments also collect income taxes.

The taxation of income, which was introduced in 1913, remains a contentious subject. Some better-off people question why they should be penalized for making money, while some poorer people ask how they can improve their situation when they have to pay tax on low earnings. Others oppose governments taking a share of their earnings in order to give handouts to people they believe are undeserving. Some people think a government has no business attempting to redistribute wealth, which is a policy they associate with left-wing politics such as socialism. However, governments in most democratic countries practice some kind of wealth redistribution, largely through income taxation, in order to achieve a more balanced society.

Many economists view income taxes as a fair form of taxation because they are direct and usually progressive. A direct tax refers to one that the government collects directly from the person on whom it is imposed. Since 1943 employers have been required to deduct part of an employee's pay and send it to the government to cover his or her estimated income taxes. This practice—known as withholding—has the advantages of making income tax one of the easiest taxes to collect and of supplying the federal government with a steady flow of revenue.

"Taxes are what we pay for a civilized society."
—OLIVER WENDELL HOLMES, JR.
(1841–1935), SUPREME
COURT JUSTICE

A progressive tax is one that places a greater tax burden on those of affluent means than on those of lesser means. For example, in 2004 the federal government taxed the highest-income earners at 35 percent of their income; the lowest earners were taxed at 10 percent. Thus, advocates maintain, a progressive tax reduces inequalities in the distribution of income. In contrast, sales taxes, which many states use to raise revenue, are seen as regressive: That is, they impose a heavier tax burden on those less able to bear it. For example, the tax on an item of clothing is the same for everyone, but in terms of proportion of income poor people pay more than wealthier ones.

However, critics say that progressive income taxes act as a disincentive for people to work hard and improve their earnings. The fact that the wealthiest 1 percent of U.S. taxpayers—those who earn more than about $300,000 a

year—pay more than a third of all income taxes, proves, some claim, that the system simply punishes the rich. Libertarians, whose doctrine stresses the rights of the individual, go further in their criticism. They oppose state intervention in the economy and view taxation as theft of private property. In the late 20th century libertarian economists such as Milton Friedman, Friedrich Hayek, and Ludwig von Mises argued that an economy functions best not when it is regulated by government but when market forces determine factors such as prices and wages. Inequality of wealth is an essential feature of the free-market economy, they believed, because it provides poor people with an incentive to improve their lives through hard work and to contribute to national prosperity.

Free-market economists claim their views were validated by the collapse of planned—government-controlled— economies in the Soviet Union and other communist countries in the late 20th century. These economies were regulated to effect a fairer distribution of wealth; however, while they eliminated extremes of wealth, they did little to ease life for the poor.

Some critics say that rather than being forced to pay high taxes, wealthy people should be encouraged to help the poor through charitable donations and other types of philanthropy. They argue that private charity is more efficient than public welfare because fewer resources are spent on overheads and tax collection. Commentators point out, however, that the federal tax system already promotes charitable giving by making contributions deductible from income taxes.

The two articles that follow debate the federal income tax system.

TAX FACTS AND FAIR SHARES
Dave Thomer

Dave Thomer is studying for a doctorate in philosophy at Temple University, Philadelphia. This article, dated May 2001, is taken from This Is Not News (www.notnewsorg), a website inspired by the works of the American philosopher John Dewey (1859–1952).

YES

The United States House of Representatives recently rejected a constitutional amendment that would have required all future revenue increases to be passed by a two-thirds supermajority of both the House and the Senate. Since few, if any, revenue increases ever pass by a two-thirds majority due to their unpopularity, the amendment would effectively forbid Congress from closing tax loopholes or raising tax rates in the future. Although the amendment failed, a majority in Congress supported it; the final vote was 232–189, short of the two-thirds majority required to amend the Constitution. Given the high degree of support, it stands to reason a measure like this will come before the House again; that support, along with the news that Republicans in Congress plan to pass a massive tax cut that will likely be weighted more toward the wealthiest taxpayers, tells me that we need to have an informed discussion of the nature and function of the federal tax system.

Progressive taxation

An example of a tax credit is the Earned Income Tax Credit (EITC). Available to low-income workers, the credit reduces the amount of tax an individual owes and is often returned in the form of a refund (rebate).

To lay my cards out on the table, I believe in a progressive, redistributive tax system. By progressive I mean a system in which wealthier citizens pay a greater share of their wealth in taxes, and by redistributive I mean a system in which those tax revenues are then used to improve the resources of poor and middle-class citizens, either by directly returning to them in the form of tax credits and rebates or by providing services that they would otherwise be unable to afford. Our current system imperfectly reflects these priorities, as progressivity and redistribution seem unfair to many Americans who therefore exert political pressure to keep rates low and open loopholes; a significant minority wish to impose a flat tax or eliminate most income taxes altogether. At first glance, they have a compelling argument; America is a capitalist society, built upon the notion of individual competition and achievement. Perhaps more importantly, we have enshrined respect for private property and transformed it into a fundamental right, conferred by human nature. Given these principles, why should citizens not be entitled to keep what they earn?

A flat tax would tax all income at one flat rate. Go to www.cse.org to find out more. Do you think such a tax reform would disadvantage the poor?

The reason is that I feel that concept of individualism is hopelessly outdated in a 21st century information/industrial era. As John Dewey argues in *Individualism, Old and New*, success in the new age is not achieved by a single person moving forward and taming the land alone. Instead, individuals must gather together, pool their resources and act collectively. The actions of one unavoidably influence the fate of another. Certain individuals find themselves in a position to roughly control the actions of these collective groups. In our current system, which tries to treat each individual as if he or she exists in a vacuum, these elites are entitled to a disproportionate share of the wealth that the collective creates. The rest of the organization is so many cogs in a machine, and while the mythology of the American Dream insists that anyone can pull themselves up by the bootstraps, the reality is that the resources necessary to achieve success are shared by a relative few. Unable to strike out on their own, and unable to fully participate in the functioning of the collectives of which they are part, many Americans languish as undifferentiated individuals, what Dewey calls "lost individuals." Once Americans understand and accept this shift, they can begin to confront the new reality as skillfully as they confronted the challenges of the frontier. [He says]:

> *The adventure of the individual, if there is to be any venturing of individuality and not a relapse into the deadness of complacency or of despairing discontent, is an unsubdued social frontier. The issues can not be met with ideas improvised for the occasion. The problems to be solved are general, not local.*

Dewey's relevance

Dewey's position makes a twofold challenge to the current structure:

1. It denies, or at least weakens, the individual entitlement to private property by denying that the individual is solely responsible for his or her success. This is not a denial of the role of the individual, but an attempt to understand the individual as being inextricably part of a larger whole. Many Americans take pride in home ownership, and justifiably so. But most if not all of these homeowners have more expensive homes than they would be able to afford in a pure capitalist housing market, if they could afford homes at all, because the federal government subsidizes homeowners through the tax deduction on mortgage interest. Does this

In Individualism, Old and New, *which he wrote in 1930, Dewey characterized the "old individualism" of America's pioneers as one of self-reliance and personal independence. In contrast, Dewey's "new individualism" of the modern age centered on monetary gain and enslavement to economic greed.*

According to some estimates, more than two-thirds of Americans are home owners. The right to own property is treated as equal to the right to life and to liberty in the Fifth Amendment of the Bill of Rights. Do you think there is too much pressure on people to own their home as part of the "American Dream"? Go to http://www.bizjournals.com/dayton/stories/2002/09/30/focus3.html to read an argument against raising home-ownership levels.

mean that homeowners should be less proud of their achievement? I don't think so. But I do think they should be aware that that achievement was assisted by a collective social action, and that therefore they have a certain obligation to the society that has assisted them.

2. It brings to the forefront the notion of equality of opportunity, the need for each individual to start from a relatively equal position in the competitive economic game. As my previous articles on the public education system attest, we fall far short on that score. Wealth buys access to education, technology, safety, better health, and who knows how many other advantages. The increasing concentration of wealth in a small number of hands denies these things to an ever-growing part of the population. Redistribution aims to address this fundamental imbalance, and give more people the capability to fulfill their potential and thus become true individuals.

Use the Internet to research statistics on the concentration of wealth in the United States. Why do you think the gap between rich and poor continues to grow?

Honest look at taxation

This is not to say I necessarily favor higher taxes, or that I believe that every federal program is a good one. Clearly, there are many wasteful programs which, if eliminated, would reduce the need for tax revenue. Those programs are protected by the same local voters who make tax hikes so hard to pass, by demanding that federal funds be spent in their area while at the same time wanting the federal government to have less funding. An honest look at how we finance our government will have to include these programs as well.

The Brookings Institution is an independent think tank based in Washington, D.C. Go to http://www.brook.edu/views/op-ed/gale/20000221.htm to read the Los Angeles Times *article by William Gale.*

A proposal by the Brookings Institution would make a good starting place for a discussion of a better, simpler, more equitable tax code. In an article in *The Los Angeles Times*, they propose that a new tax system:

April 15 is the deadline each year for taxpayers to file their tax return—a declaration of all income from the preceding year—with the Internal Revenue Service.

- Relieve between 40 million and 50 million households of the need to file tax returns. With small changes in withholding rules, this could be done for households that do not take itemized deductions and have income only from wages, Social Security, IRAs, pensions, unemployment insurance, interest and dividends.
- Cut the top rate from 39.6% to 30% and tax capital gains as ordinary income. Lowering the top rate would raise economic activity and reduce tax avoidance. Eliminating the differential between capital gains and other income would close down a significant amount of sheltering activity.

"Capital gain" is the profit earned from the sale of investments or property.

- Raise the standard deduction significantly. This would reduce the number of households that have to itemize their deductions.
- Confine the alternative minimum tax to operators of real tax shelters by drastically raising the exemption and indexing it for inflation. Do not force people onto this tax by virtue of their personal exemptions, standard deductions or state and local taxes.
- Remove the restrictions on itemized deductions and personal exemptions that affect high-income taxpayers. These are needless complications that raise little revenue.
- Make the tax credits for children, child care, education and adoption completely refundable, so that low-income households get the full value of the credit even if their income tax liability is zero. Eliminate the phase-outs of these credits as income rises.
- Consolidate and simplify all IRAs and related plans into one account with simple and clear contribution and withdrawal rules.

A "personal exemption" is a set amount that a taxpayer can claim for him- or herself to reduce the income subject to tax. The exemption amount changes each year. A website that explains tax terminology is http://www.irs.gov/app/understandingTaxes/jsp/s_tools_glossary.jsp, a glossary from the IRS.

"IRA" is an abbreviation of Individual Retirement Account.

This is a rough outline, but it is a start. It emphasizes fairness, fiscal responsibility, and simplicity. As such, it might be a system we can all support and understand, so that the next time legislators want to cripple the country's economic foundation, we'll be ready to oppose them.

LET'S ABOLISH THE INCOME TAX
Sheldon Richman

Sheldon Richman is senior fellow at the Future of Freedom Foundation, an organization that promotes individual liberty, free markets, private property, and limited government. This is an extract from his book Your Money or Your Life: Why We Must Abolish the Income Tax, published in 1999.

The United States first introduced personal income taxation as a temporary measure to help finance the Civil War (1861–1865). It was phased out by 1872. For the next 40 years most government revenue came from excise taxes and import duties. In 1894 the Supreme Court declared income taxes unconstitutional, but in 1913 the Sixteenth Amendment was ratified, allowing income tax to be imposed on individuals and corporations.

NO

Can we live without the Sixteenth Amendment, the income tax, and the Internal Revenue Service?...

[I]t might be better to ask if we can continue to live with them.... [T]he income tax is based on a fundamentally immoral notion: that the state has a prior claim on the fruits of a person's labor. That notion, which is a half-step removed from the slave principle, is at odds with the Jeffersonian idea that lies at the foundation of the American Republic: that every human being has a natural right to life, liberty, and the pursuit of happiness, which of necessity includes the right to use and dispose of honestly acquired property....

[W]hen the state is permitted to tax income a process is set in motion that inevitably reverses the traditional American relationship between citizen and government. In the original Jeffersonian vision the citizen was the master and the government was the servant. But with the advent of income taxation, that relationship began to change and eventually was reversed. When government seeks to tax income it will inevitably assume the powers required to carry out that mission. Those powers will enable it to delve deeply into people's personal affairs, destroying their financial privacy, ... and leaving them vulnerable to demands that they prove they have not violated the law....

Effect on the market economy

[I]ncome taxation undermines the market economy. By draining the people's savings and capital, the tax necessarily impedes their ability to create prosperity, to achieve financial independence, and to make a better society for everyone. Meanwhile, the income tax gives the state unprecedented access to wealth, bringing in huge revenues with which politicians and bureaucrats can attempt to shape society according to their liking and buy political support so they may stay in power and tax some more.... [P]olicymakers use the tax code to encourage and discourage behavior arbitrarily, undermining the spontaneous productive forces of society....

Since World War II, the personal income tax has been the largest source of federal revenue. In fiscal year 1997, it was expected to raise more than $791 billion, more than 45 percent of all receipts, in a budget of more than $1.7 trillion…. The corporation income tax was expected to bring in almost $198 billion more (12 percent), and the category known as "social insurance taxes and retirement receipts"— payroll taxes—was to capture more than $596 billion more (34 percent)…. The people's income has proven to be a mother lode for the U.S. government. Cut off from that kind of money, the size and scope of government would shrink fast. Imagine what would be possible with that amount left in people's pockets!…

What government should *not* do

In the original Jeffersonian, or libertarian, vision of America, the federal government had a few specified constitutional functions. Under the U.S. Constitution the federal government was permitted to exercise no powers other than those delegated by that document. All other powers were reserved to the states or the people. It is important to keep that framework in mind. If a power was not specified, the federal government could not assume it. That point was made over and over when, during the ratification debates, people demanded a Bill of Rights. Why is there a need for a Bill of Rights, defenders of the proposed Constitution asked?…

As a result of that philosophy, the federal government was limited. It has been noted that for much of the nineteenth century, an American could live his life without having contact with a federal official, except a postmaster.

The Progressive mindset

Somewhere along the line, the Founders' philosophy was turned on its head. Presidents, congressmen, judges, statist intellectuals, and later almost everyone else came to believe that the federal government should be able to do anything that is not expressly prohibited. That was the essence of the Progressive mindset. In the Progressive world-view, government needs the flexibility to respond to any contingency, to address any social problem, to right any wrong, to relieve any pain….

The early advocates of big government in America were offended that entrepreneurs were amassing fortunes in the industrial revolution. They were offended by income disparities. They were offended by new-fangled factories. They were offended by the poverty that had always existed but which the new prosperity now made more conspicuous. They failed to realize that free-market capitalism did not create poverty and was steadily reducing it. They looked at

"Mother lode" means principal source or supply.

Thomas Jefferson, third president (1801–1809), is often credited with saying, "That government is best which governs least"—a quote that is sometimes regarded as being the basic tenet of libertarianism.

Should we concern ourselves with the Framers' philosophy as long as the federal government functions effectively? Go to Volume 7, The Constitution, Topic 1 Does it matter what the original intentions of the Framers were?

the remains of the older, precapitalist world and assumed it was the fault of economic freedom and property rights....

Many of the people prospering under capitalism also wanted a new role for the state. Finding the competitive, profit-and-loss system too uncertain, businessmen often turned to government for protection from foreign and domestic competitors.... They felt more comfortable with a little insurance from the government.

But for the government to play the role of economic and social insurer, it must get into the wealth-transfer racket. Increasingly, government took wealth from producers and gave it to nonproducers because it had no resources of its own. Although from the beginning the federal government engaged in some transfer activities (the tariff primarily), the Progressives helped turn it into a veritable transfer machine....

Eventually it became accepted by almost everyone that the government was there to provide "services." Today there is no shame in seeking favors that others must pay for.... It is hard to know whether the people seeking government favors ever admit to themselves that the money first has to be taken from others before it can be given to them. Perhaps they rationalize by thinking that the money belongs to everyone. Or maybe they think that if they don't take the money someone else will. However they explain it, the moral compunction against asking the state to steal from one's neighbor gradually weakened and disappeared....

Observe the transfer state in action. Social Security imposes taxes on working people and hands the money to retired people. Medicare does almost the same thing, except the money goes to doctors and hospitals.... Welfare programs give the taxpayers' money to people who do not work. Subsidies reward well-connected business people with the hard-earned money of the middle-class and working class.... Government cultural agencies transfer wealth to artists, musicians, broadcasters, and humanities scholars. The education bureaucracy subsidizes trendy social experiments on children. The defense bureaucracy floods contractors with cash for equipment that is not needed and for missions that are improper. The list goes on and on....

The unwritten Constitution

The written Constitution was never enough to stop the growth of government. Constitutions are always interpreted by officers of the state, who usually have an interest in weakening any limits. The paper document must be

Is it fair to measure people's contribution to society purely in terms of their productivity?

A tariff is a tax on products imported from foreign countries.

Is taxation stealing? Could it equally be argued that people have a moral duty to help the needy if they have the means to do so? See Topic 1 Do wealthy members of society have a duty to help the poor?

Is the author right to label welfare recipients as "people who do not work"? Some payments go to people who are unable to work, rather than those who choose not to, as the phrase "do not work" might imply. Always be precise with your language in a debate.

buttressed by an unwritten constitution in the hearts and minds of the people. That is what provides the ultimate limits on the state....

Can the unwritten constitution be revived? If it is possible at all, it will be accomplished only through a libertarian moral revival.... When the residents of the colonies got mad at the Crown's stamp and tea taxes, they were showing a sensitivity to taxes that has not been seen in the United States for a long time. A libertarian moral revival would include that kind of high sensitivity to any talk about higher or new taxes. It would also prompt opposition to welfare-state programs, economic regulation, violations of civil liberties, and intervention in foreign conflict, on grounds that those all diminish freedom. The revival would see the megastate as the major threat in the world today.

Richman is referring to the anti-British protests that fueled the American Revolution. Go to http://www. historyplace.com/ unitedstates/ revolution/ rev-prel.htm for background information.

In sum, when people come to understand what liberty truly means, and when they value it as much as they say they do, they will be far less tolerant of government. They will be appalled at a political process that takes their money and gives it to their fellow citizens …

A libertarian crusade

The crusade has to start somewhere. What better opening target than the income tax? It combines the most egregious features of government power: theft, intimidation, violation of privacy, and arbitrariness. It is the perfect device for teaching people about the threat of power.... At the median income, a two-earner couple works eighty-seven days a year to pay their federal income and payroll taxes. Ironically, because of the structure of the income tax, that burden increases when the economy grows and falls when the economy slows. Americans are punished for being productive....

In what ways can income taxation be seen as a violation of privacy?

Abolition vs. reform

A campaign against the Sixteenth Amendment, the income tax, and the Internal Revenue Service would be doubly valuable. It would move us toward the explicit goal of abolition, and it would prepare people for the campaigns to follow against other forms of tyranny. The income tax cannot be reformed, because taxation of income has no place in a free society. It calls into being a multitude of evils that should offend anyone who values liberty....

Does the author's use of words such as "evils" and "tyranny" help or hinder his argument?

We must call for nothing less—and settle for nothing less— than the end of the Sixteenth Amendment, all taxation of income, and the IRS. That is the indispensable step on the road to freedom.

Summary

Many people disagree about whether income taxation is an effective way to redistribute wealth. In the first article Dave Thomer defends the progressive federal tax system against accusations that it contradicts the notions of individual competition and achievement on which American society is founded. Borrowing an argument from the philosopher John Dewey, Thomer claims that the concept of individualism is outdated and insists that people learn to act for the collective good. He maintains that without tax deductions on mortgage interest many home owners would not be able to afford to buy their properties, and that redistribution of wealth allows more people to "fulfill their potential and thus become true individuals." However, he agrees with some critics that reform emphasizing "fairness, fiscal responsibility, and simplicity" would garner more support for federal taxation.

In the second article Sheldon Richman argues that income taxation is based on the "fundamentally immoral notion" that government has a claim on individual earnings. This contradicts, he says, the Framers' philosophy that humans have the right to use and dispose of honestly acquired property. He claims that income tax undermines the economy by denying people the opportunity to create prosperity and thereby to make a better society. Richman outlines the growth of government and the wealth-transfer system in America, and complains that people no longer have any qualms about "asking the state to steal from one's neighbor." He concludes by urging a "libertarian crusade" against all taxation of income.

FURTHER INFORMATION:

Books:

Brownlee, W. Elliot, *Federal Taxation in America: A Short History* (2nd edition). New York: Cambridge University Press, 2004.

Friedman, Milton, *Capitalism and Freedom* (40th anniversary edition, with a new preface). Chicago: University of Chicago Press, 2002.

Slemrod, Joel, and Jon Bakija, *Taxing Ourselves: A Citizen's Guide to the Debate over Taxes* (3rd edition). Cambridge, MA: MIT Press, 2004.

Useful websites:

www.irs.gov
Internal Revenue Service site, includes a student guide to taxes and a glossary of tax terminology.

www.mises.org
Site for the Ludwig von Mises Institute, a libertarian think tank, with articles on taxation issues.

http://www.ustreas.gov/education/fact-sheets/taxes/ustax.html
Useful fact sheets on taxes from the Treasury Department.

The following debates in the Pro/Con series may also be of interest:

In this volume:
 Topic 8 Do indirect taxes discriminate against the poor?

In *Economics*:
Topic 8 Should wealth redistribution be part of government policy?

ARE INCOME TAXES AN EFFECTIVE WAY OF REDISTRIBUTING WEALTH?

YES: Revenue from income taxation funds programs that give everyone access to essentials like health care, social welfare, and education. Poor families also receive tax credits (refunds).

YES: Higher-rate taxpayers contribute the largest proportion of government revenue, which is then redistributed to those who need it more

EQUALITY
Can income taxes narrow the gap between rich and poor?

PROGRESSIVE TAX
Is a progressive system of taxation fair?

NO: People in low-paid jobs often have to pay some tax, making it difficult for them to improve their financial situation

NO: The current progressive tax system penalizes the wealthy for their hard work and initiative. The rich have to bear a disproportionate burden in taxes.

ARE INCOME TAXES AN EFFECTIVE WAY OF REDISTRIBUTING WEALTH?

KEY POINTS

YES: Compulsory income taxation provides a reliable source of revenue, enabling the government to plan and spend effectively

YES: Charity is not compulsory, and it would be difficult to ensure an equitable distribution of donations

ECONOMIC SENSE
Does income taxation make economic sense?

CHARITY
Is income taxation more effective than charity in redistributing wealth?

NO: High rates of income tax for the wealthy are a disincentive for prosperous business owners to invest and produce further wealth

NO: Charity is more efficient since money is not wasted on overheads and tax collection, so recipients gain greater financial benefit

Topic 8
DO INDIRECT TAXES DISCRIMINATE AGAINST THE POOR?

YES

FROM "TAXING HABITS"
REGIONAL REVIEW, QUARTER 1, 2003
PHINEAS BAXANDALL

NO

FROM "FAIRNESS AND FEDERAL TAX REFORM"
WWW.FAIRTAXVOLUNTEER.ORG
AMERICANS FOR FAIR TAXATION

INTRODUCTION

Taxes can be classified as either direct or indirect. A tax paid directly to the government by the person on whom it is imposed is known as a direct tax. An example is personal income tax. A tax that can be shifted to someone other than the person responsible for paying it is an indirect tax. An example is sales tax: Although it is imposed on and collected from the retailer, it is the consumer who actually pays the tax when he or she purchases a product.

Some observers believe that indirect taxes are unfair because they place a disproportionate burden on people with low incomes, who pay the same amount as those who are far wealthier. Others counter that alternatives based on direct taxation are easily exploited by people who have resources available to manipulate the system and avoid paying income taxes. In the United States there have been proposals to replace the federal income tax with a national sales tax, which, advocates

claim, would primarily tax the consumption of affluent taxpayers.

The federal government derives the bulk of its revenue from personal and corporate income taxes. Although most states and some local governments also levy income taxes, they rely largely on indirect taxes as a means of raising revenue. The majority of states impose a tax on the sale of goods and services based on a fixed percentage of retail cost. This has attracted criticism from some tax experts. They point out that a flat-rate sales tax is a regressive form of taxation: That is, the less income a taxpayer has, the higher the proportion collected in taxes. Since poor people and wealthy people both pay the same amount of tax if they buy the same item, sales taxes, critics say, are unfair on the poor, who spend most of their income on necessities. To offset this problem, some jurisdictions exempt basic goods such as food, clothing, or medicines from the sales tax.

In contrast, the federal system of graduated income taxes is a progressive form of taxation: Taxpayers are taxed at a higher rate the higher their incomes are. Thus, critics maintain, progressive taxes reduce the inequalities of income distribution, while regressive taxes increase them.

"The wisdom of man never yet contrived a system of taxation that would operate with perfect equality."
—ANDREW JACKSON, SEVENTH PRESIDENT (1829–1837)

Critics of indirect taxes claim that they discriminate against the poor in other ways. Both states and the federal government levy excise taxes—charges on the use or sale of specific products or transactions. Excise taxes on alcohol, tobacco, and gambling are commonly known as "sin taxes" since they are levied on what many people regard as unhealthy behavior or bad habits. Such taxes are generally more popular with voters than direct taxes on income and property on the grounds that they affect fewer taxpayers and can also be used to cover the high health-care costs incurred by smokers and drinkers. However, critics argue that the burden of sin taxes falls heavily on the poor, who are more likely to smoke and gamble than wealthier people. A report by the Congressional Budget Office in 2001 found that although tax on tobacco encourages people to quit smoking, those people are most likely to be middle- or high-income earners. The report concluded that affluent people can afford to try more effective antismoking programs, can turn to another vice, or simply have less reason to use smoking as a form of solace.

Some economists and politicians have long supported reform of the federal tax system. A 2003 proposal, introduced to Congress by Rep. John Linder as the FairTax Act, advocated the replacement of all income taxes, payroll taxes, and estate taxes with a 23 percent national retail sales tax. FairTax supporters claim that the federal tax system is overly complex and imposes high costs on consumers in the form of "hidden taxes" embedded in the price of goods.

While some commentators insist that income tax is the fairest kind of tax since an individual's income is the best single indicator of ability to pay, FairTax advocates counter that rich people often organize their wealth so that it is tied up in assets rather than in taxable income. A tax on consumption would be more equitable, they say, because its simplicity and transparency would make it difficult for people to avoid payment. Rather than being regressive, FairTax would protect the poor because every family would receive a monthly rebate on spending up to the federal poverty level. Those who lived on or below the poverty line would have zero taxes. However, critics argue that the loss of tax credits would hurt many families. A switch to an indirect form of taxation would also disproportionately affect the current generation of old people: After paying a lifetime of income taxes, they would be taxed for a second time on consumption.

The following articles examine indirect taxes in greater depth.

TAXING HABITS
Phineas Baxandall

Phineas Baxandall is a political scientist who teaches at Harvard University. This article appeared in 2003 in Regional Review, *an economics quarterly published by the Federal Reserve Bank of Boston.*

YES

✓   In 2002, new tobacco levies were implemented in 21 states, amounting to the largest average per-pack increase ever imposed in one year. Thanks to a new $1.50 tax hike, a pack of cigarettes bought in New York City now costs $7. New increases in alcohol taxes were passed in Tennessee and Alaska and were considered in 19 other state legislatures. Gaming taxes, casino revenue-sharing agreements, and new lotteries also brought in record levels of state revenue.

Taxes on "sin" have been an American tradition since the Puritans placed levies on morally suspect items like liquor, tobacco, tea, and immoderate foods like meat pies. But the modern sin tax advocate is more likely to be punching a calculator than thumping a bible. Today's sin taxes are propelled by the twin logics of public health and budget politics. Efforts to discourage the use of tobacco and alcohol by raising their price through taxes makes the population healthier while filling government coffers. States also raise revenues through their share of the proceeds on gambling.

But these levies have problems. They are paid disproportionately by the poor. They don't assess responsible consumers differently from irresponsible ones. And there are other policies that could also discourage harmful consumption and improve public health. Yet, given the political realities of budget constraints and the unpopularity of other types of taxes, state governments will likely continue to find it appealing to balance their budgets by taxing sin.

Smoking and public health

Modern sin taxes are born of the economists' creed that behavior responds to price, coupled with the politicians' desire to improve society while raising revenues. But the term "sin tax" is something of a misnomer. It refers almost exclusively to taxes on tobacco, alcohol, and gambling. Each has a long-standing cultural taint as vaguely naughty—if somewhat glamorous—even to those who indulge in them. By contrast, activities that are truly reprehensible, like molesting children or torturing animals, are criminally sanctioned rather than taxed.

The number of people who smoke has been declining in the United States for 20 years. What factors might influence smokers today to give up other than the price of tobacco?

The fact that a single cigarette can raise as much as 7.5 cents for state governments and another 2 cents for the federal government shows what a lightning rod tobacco has been for such taxes. And for good reason. Cigarettes are the leading cause of preventable sickness and death in the United States....

Taxes on cigarettes reduce smoking. Higher prices discourage people from starting to smoke and encourage smokers to cut back or quit.... And cigarette taxes are especially effective at discouraging teenagers—which has enormous public health benefits since three-quarters of all cigarette smokers start before their nineteenth birthday. Because teenagers have less discretionary income, their smoking habits are more sensitive to price....

Fairness is another appeal of cigarette taxes. Taxes can compensate and correct for the otherwise unpaid costs that smokers impose on nonsmokers. The health care costs of smokers are significant: an estimated $12,000 more than nonsmokers over an average lifetime, according to Thomas A. Hodgson of the National Center for Health Statistics....

The American Lung Association claims that the annual cost to the United States in smoking-related health care and lost workdays is at least $100 billion—the equivalent of $398 for every American each year. See Volume 10, Health, Topic 6 Should smokers pay for treatment for smoking-related diseases via increased taxes on cigarettes?

Just a glass of wine?

Sin taxes are levied on things that are fun. Even smokers who are interested in quitting generally find it enjoyable to light up and inhale. But while the social costs of smoking may outweigh these benefits, the calculus for alcohol is somewhat more complex. Only a fraction of those who drink abuse alcohol or suffer health problems, and many enjoy health benefits. The risks that drinkers pose to others may have less to do with how much alcohol they consume and more to do with how much they drive.

Do you think "sin taxes" should be introduced on other products that pose health risks, such as fatty foods?

An estimated 18.5 million Americans abuse alcohol. This not only affects the health of the person drinking, especially in increased liver disease, but it can also impose costs on others in the form of lost work time, higher health care costs, and strains on family relationships. As with cigarettes, taxing alcohol can improve public health to the extent that higher prices reduce excessive consumption and abuse. But medical research also shows that for many people, responsible drinking can be healthful....

According to the National Institute on Alcohol Abuse and Alcoholism (NIAAA), in purely economic terms alcohol-related problems cost society about $185 billion each year.

Moreover, while alcohol is taxed by the bottle or the drink, the same drink imposes very different risks depending on the situation. A 21-year-old college student whose weekly intake consists of seven beers while driving on Friday night, for instance, pays the same levy as a 40-year-old who drinks a beer each night with dinner....

Current medical research indicates that moderate alcohol consumption may provide protection against coronary heart disease, strokes, and dementia.

State legislators undoubtedly care about public health, but often the more pressing problem is how to close the holes in state budgets when voters are hostile to other ways of raising money. Before income taxes were introduced in 1913, for example, taxing sin was one of the main ways that government activities were financed. Alcohol and tobacco levies provided 37 percent of the federal budget in 1910, but only 2 percent today.

Over the past several decades, with demands on state governments increasing and other taxes unpopular, state legislators once again looked to sin as a way to balance their budgets.... States turned to gambling ... and especially state lotteries to raise new revenues....

[G]overnment gambling arrangements are not designed to reduce vice that provides the funding. State governments actively advertise and promote their lotteries—to the tune of $400 million per year....

> *Do you think states need to spend so much money promoting lotteries? Would gamblers play anyway?*

The allure of sin taxes has grown even greater since 2001 as state governments, facing sudden deficits, have needed new sources of funds. Legislators grew accustomed to rising tax receipts during the long boom of the 1990s, and committed state governments to higher spending levels.... When state revenues fell, states ... had to scramble to find money where they could....

Lawmakers know that new sin taxes arouse far less voter hostility than broader-based taxes. Taxes on income or property are far more visible and affect more taxpayers. They also seem to punish "good" things like making a living or owning a home. A growing number of voters since the 1990s tell pollsters that they dislike taxes; yet the majority support higher cigarette taxes. Smokers may resent being singled out, but they are a minority who garner little sympathy....

Poor sinners

One downside of balancing budgets on sin is that the money raised is paid disproportionately by the poor. The tax on a $4 bottle of wine is the same as that on a $40 bottle, so those who buy top-shelf liquor (or premium cigarettes) pay a smaller portion of the price in taxes. Poor people don't drink more than the affluent, but the alcohol taxes they pay are a far larger portion of their incomes. For cigarettes, the

> *Why do you think poor people smoke more than wealthier ones?*

problem is exacerbated by the fact that the poor do smoke more than the betteroff. According to Harvard Law School Professor Kip Viscusi, over 30 percent of people earning less than $10,000 a year were smokers in 1990, compared to less than 20 percent of those earning over $50,000 annually.

State-organized gambling acts as "an astonishingly regressive tax" that draws disproportionately from those with lower incomes, according to the 1999 National Gambling Impact Study Commission. State lotteries are the most regressive of these activities, and a disproportionate number of lottery outlets are located in poor neighborhoods. Lottery players with incomes below $10,000 spend almost $600 a year on tickets, more than any other income group.... Since those who gamble are overwhelmingly likely to lose money, some characterize gambling as a tax on bad math, or—more sympathetically—as a tax on those with limited prospects....

The commission also recommended that governments ban aggressive advertising strategies, especially those that target people in impoverished neighborhoods. Would such a ban be easy to enforce? Go to http://gov. info.library.unt.edu/ ngisc/ for the commission's report.

Addicted to sin?

There are a number of reasons to think that sin taxes could continue to grow. By international and historic standards, American sin taxes are still low.... But even if we can agree that there is too much smoking and problem drinking, and that taxes are effective at reducing consumption, increased sin taxes are not the only tool for solving these problems.

If governments are really serious about health issues, should they impose an outright ban on smoking and the consumption of alcohol?

Direct legislative restrictions can also reduce consumption and abuse, and the costs that go with them. These measures cost money to enforce and are more difficult to administer than simply raising the tax rate, but they target the consumption that is most costly to society …

Nontax measures also express social disapproval, whereas taxes can convey a kind of tacit acceptance—especially when education budgets depend on them. Tellingly, the first state-level taxes on cigarettes were not passed at the height of anti-cigarette fervor at the beginning of the twentieth century, but in the 1920s, when cigarettes first became socially acceptable.

The National Anti-Cigarette League, founded by Lucy Page Gaston in 1899, sought to ban cigarette sales. Between 1895 and 1921 at least 15 states enacted partial or total bans on cigarettes.

Setting tax levels on sin depends on weighing different goals: public health, virtue, and the desire to raise revenue, against efficiency and the impact on the poor. Sin taxes can be simplistically portrayed as "win–win" because they raise revenues at the same time as saving lives or promoting economic development.

But there are tradeoffs. Insofar as policies discourage alcohol and cigarette consumption, they also cut off potential sources of revenue. Punishing those who create social costs also disproportionately punishes the poor. And singling out a vice for taxation indirectly promotes the activity as a virtuous contributor to the public purse. Sin taxes may or may not be good policy, but so long as they remain one of the few acceptable ways to raise revenue, governments are likely to continue to depend on them.

FAIRNESS AND FEDERAL TAX REFORM
Americans for Fair Taxation

This article was published on the website of Americans for Fair Taxation, an organization that promotes the introduction of a federal retail sales tax.

NO

The notion of fairness in a tax system means many things to many people. The Webster's Dictionary defines "fairness" as "just and honest, impartial, unprejudiced," which connotes an abstract sense of equity.

The average taxpayer, however, sees fairness as much less abstract. Small businesses see fairness as the equitable distribution of compliance costs, or as similarly situated businesses being similarly treated. To those who must plan for the future, fairness means stability or consistency in the tax code. To individuals, fairness means that the tax structure imposes costs based on ability to pay, or that the system is enforced evenhandedly. By any standard of fairness we wish to apply, the FairTax is superior to the present tax system....

The FairTax is simpler

The simplicity of a tax system affects fairness in several respects. A fundamental notion of fairness is that citizens should be able to comprehend the laws that affect them. However, current tax law is beyond the comprehension of most taxpayers, including many of those who devote their entire professional lives to it. Today, we hold taxpayers accountable for knowing and complying with an intricate web of more than 7,000 individual Internal Revenue Code Sections, 10,000 pages of text, hundreds of thousands of pages of regulations and other pronouncements, and an equally weighty verbiage of court opinions interpreting the law.... The complexity of the tax code disproportionately affects smaller businesses that do not have the time or the resources to delve into its mysteries. When taxpayers fail to adhere to the complexities of the law—often through innocent mistakes—they are punished with penalties, interest, and a great deal of frustration.

The complexity of current tax law disproportionately rewards those who can afford to aggressively pursue tax planning.... Skillful manipulation of the tax code can lead to huge gains in competitiveness, or to substantial increases in individual wealth. The ongoing manipulation of the tax code for financial gain can be seen in estate planning, in trust planning for children's education, in pension coverage and in

The Internal Revenue Service (IRS) is the agency of the Treasury Department charged with overseeing the collection of taxes as laid down in the U.S. tax code, the official body of tax laws and regulations. When the federal income tax system was introduced in 1913, The New York Times published all of the required forms on one page. At that time the IRS had 3,000 employees. Today the tax code comprises more pages than the Encyclopaedia Britannica, and there are over 100,000 IRS employees to interpret and enforce the code.

many other facets of tax planning. In contrast, the FairTax is a highly visible tax system that cannot be avoided by sophisticated devices. Under the FairTax only one question is typically relevant: how much did the consumer spend on the purchase of a final good or service?

The complexity of the current system adds to unfairness in at least one more respect. By necessity under the current system, different industries, different sizes of firms, and different taxpayers will be treated differently, adding unfair distortions to the economy....

Current system injures savers and the poor

The income tax is unfair because it taxes the principal means by which Americans can improve the standard of living for themselves and for their children. The income tax is biased against those who are seeking to improve their families' lot in life through savings, investment, and hard work, while it favors those with assets to consume.

The FairTax would improve the standard of living of the vast majority of Americans by rewarding an individual's decision to work, save and invest. Under current law … consumption of goods and services is favored over savings and investment. A taxpayer often enjoys no immediate benefit from savings and investing, and the fact that the taxpayer has already been taxed on his or her income means that there is also no incentive not to consume. … Under the FairTax, those who benefit from tax-sheltered income, as well as those who profit handsomely from the complexities and confusion of the tax system, would no longer benefit from advantages that are not available to most taxpayers.

The FairTax would additionally benefit lower income families through increased economic growth. Slow economic growth or recessions have a disproportionately adverse impact on the poor. Breadwinners in these families are more likely to lose their jobs, are less likely to have the resources to weather bad economic times and are more in need of the initial employment opportunities that a dynamic, growing economy provides. The FairTax would dramatically improve economic growth and improve wage rates …

A fairer measure of the "ability to pay"

The FairTax plan is fairer because … it is based on "ability to pay." Under an income tax, taxing income at graduated rates has been the means for achieving progressivity in taxation. A tax on income, however … does not necessarily make an income tax progressive over the course of one's lifetime.

Tax planning—that is, seeking to minimize tax payments—is legal. Do you think there is a clear moral distinction between tax planning and tax evasion—that is, avoiding paying taxes through fraudulent means?

Are those people who can afford to save arguably those same people who should be paying higher taxes, compared to those who have no income left over to save or invest?

"Tax-sheltered income" refers to income that is exempt from taxation or on which taxes are deferred.

Go to http://www.fairtaxvolunteer.org/smart/wages.html for an explanation of how the proposed FairTax may have a positive effect on wages.

The ability to pay is not properly defined solely by how much income someone happens to make in any given period, such as a year. On the contrary, income is merely the means by which productive members of society try to increase their personal wealth so that they have better economic security, can provide better for their family and have the ability to pay for things they wish to purchase. Often wealth—which in and of itself may not be a fair determination of the ability to pay—is not captured by an income tax. Individuals rich in personal wealth may actually have very little income, because wealth is defined in assets that they hold … which may or may not have been earned by them and which may or may not generate taxable income streams. These wealthy individuals can often choose whether or not to create taxable income, since they can restructure their affairs to avoid receiving current taxable income.

What problems might there be in assessing exactly what constitutes consumption for "personal enjoyment"?

The FairTax, far more than an income tax, is based upon a taxpayer's ability to pay *precisely* because it is based upon consumption. Whether or not a taxpayer can consume for personal enjoyment is a more accurate litmus test for whether or not that taxpayer has the ability to pay. When taxpayers do not consume for personal enjoyment, but have income, they must be saving or investing those resources. When taxpayers save and invest, they contribute to the public welfare. They generate benefits to the community, for their future and their children's future, well beyond personal gratification.

Hidden taxes

"Compliance costs" refer to the costs to taxpayers of complying with the federal income tax system. According to the Tax Foundation, individuals and businesses spent an estimated 5.8 billion hours complying with the federal income tax code in 2002— an estimated compliance cost of over $194 billion. Go to http://www. taxfoundation.org/ compliance2002. html for details.

In addition to compliance cost burdens, the income tax is already invisibly embedded in the price of the goods we consume. In addition to the payments we make directly to the government, we are already paying hidden income taxes that are incorporated into every product we buy. We just do not see them. Almost every product or service we purchase has already been taxed once and often numerous times. When we purchase bread for our sustenance, we are paying a price to recover the income tax imposed on the farmer that produced the wheat, on the miller that milled the wheat, the baker that baked the dough, and on the retail outlets that brought the final product to your grocery shelf. Therefore, an accurate appraisal of the burden of the income tax must examine the hidden taxes paid on consumable items. The income tax system literally cloaks the cascading nature of the tax, its true economic effects, and its real burdens on the purchase price of the final goods and services.

The FairTax is progressive

The distribution of the FairTax proposal is fairer than present tax law because the FairTax only taxes consumption above the poverty line, assuring each family the ability to spend, tax-free, for their basic needs. In this way, the FairTax, unlike the current system, exempts from taxation the basic necessities of life. This is accomplished by providing a rebate to each family equal to the taxes paid on the purchase of essential goods and services as determined by the HHS Poverty Level. The rebate would be paid monthly in advance to every family....

The FairTax would also replace the payroll tax. The payroll tax is imposed on the first dollar of wages earned, and therefore has a disproportionate impact on lower wage earners. In contrast, the FairTax would exempt all expenditures up to poverty level through a rebate system. Additionally, unlike the Social Security component of the payroll tax, which is only imposed on the first $76,200 of wages (2000), the FairTax would be imposed on all consumption over the poverty level, and would tax the consumption of affluent taxpayers.

The FairTax would eliminate the graduated income tax rate structure that penalizes people as they strive to earn more for their families. Because of the rebate system, however, high-consumption families would pay higher average tax rates....

The FairTax is visible to all

The Americans for Fair Taxation plan is also fairer because it is more visible. One of the greatest attributes of a sales tax regime ... is its resolute clarity. The FairTax allows ... each and every taxpayer to take notice of the actual burden of government in every purchase that taxpayer makes. In this way, the FairTax is notably distinguished from an income tax and virtually every other form of tax.

The transparency of the FairTax adds to the reality and perception of fairness and compliance in one final respect: the tax paid by others is easily seen. When one purchases a good or service for personal consumption, it is clear at the retail level that each taxpayer is pulling his or her load for the tax system. Currently, the IRS estimates that the "tax gap"—unpaid taxes—amounts to about $200 billion per year under current law. This gap will never be fully closed, but it is more likely to be reduced under the FairTax, because the FairTax will be understood and viewed as fair and legitimate by most Americans.

Each year the Health and Human Services Department issues poverty guidelines, sometimes referred to as the federal poverty level. The guidelines are used to determine whether an individual or family is financially eligible for assistance under a federal program. In 2004 the poverty guideline for a family of four was $18,850.

In another effort to simplify the current tax system, Rep. Dick Armey and Sen. Richard Shelby introduced the Flat Tax bill into Congress in 1997. They proposed to replace the graduated income tax with a flat income tax of 17 percent. They claimed this would greatly reduce compliance costs. Go to http:// usgovinfo.about. com/library/weekly/ aa031398.htm for an analysis of the pros and cons of the Flat Tax.

Summary

In the first article Phineas Baxandall suggests that taxes levied on cigarettes, alcohol, and gambling—"sin taxes"—are problematic. They disproportionately affect the poor, he says, and they do not distinguish between responsible and irresponsible consumers. While cigarette taxes discourage smoking and compensate for the health-care costs that smokers impose on nonsmokers, alcohol taxes are more complex to assess since moderate drinking may have health benefits, and drinkers do not all pose an equal risk to society. Baxandall describes how state governments have increasingly turned to sin taxes to balance their budgets. Although such taxes are generally popular, they hit the poor hardest owing to their regressive nature and the fact that poor people smoke and gamble more than wealthier ones. He concludes by outlining ways to reduce consumption that do not penalize the poor, such as legislation.

In the second article the organization Americans for Fair Taxation puts forward its case for a federal tax on consumption—FairTax. The authors contend that FairTax would be much simpler than the present income tax system, which they criticize for punishing people who work hard to save and invest. They claim that FairTax would benefit poor families by encouraging economic growth. A tax based on consumption would be, the authors say, a much fairer way to assess a taxpayer's ability to pay. Moreover, by paying monthly rebates to families, it would only tax consumption above the poverty level. The authors conclude by emphasizing the transparent nature of FairTax.

FURTHER INFORMATION:

Books:

Murray, Matthew N., and William F. Fox (eds.), *The Sales Tax in the 21st Century*. Westport, CT: Praeger, 1997.

Stiglitz, Joseph E., *Economics of the Public Sector* (3rd edition). New York: W.W. Norton, 2000.

Zodrow, George R., *State Sales and Income Taxes: An Economic Analysis*. College Station, TX: Texas A&M University Press, 1999.

Useful websites:

http://www.brookings.org/comm/policybriefs/pb31.htm
"Don't Buy the Sales Tax" by William G. Gale.
http://www.cato.org/dailys/10-17-97.html
"Considering a National Sales Tax" by Dean Stansel.
http://www.irs.gov/app/understandingTaxes/servlet/IWT4L4ol
Student guide to direct and indirect taxes from the IRS.

http://www.johnlinder.com/IssueDetails.asp?IssueID=9
Congressman John Linder explains FairTax.
www.taxopedia.com
Useful glossary of tax terms.

The following debates in the Pro/Con series may also be of interest:

In this volume:
Topic 7 Are income taxes an effective way of redistributing wealth?

In *Economics*:
Topic 8 Should wealth redistribution be part of government policy?

DO INDIRECT TAXES DISCRIMINATE AGAINST THE POOR?

YES: Income tax is the fairest kind of taxation because an individual's income is the best single indicator of ability to pay

YES: Sin taxes are paid disproportionately by poor people, who are more likely to smoke and gamble

ABILITY TO PAY
Are direct taxes a fairer measure of ability to pay than indirect taxes?

SIN TAXES
Are sin taxes unfair?

NO: Income is not necessarily a true indication of wealth. Consumption is therefore a far better indicator of ability to pay.

NO: People who do not smoke or drink heavily should not be liable for the significant health-care costs incurred by those who do

DO INDIRECT TAXES DISCRIMINATE AGAINST THE POOR?

KEY POINTS

YES: Tax credits would disappear with the elimination of the federal income tax. This would leave many families struggling with finances.

YES: The current generation of seniors would in effect be taxed twice—once on income, then again on consumption

NATIONAL SALES TAX
Would people be worse off paying a national sales tax?

NO: A flat-rate tax on consumption would remove hidden income taxes embedded in the price of goods

NO: Under the proposed FairTax families would receive a monthly rebate based on the federal poverty level to cover necessities

READING DIFFICULT MATERIALS

"What we don't understand, we don't possess."
—JOHANN WOLFGANG VON GOETHE (1749–1832),
GERMAN DRAMATIST

Reading material related to your coursework is a fact of life. Sometimes the books or articles concerned are very easy to understand, but at times the material may seem—initially at least—incomprehensible, leading to feelings of inadequacy in the reader. It is easy to become distracted and to lose faith in your ability to learn, but there are ways to make difficult reading materials more accessible.

A plan of action

Most people approach reading a difficult book, such as a school textbook, in the same way that they would read a book for pleasure, such as a novel. They begin at the first page and read the work all the way through without stopping. While this is a good method for reading a piece of fiction, it is not as useful when reading a text that contains a lot of conceptual material since it does not help comprehension or the retention of information.

The following points may help in your reading of difficult texts:
• Read the table of contents, introduction, and summary. They will give you a good idea of the main themes and concepts.
• Look at titles, headings, and subheadings, and study graphs, diagrams, and charts for the main themes and ideas. Ask yourself what the central point is.
• Research. Have a good dictionary and encyclopedia available. Look up words or concepts you do not understand if you cannot get a sense of their meaning from the text.
• Comprehension. Stop every so often and ask yourself, "What have I learned?" and "How does this relate to what I already know?"
• Reread. If you are finding it difficult to understand an idea, go back over it slowly. Reread it, read it out loud if necessary, and then try and restate it in your own words.
• Read to the end. You must read the text completely. It is easy to be discouraged if you are having difficulties, but the premise or argument may become clearer the more you read.
• Highlight/jot down key text. Note or mark key concepts and ideas you do not quite understand. You can jot down notes on a pad or computer, or use highlighters or Post-it® flags to mark things you want to note or look up later.
• Try not to get discouraged. Ideas can become clearer the more you read. When you finish reading the whole text, look at your notes or the marked material to see what the key issues are. Note the areas that need further explanation or research.

• Research. If you need further clarification or explanation, you might get more information from the references or bibliography. The Internet also provides a wealth of easily accessible information, but it is important to use reliable sources (see Volume 2, *Government*, *Research skills*, pages 58-59).

• Ask. If you are still confused or unclear, talk to your teacher and peers—they may be able to help. Try not to panic or become stressed (see Volume 21, *U.S. Judiciary*, *Stress management*, pages 124-125).

SQ3R

In a book entitled *Effective Study* (1946) educator F.P. Robinson used the acronym SQ3R to describe an effective way of reading difficult texts. SQ3R, which stands for Survey, Question, Read, Recite, and Review, is still advocated by many teachers today. It focuses on making the reader understand the text, but critics argue that it is suitable only for certain subjects, such as math. Supporters counter that the method has been highly successful in helping students read materials that provide a lot of in-depth information, such as biology texts.

The structure

• Survey: The first stage ensures that you gather information and formulate questions. Surveying involves reading the title, introduction, or summary; reading every bold word, heading, and subheading; examining any visual aids; and reviewing reading aids such as definitions, questions, and chapter objectives. Surveying the text gives you an overall framework within which to work.

• Question: Examine bold headings, and write them down as questions. For example, there might be a heading on mnemonics in a piece on memory skills, and you could phrase this as "What are mnemonics?" As you read, look for answers to the question. In doing this, the brain becomes engaged in the learning process, which helps with comprehension and remembering the information later (see Volume 22, *International Law*, *Improving your memory*, pages 122–123). This step and reading and reciting are repeated as you look at each section of text.

• Read: It is important to read one section at a time. You can jot down questions and answers in your own words by paraphrasing parts of the text. Reading out loud will help your mind concentrate, learn, and retain information (see Volume 24, *Work and the Workplace*, *Improving your concentration*, pages 150–151).

• Recite: At the end of each section you should try to recite the answers you have jotted down in response to your questions. If you cannot remember information, you should reread the text with which you have had difficulty. Once you have understood a section, repeat the process of question, read, and recite for each new piece of text.

• Review: Once you have read the whole chapter or text using the first four steps, go back over all the questions you have jotted down to see how much information you have retained. This helps you remember what you have learned.

Topic 9
DOES WELFARE PERPETUATE POVERTY?

YES

FROM "WHY THE WAR ON POVERTY FAILED"
THE FREEMAN, VOL. 49, NO. 1, JANUARY 1999
JAMES L. PAYNE

NO

FROM "MYTH: WELFARE INCREASES POVERTY. FACT: THE MORE WELFARE, THE LESS
POVERTY—BOTH HISTORICALLY AND INTERNATIONALLY"
HTTP://HOME.ATT.NET/~RESURGENCE/L-WELFAREPOVERTY.HTM
STEVE KANGAS

INTRODUCTION

In many developed countries the government provides help for people who, for reasons such as old age and unemployment, are unable to support themselves. This assistance is called welfare. In the United States welfare commonly refers to a variety of government-funded programs offering either cash payments or in-kind benefits —goods or services such as food stamps or medical care—to the unemployed or underemployed.

The primary purpose of welfare is to provide a "safety net" to prevent people from suffering poverty in specific and usually temporary circumstances such as illness. Welfare is mostly intended to help people solve their problems and become self-sufficient again. However, some critics argue that welfare actually traps recipients in a cycle of poverty by discouraging them from finding work and supporting themselves.

In the United States advocates claim that the welfare system has made great progress in the fight against poverty.

They point in particular to the success of welfare reforms enacted in 1996 that emphasize employment and personal responsibility. But critics say that there is evidence that the most needy families are faring badly under the reforms.

The modern federal welfare system has its roots in the Great Depression of the 1930s. With as much as one-quarter of the labor force out of work, Congress passed the Social Security Act in 1935 as part of President Franklin D. Roosevelt's (1933–1945) New Deal. The act and its 1939 amendments created a number of welfare programs that targeted different sections of society, such as the elderly, the unemployed, and children of poor families.

The system grew rapidly after 1965, when President Lyndon B. Johnson's (1963–1969) "Great Society" reform program introduced legislation to tackle poverty. His administration founded Medicare and Medicaid (medical assistance for the elderly and needy), food stamps, and housing programs.

These programs succeeded in reducing the percentage of people living below the poverty level from 22 percent in 1959 to around 11 percent by the late 1970s. However, critics became increasingly concerned about one particular cash-assistance program aimed at families headed by a single parent or guardian—Aid to Families with Dependent Children (AFDC). In 1960 AFDC provided support to 1 million families, but at its peak in 1994 that figure had risen to 5.1 million.

> *"I think the best possible social program is a job."*
>
> —RONALD REAGAN, 40TH PRESIDENT (1981–1989)

In 1996 President Bill Clinton (1993–2001) signed into law the Personal Responsibility and Work Opportunity Reconciliation Act, which replaced the federal AFDC program with a state-run program, Temporary Assistance for Needy Families (TANF). To discourage long-term dependence, TANF imposed a five-year limit on cash benefits and required most recipients to work after two years ("welfare to work").

Advocates of welfare reform maintain that it is inherently better for the poor to work than to receive handouts since employment motivates people to better themselves. Some studies cite evidence that welfare-to-work programs boost participants' self-esteem. In contrast, many people regard handouts as self-defeating: They condition recipients to become dependent on others, provide no incentive to work, and encourage irresponsible behavior such as starting a family without having adequate finance.

Government sources indicated that by 2001 the number of families receiving economic assistance had dropped to 2.1 million. Supporters claim that this decline in caseloads is proof of the reforms' success. However, others argue that statistics do not give the full picture. Census Bureau figures for 2002 showed that of 75 million families in the United States, 7.2 million had incomes below the poverty threshold. Only around 29 percent of these families were supported by welfare programs. Critics of TANF contend that reducing poverty should be a higher priority than limiting welfare dependence. Although poverty rates have dropped since 1996, they argue, they have not declined as much as welfare enrollment. This suggests that people in need are not being helped. Critics say the reforms have merely created an underclass of "working poor" who are trapped in badly paid jobs. Employed at a minimal wage and liable for taxes and childcare expenses, some single mothers in particular claim they are worse off than when they received benefits. Observers also argue that TANF leaves low-income families vulnerable to any economic downturn and rise in unemployment.

In 2002 President George W. Bush (2001–) announced a proposal for reauthorization of the welfare reform legislation. He proposed extending the required number of hours spent on work activities from 30 to 40 hours a week for 70 percent of participants. As of mid-2004 the Senate had yet to approve the bill.

The following two articles debate the success of the U.S. welfare system.

WHY THE WAR ON POVERTY FAILED
James L. Payne

James L. Payne is a writer and political analyst. This article first appeared in 1999 in The Freeman, a publication of the Foundation for Economic Education, a research organization that promotes free-market economics.

"SSI" stands for Supplemental Security Income, a federal income supplement for poor elderly, blind, or disabled people. Many states add to SSI benefits from their own revenues.

Michael Harrington's book The Other America (1962) was a groundbreaking study that revealed that one out of four Americans was trapped in poverty. In particular, Harrington highlighted the plight of the rural poor living in the Appalachian Mountains.

YES

✓ Well, it's now official: the war on poverty was a costly, tragic mistake. Ordinary people have suspected that for decades, of course, but we had to wait for the *New York Times* to decide this news was fit to print—which it finally did on February 9, 1998. In a front-page story on poverty in rural Kentucky, Michael Janofsky detailed the failure of this effort in the one region that was supposed to be the centerpiece of reform. "Federal and state agencies have plowed billions of dollars into Appalachia," he wrote, yet the area "looks much as it did 30 years ago, when President Lyndon B. Johnson declared a war on poverty, taking special aim at the rural decay."

Janofsky visited Owsley County, Kentucky, and found a poverty rate of over 46 percent, with over half the adults illiterate and half unemployed. "Feelings of hopelessness have become so deeply entrenched," he reported, "that many residents have long forsaken any expectation of bettering themselves." For years, the government has been trying to treat the despair with welfare programs: two-thirds of the inhabitants receive federal assistance, including food stamps, AFDC, and SSI disability payments. This, it now appears, is part of the area's problems....

Why did the war on poverty fail? What was wrong with the programs under which the nation spent over $5 trillion attempting to solve the problems of the poor, only to come up empty? It's an important question to ask in these days of welfare reform. The first step toward a sound policy ought to be to identify the errors of the past.

Perhaps the best way to answer the question is to take a close look at the book that inspired the war on poverty, Michael Harrington's *The Other America*, published in 1962.... In it we find the fallacies that sent reformers down dark and tangled paths into today's social tragedies....

Curing poverty through algebra

Harrington's premise was that poverty is a purely economic problem: the needy simply lack the material resources to lead productive, happy lives. Supply these resources, the theory runs, and you will have solved the problem of poverty....

Sargent Shriver, the administration's leading anti-poverty warrior, told Congress that the nation had "both the resources and the know-how to eliminate grinding poverty in the United States." President Lyndon Johnson echoed the claim. "For the first time in our history," he declared, "it is possible to conquer poverty."

Sargent Shriver (1915–) headed President Johnson's war on poverty, which led to the formation of various welfare programs.

A cluster of problems

To most people, these claims seemed incredibly naïve. While the state of neediness we call poverty does involve a lack of material resources, it also involves a mass of psychological and moral problems, including weak motivation, lack of trust in others, ignorance, irresponsibility, self-destructiveness, short-sightedness, alcoholism, drug addiction, promiscuity, and violence. To say that all these behavioral and psychological problems can be "abolished" seems a denial of the common-sense Biblical teaching that the poor will always be with us.

Do you agree with the writer's assertion that poverty is associated with behavioral and moral problems? Do such problems affect only the poor?

Abolishing poverty did not seem far-fetched to the activists, however. Indeed, one book from that era boldly challenged the Biblical wisdom with its title: *The Poor Ye Need Not Have With You*. This 1970 volume was written by Robert Levine…. Levine adhered to the simple materialistic view of poverty. "Even a quick look can convince us that poverty as it is currently defined in the United States is a completely solvable problem," he wrote. "If we were to provide every last poor family and individual in the United States with enough income to bring them above the level of poverty, the required outlay would be less than $10 billion a year." In this perspective, curing poverty was simple algebra: add government's x dollars to the poor's y dollars and the result would be the end to poverty….

Robert Levine served in the Office of Economic Opportunity, the federal government's antipoverty agency. In an article for the International Herald Tribune in 2002 he wrote, "We did not end poverty. But … we helped many to get out of poverty."

The ideology of handouts

The simple economic theory of poverty led to a single underlying principle for welfare programs. Since the needy just lacked goods and services to become productive members of the community, it followed that all you had to do was give them these things. You didn't have to see that they stopped engaging in the behavior that plunged them into neediness. You didn't have to ask them to apply themselves, or to work, or to save, or to stop using drugs, or to stop having babies they couldn't support, or to make any other kind of effort to improve themselves. In other words, the welfare programs the war-on-poverty activists designed embodied something-for-nothing giving, or what we usually call "handouts."

Is it fair to blame the poor for their own behavior? Are some people just unlucky?

The handout feature characterized not only the programs that gave away cash and material resources like food and housing; it was also incorporated in programs that provided training, education, and rehabilitation. Recipients did not have to make any significant sacrifice to be admitted to them, and they did not have to make any significant effort to stay in them. Swept up by the rhetoric of the day, program organizers simply assumed that all that recipients needed was "opportunity," especially the opportunity to learn a trade and to get a job.

What might welfare recipients' response be to the charge that they lack motivation?

Alas, this was mainly untrue. One of the first things the needy lack is motivation; that is, they lack the ability to sacrifice and to discipline themselves, to defer present gratification for future benefit. Most of the recipients in the anti-poverty training and education programs were poorly motivated, and their lack of commitment meant that they couldn't make good use of the opportunities put before them....

The healthy way to give

In adopting the handout approach for their programs, the war-on-poverty activists failed to notice—or failed to care—that they were ignoring over a century of theory and experience in the social welfare field. Charity leaders of the nineteenth century had lived with the poor and had analyzed the effects of different kinds of aid. They discovered that almsgiving—that is, something for nothing—actually hurt the poor. First, it weakened them by undermining their motivation to improve themselves.... Second, handouts encouraged self-destructive vices by softening the natural penalties for irresponsible and socially harmful behavior. If you gave a man coal who had wasted his money on drink, you encouraged him to drink away next month's coal money, too. Finally, the nineteenth-century experts argued, handouts were self-defeating. People became dependent on them, and new recipients were attracted to them....

Do you think people give to charity expecting something in return for their donation? If not, why do they give?

The correct way to help the needy, they said, was to expect something of recipients in return for what was given them. Instead of giving poor people what they needed, the charity leaders organized programs that enabled the needy to supply their own wants....

Failing in the field

The war-on-poverty activists not only ignored the lessons of the past on the subject of handouts; they also ignored their own experience with the poor. The case of Harrington himself is especially revealing.

In the early 1950s Harrington worked at the St. Joseph's House of Hospitality, a shelter for the homeless in New York's Bowery district. The philosophy of the shelter was pure handout.... In *The Other America* Harrington described at length the tragic lives of the alcoholics served by the shelter, the degradation, exposure, disease, theft, and violence that made up their lives. Yet he didn't report having any strategy to uplift them, and didn't report rehabilitating a single one.... Summarizing his experience, he concluded that alcoholic poverty was not an economic problem but "deeply a matter of personality." In a revealing aside, he added, "One hardly knows where to begin."

For someone so ready to hector others about how easily poverty could be "abolished," Harrington was astonishingly unreflective about his own performance.... The man who "hardly knew where to begin" in treating the problems of poverty—and who failed when he tried—became the guru for a massive array of government handout programs that ... only deepened the culture of poverty.

The road back to common sense

In the 1996 welfare reform, the nation began to undo the damage caused by the war on poverty's misguided approach. Most lawmakers finally grasped the point that handout programs are harmful and self-defeating. They began to see that welfare ... recipients have to be asked to take steps toward self-improvement and self-sufficiency....

Lawmakers have yet to discover that government agencies are ill-suited to carry out the subtle task of personal uplift. This mission requires helpers who become personally involved in the lives of their clients. It requires that helpers be mentors who project healthy values. It also requires treating each client as an individual, subject to a different set of expectations and rewards. All this runs against the grain in government, where the pressures of law and regulation push agencies toward behaving in an impersonal, value-free, and uniform manner. In the long run, this leads to handout programs, because handouts are impersonal, value-free, and uniform....

The 1996 welfare reform was therefore just a first step in undoing the harmful anti-poverty policies of the 1960s. It did introduce the idea that handouts are wrong. But it missed the deeper point that ... government agencies aren't very good at anything but handouts. It remains for future generations to lay the government programs entirely aside and to promote the personal, voluntary arrangements that make for truly effective social assistance.

Is the point of a shelter such as the one that Harrington worked in to provide rehabilitation or simply to keep people from living on the streets?

Payne has acknowledged that Harrington had direct experience of working with the poor. Would his case be stronger if he revealed that he had such experience himself?

Voluntary agencies proved incapable of coping with the levels of poverty in the Great Depression of the 1930s, which is why welfare was introduced. Why might they cope better today?

MYTH: WELFARE INCREASES POVERTY...
Steve Kangas

Steve Kangas was studying for a PhD in economics and political studies before he died in 1999. This article first appeared on his Liberalism Resurgent website.

NO

X Many conservatives believe that welfare does not accomplish what it sets out to do; that, despite decades of massive anti-poverty spending, poverty is still with us, and perhaps even worse than before. In fact, some conservatives make even more ambitious claims: poverty was not a problem in America until President Johnson declared war on it. Some hearken back to a golden age that never was, claiming that charity was sufficient to solve what little poverty there was.

See Volume 13, U.S. History, Topic 8 Was the New Deal "new"?

Neither history nor the statistics bear out these myths. Poverty was greater in the U.S. before Roosevelt established the New Deal. Since then, welfare has been an important tool in alleviating poverty, not just in America but abroad as well.

Economic polarization in the early 20th century
Before 1964, official statistics on poverty did not exist, and it was not the focus of government attention. However, mainstream scholars disagree little over the broad generalizations of decades prior. By one estimate, 56 percent of all American families lived in poverty in the year 1900. The so-called "Roaring 20s" were a period of economic polarization, with less than 1 percent of the population earning a "rich" salary of $100,000 a year, about 15 percent earning a "middle class" income, and about half of all Americans struggling to make ends meet....

President Herbert Hoover (1929–1933) was reluctant to embrace the idea of federal relief for the unemployed at the start of the Great Depression.

The Great Depression brought much deeper poverty, of course, but almost all the damage was done on Hoover's watch. Under Hoover, the economy shrank an average of –8.4 percent a year; under Roosevelt, it grew an average of 6.4 percent a year until 1940, the year it finally returned to its 1929 level. During this recovery, Roosevelt launched the New Deal, essentially creating the modern American welfare state. Dozens of programs were instituted that redistributed wealth from the rich to the poor....

The U.S. emerged from World War II with a supercharged economy.... The poverty rate for the 50s is estimated to have been about 20 percent, still high by today's standards, but a major improvement over the 1920s. Still, with a booming economy, it was easy to forget the bottom 20 percent.

Michael Harrington had to write a bestseller entitled *The Other America* to remind the middle class that not all Americans were enjoying the good times. This book caught the attention of President Kennedy.... Consequently, he instructed his Council of Economic Advisors to study the problem and recommend policies.

After Kennedy's assassination, President Johnson greatly accelerated the Council's work. In his first State of the Union address, Johnson declared war on poverty, and launched his "Great Society" program. Between 1964 and 1975, total real outlays for means-tested assistance (medical, housing, food and cash) rose nearly 400 percent. Between 1960 and 1973, real spending on federal, state and local AFDC soared over 400 percent.

In the mid-70s, however, a sea-change in federal government occurred. The 1975 SUN-PAC decision legalized corporate political action committees, and corporate activism in Washington soared. Corporate lobbyists wasted no time scaling back the New Deal and the Great Society. Total real spending on cash assistance—including the Earned Income Tax Credit—peaked in 1976, but fell 14 percent over the next eight years. It would eventually surpass its 1976 level, but by then the population had grown, and individual benefits had been sharply reduced. By 1991, the typical AFDC family had seen the purchasing power of their benefits fall 42 percent from their 1970 level, primarily as a result of state and federal cuts....

The ... chart [on page 122] shows how this history of welfare affected the poverty rate. Keep in mind that welfare is not the only factor that affects poverty; the unemployment rate is also an important influence. Typically, unemployment spikes during a recession, and takes several years to gradually fall back to its pre-recession level.... Generally, poverty trends follow these unemployment trends.... [I]f you look at the general trends between recessions, you can see that poverty rates were lower in the 70s than in the 80s. This is largely due to deepening cuts in individual welfare benefits....

[A]fter taking recessions into account, a history of welfare in America is also its history of poverty: the more, the less....

The conservative response

In 1984, Charles Murray published a bestseller entitled *Losing Ground.* In it, he argued that the success of welfare in reducing poverty was really illusory. The official poverty statistics measured poverty only *after* welfare benefits had already been paid. Murray was much more interested in what he called "latent poverty," namely, the amount of poverty that

A "means test" is an examination of an individual's financial situation to determine his or her suitability for public assistance.

Political action committees (PACs) are organizations that lobby Congress. In 1975 the Federal Election Committee ruled that corporations could organize PACs just as labor unions had done for years.

In 1979 the unemployment rate in the United States was 5.9 percent. It briefly rose above 10 percent in the early 1980s and fell back to 5.5 percent in 1988. Go to the Bureau of Labor Statistics website at www.bls.gov to find the current rate of unemployment.

Charles Murray (1943–) also coauthored The Bell Curve (1994), which controversially argued that African Americans are genetically intellectually inferior to white European Americans.

POVERTY RATE IN THE UNITED STATES

Year	Rate	Note	Year	Rate	Note
1959	22.4%		1977	11.6	
1960	22.2	< recession year	1978	11.4	
1961	21.9		1979	11.7	
1962	21.0		1980	13.0	< recession year
1963	19.5		1981	14.0	< Reagan-era cuts in individual benefits
1964	19.0	< Johnson's Great Society begins	1982	15.0	< recession year
1965	17.3		1983	15.2	
1966	14.7		1984	14.4	
1967	14.2		1985	14.0	
1968	12.8		1986	13.6	
1969	12.1		1987	13.4	
1970	12.6	< recession year	1988	13.0	
1971	12.5		1989	12.8	
1972	11.9		1990	13.5	< recession year
1973	11.1		1991	14.2	< recession year
1974	11.2	< recession year	1992	14.8	
1975	12.3	< recession year	1993	15.1	
1976	11.8	< individual benefits level off, decline			

would have existed without these transfers. It was his argument that the welfare state had increased latent poverty.

To support his argument, Murray noted that latent poverty decreased fastest in the 1950s and early 60s, when welfare outlays grew slowest. However, latent poverty leveled off and actually began rising again in the late 60s and 70s, when welfare outlays grew fastest. Murray argued that increased welfare outlays had caused latent poverty to grow, because the poor had been lured out of the workplace and into welfare dependency.

That was just an observation about latent poverty; another was possible about official poverty too. Despite increasing the amount of social spending in the 70s, official poverty remained

What do you think would be the attraction of "welfare dependency" over having a job? What would the drawbacks be?

stuck at about 11–12 percent. Murray therefore argued that poverty was intractable, and not worth wasting money on.

These arguments provided the Reagan administration with the intellectual cover needed to cut welfare spending in the 80s.

The problem with Murray's analysis is twofold: it seriously downplays the economic slowdown of 1973, and it completely ignores the dramatic success in poverty reduction caused by relatively minor welfare transfers....

The economic slowdown

As most people know, the economic juggernaut that was the U.S. economy shifted into low gear in 1973....

When an economy is experiencing rapid growth, poverty tends to fall. When growth slows down, poverty tends to rise. We have seen this not only in American history, but the history of other rich nations as well. And this happens regardless of the amount of social benefits being handed out....

If rapid economic growth diminishes latent poverty, then we should expect to see diminishing latent poverty even in the presence of modest welfare programs. But if slow economic growth increases latent poverty, then welfare spending will be fighting against a head wind, and much greater efforts will be needed to achieve the desired effect. To conservatives who object that it is *welfare* that is responsible for slowing down growth, we should point out the example of Europe, which is growing faster than the U.S. despite higher welfare benefits....

The inexpensive success of anti-poverty programs

Conservatives often speak of welfare as a terrible monster burgeoning out of control. But the actual expenses have been surprisingly modest, especially when compared to the welfare programs of other nations. In 1960, U.S. welfare programs comprised 4.4 percent of the GDP. By 1992, that had grown to 12.9 percent. But even this overstates the amount spent on relieving poverty, because a third of this latter figure is Medicare, Medicaid and other health care, which represents windfall profits for hospitals, doctors and other health care providers. So a more correct set of figures for anti-poverty spending would be from 4.4 percent to roughly 8–9 percent.

But consider what these modest outlays have accomplished: the poverty rate was cut in half between 1959 and 1973, from 22 to 11 percent. Between 1959 and 1969, welfare was largely responsible for cutting black poverty from 55 to 32 percent (where it has remained to this day)....

The administration of Republican President Ronald Reagan (1981–1989) introduced tax and welfare cuts while massively increasing military spending.

A global economic downturn was triggered in 1973 when Arab members of the Organization of Petroleum Exporting Countries (OPEC) announced an embargo on oil exports to nations that supported Israel in its conflict with Egypt. This affected the United States and other western nations. By 1974 the price of oil had quadrupled, and an energy crisis had developed.

Gross domestic product (GDP) is the value of goods and services a country produces. Many western European countries spend more on welfare as a percentage of their GDP than the United States does.

Go to http://www.census.gov/hhes/www/poverty.html for current statistics from the Census Bureau on poverty rates. See also Topic 5 Is income inequality related to race?

Summary

The authors of the two articles have differing views on whether welfare perpetuates poverty. In the first article James L. Payne argues that the war on poverty instigated by the Johnson administration in the 1960s was a costly mistake. The reason it failed, he says, is that politicians believed poverty was a purely economic problem that could be solved by providing welfare handouts. Payne contends that this view was naive: Poverty also involves problems such as ignorance, drug addiction, promiscuity, and violence. Thus welfare simply discourages poor people from taking steps toward self-improvement and self-sufficiency. Poverty, he asserts, goes hand in hand with negative behaviors such as weak motivation and poor self-discipline, which cannot be addressed by charity. Payne believes that the most effective way of fighting poverty is by using volunteers to act as mentors to encourage poor people to improve their lives.

Steve Kangas, the author of the second article, argues that the viewpoint "welfare increases poverty" is supported by neither history nor statistics. He describes how the U.S. government quadrupled means-tested assistance to the poor between the mid-1960s and mid-1970s. Accordingly, the number of poverty-stricken Americans dropped from 19 to about 11 percent of the population. Kangas uses statistics to support his argument that, after taking economic recessions into account, the history of welfare in America is also its history of poverty—the more welfare there is, the less poverty there is. He counters the conservatives' argument that welfare slows growth by pointing out that other factors affect growth besides welfare spending.

FURTHER INFORMATION:

Books:

Albelda, Randy, and Ann Withorn (eds.), *Lost Ground: Welfare Reform, Poverty, and Beyond*. Cambridge, MA: South End Press, 2002.
Payne, James L., *Overcoming Welfare: Expecting More from the Poor and from Ourselves*. New York: Basic Books, 1998.

Useful websites:

http://www.acf.dhhs.gov/programs/ofa/
Site for the Administration for Children and Families Office of Family Assistance, with information on TANF.
http://www.financeprojectinfo.org/win/
Welfare Information Network provides information, policy analysis, and technical assistance related to welfare.
http://www.policyalmanac.org/social_welfare/welfare.shtml
Information and links on TANF and federal welfare policy.

The following debates in the Pro/Con series may also be of interest:

In this volume:
Topic 3 Is begging wrong?

In *Economics*:
Topic 6 Should welfare be abolished?

In *Family and Society*:
Topic 13 Does the welfare system provide enough support for the family?

DOES WELFARE PERPETUATE POVERTY?

YES: Handouts are a disincentive for the poor to seek employment and become financially self-sufficient

YES: Work improves people's self-esteem; public works projects can also benefit the community

DEPENDENCE
Does welfare encourage dependence on handouts?

WORK
Is it better to force people into work than to provide financial assistance?

NO: Very few people want to be reliant on welfare payments, which provide a very basic income at best

NO: Compulsory work simply moves the poor into badly paid, dead-end jobs, trapping them in a "working underclass"

DOES WELFARE PERPETUATE POVERTY?
KEY POINTS

YES: The decrease in poverty rates is nowhere near proportionate to the massive increases in welfare spending

YES: In the past spending on welfare has spiraled out of control, causing the economy to slow down

STATISTICS
Do statistics provide evidence that welfare perpetuates poverty?

ECONOMIC GROWTH
Does welfare spending harm economic growth?

NO: After the enlargement of the welfare system in the 1960s the percentage of people in poverty had almost halved 10 years later

NO: Many European countries spend proportionately more on welfare, yet their growth rates exceed that of the United States. Growth is affected by other factors besides welfare.

Topic 10
SHOULD PEOPLE HAVE TO PAY FOR NATURAL RESOURCES?

YES
"WATER IS NOT 'DIFFERENT'"
TECH CENTRAL STATION, DECEMBER 9, 2003
RICHARD TREN

NO
FROM "WHO OWNS WATER?"
THE NATION, SEPTEMBER 2, 2002
MAUDE BARLOW AND TONY CLARKE

INTRODUCTION

The planet's natural resources include water, oil, copper, lead, coal, and air, among other things. They are essential to the survival and development of humankind. These resources are usually classified as renewable and nonrenewable. Renewable resources are energy sources that have the capacity to be naturally replenished in theory—wind, solar, plants, and animals, for example. In some cases, however, human overexploitation can prevent this from happening, leading certain wildlife species to die out or water sources to become depleted. Nonrenewable resources include mineral ore and fossil fuels. The planet has only a finite supply of them: Once they are used up, they are gone.

Over the last one hundred years or so experts have become concerned about the global population, which grew from 1.6 billion in 1900 to just over 6.3 billion in 2004. Many believe that there are not enough natural resources to sustain it. While governments and the international community have tried to encourage sustainable development—economic growth through the use of renewable resources rather than finite ones—this has not always been successful. Some environmentalists argue that globalization and the rise of massive corporations,with little concern for anything other than profit maximization, have exacerbated the problem. Global entities such as Coca-Cola and McDonalds have been accused of such offenses as poisoning local water supplies in India and of causing deforestation in Brazil while operating their businesses. Although various laws have been passed to protect the environment, some observers believe that the best way to make citizens use resources efficiently and responsibly is by making them pay for them.

Among the arguments against payment is that essential resources, such as air and water, are "global commons"—they belong to everyone, and critics believe that it would be wrong for them to be owned by one particular company or country. They believe that everyone has a natural right to a basic resource such as water, for example, and that morally it should be free. Critics, however, counter that while this argument can possibly be applied to renewable resources, that is not a realistic approach to scarce resources. They also suggest that making people pay for resources is essential to making them behave more responsibly in their consumption.

> *"The nation behaves well if it treats ... natural resources as assets which it must turn over to the next generation."*
> —THEODORE ROOSEVELT, 26TH PRESIDENT (1901–1909)

Some environmentalists and economists reject this argument. They insist that treating natural resources like the property of firms or nations creates an inherently unfair situation. They also contend that it would exacerbate the divide between rich and poor countries since many developed nations—through colonialism or trade liberalization, for example—would be able to control the supply of key natural resources in poor countries.

If people do have to pay for natural resources, that also raises the question of whether it is preferable for the supplier to be a private firm or a

public, state-owned enterprise (SOE). Many people argue that natural resources should be in the hands of publically owned industries, which are subject to government control to ensure fair pricing and distribution. Citizens pay a fair rate for, say, water or natural gas. Any large spending on capital projects can be subsidized by government funds, while any profits are either reinvested into the SOE or transferred by the government to subsidize other SOEs. Among the criticisms leveled at SOEs, however, are that they are inefficient and bureaucratic. Opponents believe that private companies actually do a far better job and can supply resources to citizens more efficiently and at more competitive rates.

The alternative to SOEs is private business. However, many people are wary of the rise of transnational corporations (TNCs) with business operations in more than one country. They highlight "debt-for-equity" deals that became popular in the 1990s when developing nations, particularly in Latin America, were encouraged to exchange national assets to pay debts or acquire loans from organizations such as the World Bank. The supply of, say, water, then passed in some cases to TNCs with no great commitment to their customers. Critics have claimed that local people were often cut off from vital resources since they either could not or would not pay the high rates charged. The companies that have taken over these resources, however, insist that they have acted responsibly, invested in essential infrastructure, helped conservation efforts, and charged reasonable prices.

The following two articles look at the debate with particular regard to water.

WATER IS NOT "DIFFERENT"
Richard Tren

Richard Tren is director of the South African-based nongovernment organization Africa Fighting Poverty. He has written many articles on water privatization in South Africa. This 2003 article appeared on Tech Central Station, a website where "free markets meet technology."

YES

✓ "Water must be declared and understood for all time to be the common property of all. No one has the right to appropriate it for profit." These are the words of the Canadian water activist Maude Barlow, but they could have been said by any number of leftist commentators and organisations that oppose any private water ownership or private provision of water services. Yet constantly repeating these water mantras is not going to magically improve the access the people have to clean water; in fact it will do quite the opposite and encourage the misuse and waste of a precious resource.

The one fundamental problem with declaring anything a public good or common property is that it provides no incentive to any individual to conserve that good. Well intended water conservation campaigns may lead to some improved water use at the margin, but unfortunately do not address the fundamental problem. Human beings respond to incentives and where those incentives encourage the wasteful use of water, no amount of pleading from water conservation groups will change that behaviour. The only way to use water more efficiently is to ensure that it is privately owned and its use is monitored and paid for.

Do you think that adequate and fair access to water is a basic human right? What other resources may be considered as basic rights?

The case of South Africa
South Africa has a long and interesting history of water allocation and use. For most of our 300 year history, raw water was allocated to users on a political basis, rather than an economic basis. At varying points in our history, either English speaking or Afrikaans farmers were allocated most of the country's water resources. Unsurprisingly, for the most part, blacks were out of favour when it came to accessing water for agriculture or anything else for that matter.

Should race, gender, or other minority status influence whether people have access to natural resources?

In Africa around half of the water resources are used in agriculture. Addressing the way in which farmers use water is key to improving access to clean water and sanitation for South Africa's poor who are subjected to dirty and dangerous water supplies. The post-Apartheid government had its work cut out for it in attempting to correct the wrongs of the past. The 1998 National Water Act is a rather mixed bag of

Villagers use a water pump in Cotonou, Benin, to get their fresh water.

legislation; it improves control over water by setting up local Water User Associations (WUAs). This move empowers local water users and reduces Pretoria's influence. But the Act also nationalises water resources and forces water users to apply for temporary water use licences. This increases the discretionary power of bureaucrats to decide who should and shouldn't use water—repeating the errors of the past.

Nevertheless, in several catchments in South Africa, water users are trading water rights. Those that have water rights and either don't need them or can't put them to a high value use are selling those rights to other users who can use the water more efficiently and profitably. By allowing the market to allocate water, the resource is used more efficiently which is not only good for the economy, but for the environment and people as well.

The idea of water markets fills some people with horror as they imagine greedy speculators trading in water, while poor people are priced out of the water market, left to drink untreated and unhealthy water from streams. The reality is somewhat different.

In 1998 Chile embarked on a campaign to privatize its water supply. Go to http://www.trade partners.gov.uk/ water/chile/profile/ overview.shtml to read more about this subject.

How it can work

When Chile privatised its water resource and allowed water trading, municipalities could enter the market and buy up water from farmers so that they could improve supplies to their population. The upshot is that in a few short years, 99% of the urban poor and 94% of the rural poor had access to clean water. To a limited extent this is happening in South Africa, but the Department of Water Affairs (DWAF) has been tying up potential trades in red tape and has not approved any trades since February. The government should be applauded for allowing trades to take place, but by dragging its bureaucratic feet it is now harming agriculture and limiting access to water for the poor. In addition to sorting out the red tape issues, DWAF should give greater certainty over water rights so that trades can be done more efficiently and fairly. It is difficult and risky to attempt to trade something if the buyer thinks government will at some stage remove the right he wants to buy.

Many people criticize "red tape" bureaucracy, but is it necessary to have some kind of control over the use of resources? How else could this be achieved if not in this way?

If some people accept the benefits of trading raw, untreated water, they often balk at the idea of a private company treating and providing water and sanitation services in towns. The assumption that the state is better placed to deliver water is false. In almost every instance, the state is less efficient at supplying services than the private sector, and those costs are borne by all taxpayers. In the past, most state controlled water schemes in most poor countries favoured the urban elite, while the poor have to pay exorbitant sums to water sellers. Yet supplying safe water to the millions who need it is often beyond the budget of the state or the largesse of charities.

The private sector, however, can play a crucial role by investing in infrastructure and delivering safe, potable water. Examples are often cited where private water supply has gone wrong, such as in Cochabamba, Bolivia. Here the private water supplier hiked prices and didn't deliver the goods, leading to violent street riots. Yet if the proper institutions of the free market, such as the rule of law, are in place that can enforce contracts and ensure that a supplier delivers, then the private supply of water has a far better chance of working—just like the private supply of all other goods and services. Of course the supply of water services is a natural monopoly and so a regulator could ensure that it doesn't abuse its position while still making a profit. And if one is worried about the very poor not having access to water (and we should be) then the government can and should provide vouchers that can be exchanged with a private supplier for clean water and sanitation services.

Those that campaign against private water ownership and supply on the grounds that somehow water is "different" should think again. It is precisely because water has been treated unlike other goods that it is used inefficiently in agriculture and why poor people still lack safe access to the resource. Food, like water, is essential for human survival, yet no one seriously considers that the only way to reduce hunger is for the state to seize control of agriculture and then manufacture and distribute all food. Countless communist countries have done this and it only lead to mass starvation. It is high time we recognise that markets and the private sector are the friend of the poor and an essential tool for providing water to those who need it.

See the box on page 144 for more information about this and how the local population drew together to fight the privatization of their water supply.

Natural monopolies are industries in which advantages of large-scale production make it possible for one firm to produce the entire output of the market at a lower cost than a number of competing firms.

It is estimated that around one-sixth of the world's population lacks safe, secure, and adequate access to fresh water.

WHO OWNS WATER?
Maude Barlow and Tony Clarke

Maude Barlow heads a group of 60 activist organizations called Water For All. Tony Clarke is director of the Polaris Institute, an organization that helps citizen movements work for social change. This article appeared in the magazine The Nation in 2002.

NO

As the World Summit on Sustainable Development draws closer, clear lines of contention are forming, particularly around the future of the world's freshwater resources. … The world is running out of fresh water. Humanity is polluting, diverting and depleting the wellspring of life at a startling rate. With every passing day, our demand for fresh water outpaces its availability, and thousands more people are put at risk. Already, the social, political and economic impacts of water scarcity are rapidly becoming a destabilizing force, with water-related conflicts springing up around the globe. Quite simply, unless we dramatically change our ways, between one-half and two-thirds of humanity will be living with severe freshwater shortages within the next quarter-century.…

The earth's fresh water is finite and small, representing less than one half of 1 percent of the world's total water stock. Not only are we adding 85 million new people to the planet every year, but our per capita use of water is doubling every twenty years, at more than twice the rate of human population growth. A legacy of factory farming, flood irrigation, the construction of massive dams, toxic dumping, wetlands and forest destruction, and urban and industrial pollution has damaged the Earth's surface water so badly that we are now mining the underground water reserves far faster than nature can replenish them.…

Today thirty-one countries and over 1 billion people completely lack access to clean water. Every eight seconds a child dies from drinking contaminated water. The global freshwater crisis looms as one of the greatest threats ever to the survival of our planet.

Washington Consensus

Tragically, this global call for action comes in an era guided by the principles of the so-called Washington Consensus, a model of economics rooted in the belief that liberal market economics constitutes the one and only economic choice for the whole world. Competitive nation-states are abandoning natural resources protection and privatizing their ecological commons.…

Do you think American consumers are aware enough of the reasons why water needs to be conserved? Do you and your family use any water conservation measures at home, such as collecting rain water in barrels to use to water your garden?

What other factors do you think might threaten the survival of the planet?

Go to http://www.cid. harvard.edu/ cidtrade/issues/ washington.html to read about this concept.

Faced with the suddenly well-documented freshwater crisis, governments and international institutions are advocating a Washington Consensus solution: the privatization and commodification of water. Price water, they say in chorus; put it up for sale and let the market determine its future. For them, the debate is closed. Water, say the World Bank and the United Nations, is a "human need," not a "human right." These are not semantics; the difference in interpretation is crucial. A human need can be supplied many ways, especially for those with money. No one can sell a human right.

Do you think that a distinction can be made between these two things?

So a handful of transnational corporations, backed by the World Bank and the International Monetary Fund, are aggressively taking over the management of public water services in countries around the world, dramatically raising the price of water to the local residents and profiting especially from the Third World's desperate search for solutions to its water crisis.... The agenda is clear: Water should be treated like any other tradable good, with its use determined by the principles of profit....

Food is a tradable good. Why should water be considered any different?

According to *Fortune*, the annual profits of the water industry now amount to about 40 percent of those of the oil sector and are already substantially higher than the pharmaceutical sector, now close to $1 trillion. But only about 5 percent of the world's water is currently in private hands, so it is clear that we are talking about huge profit potential as the water crisis worsens....

Water lords

There are ten major corporate players now delivering freshwater services for profit. The two biggest are both from France—Vivendi Universal and Suez—considered to be the General Motors and Ford of the global water industry. Between them, they deliver private water and wastewater services to more than 200 million customers in 150 countries and are in a race, along with others such as Bouygues Saur, RWE-Thames Water and Bechtel-United Utilities, to expand to every corner of the globe.... They are aided by the World Bank and the IMF, which are increasingly forcing Third World countries to abandon their public water delivery systems and contract with the water giants in order to be eligible for debt relief. The performance of these companies in Europe and the developing world has been well documented: huge profits, higher prices for water, cutoffs to customers who cannot pay, no transparency in their dealings, reduced water quality, bribery and corruption....

Does this seem fair? Should the World Bank and IMF be allowed to make these kinds of conditions?

International trade

See Volume 18, Commerce and Trade, Topic 8 Do transnational corporations have more influence on the world economy than national governments?

At the same time, governments are signing away their control over domestic water supplies to trade agreements such as the North American Free Trade Agreement, its expected successor, the Free Trade Area of the Americas (FTAA), and the World Trade Organization. These global trade institutions effectively give transnational corporations unprecedented access to the freshwater resources of signatory countries. Already, corporations have started to sue governments in order to gain access to domestic water sources and, armed with the protection of these international trade agreements, are setting their sights on the commercialization of water....

The case against privatization

Why do you think some rich nations have refused to cancel the Third World debt? See Topic 12 Should developing nations take more responsibility for their own poverty?

If all this sounds formidable, it is. But the situation is not without hope. For the fact is, we know how to save the world's water: reclamation of despoiled water systems, drip irrigation over flood irrigation, infrastructure repairs, water conservation, radical changes in production methods and watershed management, just to name a few. Wealthy industrialized countries could supply every person on earth with clean water if they canceled the Third World debt, increased foreign aid payments and placed a tax on financial speculation. None of this will happen, however, until humanity earmarks water as a global commons and brings the rule of law—local, national and international—to any corporation or government that dares to contaminate it. If we allow the commodification of the world's freshwater supplies, we will lose the capacity to avert the looming water crisis. We will be allowing the emergence of a water elite that will determine the world's water future in its own interest. In such a scenario, water will go to those who can afford it and not to those who need it.

Many people believe that too much pressure is put on low-income countries to achieve good governance. Some argue that it is unattainable. Go to Volume 14, International Development, Topic 3 Is good governance key to poverty reduction? What do you think?

This is not an argument to excuse the poor way in which some governments have treated their water heritage, either squandering it, polluting it or using it for political gain. But the answer to poor nation-state governance is not a nonaccountable transnational corporation but good governance. For governments in poor countries, the rich world's support should go not to profiting from bad water management but from aiding the public sector in every country to do its job.

The commodification of water is wrong—ethically, environmentally and socially. It insures that decisions regarding the allocation of water would center on commercial, not environmental or social justice considerations. Privatization means that the management of water resources is based on principles of scarcity and profit maximization rather than long-term sustainability. Corporations are dependent on increased consumption to generate profits and are much more likely to invest in the use of chemical technology, desalination, marketing and water trading than in conservation....

A new water ethic

...Water must be declared and understood for all time to be the common property of all.... Simply, governments must declare that water belongs to the earth and all species and is a fundamental human right. No one has the right to appropriate it for profit. Water must be declared a public trust.... Already, a common front of environmentalists, human rights and antipoverty activists, public sector workers, peasants, indigenous peoples and many others from every part of the world has come together to fight for a water-secure future based on the notion that water is part of the public commons. We coordinated strategy at the World Social Forum in Porto Alegre, Brazil, last January. We will be in South Africa for the World Summit on Sustainable Development in September and in Kyoto, Japan, next March, when the World Bank and the UN bring 8,000 people to the Third World Water Forum. There, we will oppose water privatization and promote our own World Water Vision as an alternative to that adopted by the World Bank at the Second World Water Forum in The Hague two years ago. We will stand with local people fighting water privatization in Bolivia, or the construction of a mega-dam in India, or water takings by Perrier in Michigan, but now all of these local struggles will form part of an emerging international movement with a common political vision.

Steps needed for a water-secure future include the adoption of a Treaty Initiative to Share and Protect the Global Water Commons; a guaranteed "water lifeline"—free clean water every day for every person as an inalienable political and social right; national water protection acts to reclaim and preserve freshwater systems; exemptions for water from international trade and investment regimes; an end to World Bank and IMF-enforced water privatizations; and a Global Water Convention that would create an international body of law to protect the world's water heritage based on the twin cornerstones of conservation and equity. A tough challenge indeed. But given the stakes involved, we had better be up to it.

Sustainable development is the process of achieving economic growth in a way that does not outstrip the supply of natural resources. Some development specialists believe that corporations are only playing lip-service to working in this way since they ultimately want to maximize profits. Do you think governments should do more to encourage sustainable development?

Hundreds of water specialists met at the Second World Water Forum, held in Hague from March 17 to 22, 2000. Go to http://www.waternunc.com/gb/secWWF.htm to look at articles on the subject and to find links to other water sites.

The July 21, 2001, treaty stated that the world's fresh-water supply is a global common, "it cannot be sold by any institution, government, individual, or corporation for profit." Do you think that this is realistic?

Summary

Economists have debated for years about whether people should have to pay for natural resources. The preceding articles examine the issue with regard to water. Richard Tren, in the first, insists that viewing water as the property of everyone encourages waste and discourages development. He says that there has to be an incentive to conserve the world's water supply and argues that people will value water more when they pay for it. He believes that it is wrong to automatically assume that the state is better positioned to provide fresh water for its citizens. Tren claims that the private sector is more financially solvent and is better placed to invest in much-needed infrastructure. Problems with privatization can be sidestepped as long as the business is properly regulated, and making a profit and providing a good, affordable service are not mutually exclusive, he argues.

   Maude Barlow and Tony Clarke disagree. They claim that the world is running out of fresh water and that big business is partly to blame thanks to the legacy of industrialization. By making water a commodity, these businesses make huge profits while poorer countries are forced into restrictive contracts that do not really benefit their people. They argue that a water elite is emerging that will determine the future of the world's water but that will work in its own interest. They insist that the only way forward is for rich countries to help poor nations both develop their own public sectors and establish a legal framework to protect water rights. Barlow and Clarke conclude that the "commodification" of water is ethically, environmentally, and socially wrong, and the only way out of this trap is to decommodify water and declare it the common property of all.

FURTHER INFORMATION:

Books:

Sclar, Elliot D., and Richard C. Leone, *You Don't Always Get What You Pay For: The Economics of Privatization*. New York: Cornell University Press, 2000.
Ward, Diana Raines, *Water Wars: Drought, Flood, Folly, and the Politics of Thirst*. New York: Riverhead Books, 2002.

Useful websites:

www.nrcs.usda.gov
Natural Resources Conservation service.
http://www.whirledbank.org/development/private.html
Article that examines the World Bank and privatization and how certain countries are being forced to sell off their public industries.

The following debates in the Pro/Con series may also be of interest:

In this volume:
Part 3: International development

In *International Development*:
Topic 16 Does water scarcity prevent economic development?

Water: A crisis situation?, pages 212–213

SHOULD PEOPLE HAVE TO PAY FOR NATURAL RESOURCES?

YES: Most natural resources have a finite supply: Charging for usage encourages people to use them efficiently and to treat them with respect

YES: Private companies have the money to invest in the infrastructure needed to ensure more people can enjoy fresh water

MORALITY
Is it right to charge for natural resources?

ACCESS
Does privatization aid access to resources such as water?

NO: Resources, such as water, are the common property of all: They should be free

NO: Several attempts to privatize water supplies have ended in disaster. Access to certain natural resources should be a basic right, and privatizing them often prices them out of the range of poor people.

SHOULD PEOPLE HAVE TO PAY FOR NATURAL RESOURCES?
KEY POINTS

YES: As part of a structural adjustment program, the World Bank has encouraged some nations to privatize natural resources supply in exchange for loans and aid. Water quality, sanitation, and distribution have improved, particularly to remote communities.

YES: Many resources need expensive infrastructure to bring them to local communities, but ownership should be limited to local industry and be governed by strict laws

RIGHTS
Have institutions like the World Bank helped promote equitable resource distribution?

OWNERSHIP
Should natural resources be home-owned?

NO: In Latin America the World Bank was criticized for brokering deals that adversely effected local populations by putting water rights in the hands of exploitative foreign companies

NO: Many poor nations—where such resources are found—simply do not have the financial or technical resources to provide adequate, efficient, and cheap supplies of them

137

PART 3
INTERNATIONAL DEVELOPMENT

INTRODUCTION

In any analysis of poverty and wealth the issue of international development arises. Development helps societies progress in three main ways: First of all, it facilitates the availability and distribution of essentials such as food, water, and shelter; second of all, living standards are improved through access to better education and employment, and the fostering of individual and national pride, for example; and finally, development also increases the range of choices available to both individuals and nation-states.

Many governments, including that of the United States, with the help of international organizations such as the United Nations and World Bank, are trying to help poor nations develop by such means as investment in education programs, funding small businesses, and promoting good governance in unstable nations. Some economists and politicians have also claimed that globalization, new technology, and the opening up of new markets through trade liberalization are also helping developing nations' economies.

Despite this, critics claim that the divide between rich and poor nations and the fact that more than one-fifth of the world's population lives in extreme poverty, with little or no access to food, water, and other essential resources, is proof that more has to be done to help.

But whose responsibility is it? Do rich nations have a duty to help the poor, especially countries that were former colonies? Would forcing rich nations to pay a percentage of their gross national product (GNP) toward development aid and loans help or hinder economic growth in low-income countries? Or are poor nations too dependent on foreign help to solve their problems? Should they in fact be forced to take responsibility for their own poverty and bad governance? This section discusses some of these key questions.

Globalization

The issue of globalization is always raised when examining international development. For many economists globalization means the opening up of world markets to international trade so that capital, goods, and services can flow unhindered between nations. This trade liberalization, or "free trade," has been a basic principle of post-1945 economic policy. International organizations, including the World Trade Organization, which arose out of the General Agreement on Tariffs and Trade, exist to help reduce trade barriers between countries. But some experts believe that globalization has in fact helped exacerbate the rich–poor divide, working to the advantage of wealthy nations. For example, western firms now find it easier to move their business operations to developing countries where labor and natural resources are cheaper, and human and environmental rights laws are often far more lax. This has helped create a group of hugely powerful transnational organizations. Some of these business enterprises have more economic and political clout than many nation-states; people living on the planet has almost tripled to reach its current level of over six billion people—four billion of this figure reside in developing nations. Some observers believe that the world has reached its natural carrying capacity, and that the world will soon reach a stage where population outstrips the natural resources needed to sustain it. Overpopulation,

> *"The human family can only advance collectively if there are fair relations for all its members."*
> —KENNETH KAUNDA, PRESIDENT OF ZAMBIA (1964–1991)

they are often accused of abusing their power to the cost of local populations and the environment. Others claim that since TNCs are responsible for large sums of foreign direct investment—now the largest form of private capital inflow to developing countries—they are therefore easy targets when problems arise. Some economists also claim that TNCs have helped poor nations develop by investing in local infrastructure and providing training in new industries and employment. Topics 11 and 15 in this section look at globalization and transnational corporations and their relationship to poverty.

Population and bad governance

Although the aforementioned issues are without doubt important, some commentators believe that the causes of poverty, underdevelopment, and slow economic growth are far more basic. Population growth, for example, is a matter of concern, especially since in the last 50 or so years the amount of particularly in poor nations, has, some argue, hindered economic growth, and some governments have introduced policies to control birthrates. Many commentators believe that such steps are positive examples of poor nations taking responsibility for their own problems. Similarly, investment in new industry, the promotion of democratic principles, and the rule of law are other measures that the governments of poor nations have introduced.

Critics of this viewpoint say that poor nations cannot evolve without help. They maintain that rich countries, particularly former colonial powers, have a duty to help low-income nations in any way they can. Any state that has profited from exploiting the natural resources of a poor nation must give back in kind, they claim. But what is the best way to do this? Is investment in education or the promotion of new technology enough when millions are starving or suffering the effects of malnutrition? Topics 12, 13, 14, and 16 examine some of these issues.

INTRODUCTION

Globalization is one of the most controversial issues in international economics. It can be defined as the progressive integration of economies around the world, particularly through the lifting of restrictions on trade or the flow of investment. The term globalization, however, also has a wider use in which it refers to the movement of workers, technology, culture, and knowledge across international borders. While many economists and politicians believe that globalization has a positive effect on the world economy—and that it is also inevitable—others insist that in practice globalization helps rich nations increase their power and wealth at the cost of poorer nations.

The basis of globalization is free trade, or the removal of restrictions on the flow of goods and capital in the shape of, for example, protective tariffs on imports. Free trade itself has been the fundamental principle of neoclassical economic theory since its formulation by Scottish economist Adam Smith (1723-1790) in the 18th century. Free trade underlies the policies of influential global economic organizations such as the General Agreement on Tariffs and Trade (GATT) and its successor the World Trade Organization (WTO). It has also encouraged the emergence of regional free-trade areas, such as the North American Free Trade Agreement (NAFTA) and the European Union (EU).

Supporters of free trade argue that it allows national economies to specialize in providing those goods and services for which they have a comparative advantage: That is, they can provide them more cheaply or efficiently than other countries. They can then use the proceeds to buy other goods and services they need from other countries. According to orthodox economic theory, this will increase the volume of global trade, which will in turn benefit national economies.

Supporters of globalization, who include observers from both industrialized and developing countries, argue that the lifting of restrictions will enable poor countries to trade more effectively and thus increase their GDP (gross domestic product). They also maintain that poor countries will benefit from the increased flow of knowledge and technology among countries. One example they cite is India, which went from being a relatively poor nation to a world leader in the IT sector in less than a decade.

> *"It has been said that arguing against globalization is like arguing against the laws of gravity."*
>
> —KOFI ANNAN,
>
> UN SECRETARY-GENERAL (2001)

Critics of globalization argue that although jobs may have been created in countries such as India, they tend to benefit foreign rather than domestic labor and firms. Some experts refer to statistics from the International Monetary Fund (IMF) to show that although the wealthiest quarter of the world population saw its per capita GDP increase nearly sixfold during the 20th century, the poorest quarter experienced a less than threefold increase. They assert that while developing countries may increase their economic activity through the lifting of trade restrictions, for example, trade liberalization in practice usually gives greater benefits to more developed nations. This means that rather than allowing poor countries to achieve parity and join the "developed" world, they are in fact often being left even further behind.

Advocates of globalization, however, insist that such simple indicators do not tell the whole story. They claim that broader measures, such as the human development indicator (HDI), which takes into account factors such as life expectancy and education, show that the rich–poor divide is narrowing both between countries and within certain countries. They also suggest that the main problem is not globalization itself but that of how to best achieve fair or equitable distribution of its benefits. Such factors as sound financial institutions, fair trade legislation, medical and educational initiatives, facilities for technological dissemination, ecological and environmental restraints, and fair treatment of accumulated debt are necessary for this to occur, they claim.

The IMF, among others, believes that developed economies can play a vital part in facilitating the integration of poor nations into the global economy, by, for example, helping them develop more equitable trade distribution, and encouraging flows of private capital into such nations. For other observers this is an unrealistic suggestion. They assert that it is simply not in the best interests of rich nations to share their advantages: Their main priority and that of the international organizations they dominate is to exploit the resources of poor nations, such as cheap labor, in such a way as to maximize their own profits.

Jim Shultz and Maria Livanos Cattaui examine globalization further.

GLOBALIZATION RESISTANCE BRINGS DOWN A PRESIDENT
Jim Shultz

Jim Shultz is the executive director of the Democracy Center (www.democracy ctr.org), which publicized the water issue in Bolivia. This 2003 article was published in the New Internationalist.

YES

On the night of 17 October, those Bolivians who own TVs were witness to a split-screen image of history unfolding. At the bottom was a Boeing 767 taking off for an overnight flight to Miami, carrying aboard Gonzalo Sànchez de Lozada, who had just resigned the Presidency. At the top was a live broadcast from the national Congress where Vice-President Carlos Mesa Gisbert was being sworn in to replace him. A month-long series of protests, sparked by a proposal to export Bolivian natural gas to California, had ended with the toppling of the Government.

Bolivia shows the world

See the box on page 144 for more information about Bechtel's takeover of Cochabamba's water supply and its implications for the city's poor.

For the third time in as many years, Bolivia has offered to the world a powerful symbol of popular resistance to globalization imposed from abroad. In 2000 the people of Cochabamba captured world attention when they took back their privatized water from the corporate giant Bechtel. Last February nationwide protests succeeded in blocking an IMF imposed belt-tightening package, but only after troops killed more than 30 people.

Historic resentments

The September–October uprising was a response to plans to export part of Bolivia's mammoth natural-gas reserves through a British-led consortium called Pacific LNG. Under the company's plan the gas would have been shipped from landlocked Bolivia to the Pacific via Chile, then on to Mexico for processing and finally to its lucrative end market in California. Popular opposition to the plan is strong. Piping the gas through Chile arouses deep historical resentment over that country's seizure of Bolivia's last remaining access to the sea in 1879. But a majority opposes the gas deal via any route. "The money will all just end up in the pockets of the president, the ministers and other politicians," says Lourdes Netz, a former Roman Catholic nun. "Look at all the public companies that have been privatized. Have the people benefited?"

Should natural resources be managed by public-owned companies? Go to www.bbc.co.uk and www.cnn.com, and look up articles on nationalized industries.

Bolivian President Carlos Mesa Gisbert (1953–) on his first day in office on October 17, 2003. Mesa replaced President Lozada after riots and protests.

COMMENTARY: Bechtel, water, and Bolivia

Although rich in natural resources, Bolivia is one of Latin America's poorest nations, and many of its citizens live in abject poverty. In 1996 the World Bank offered Cochabamba, Bolivia's third largest city, a $14 million loan to extend its water services on the condition that it privatize its water supply; less than a year later it offered Bolivia $600 million in debt relief on the same condition. In 1999 a company called Aguas del Tunari was given a 40-year lease on the water system of Cochabamba; a California engineering company, Bechtel, was its major shareholder. Bolivian President Gonzalo Sànchez de Lozada, Bechtel, and the World Bank were all heavily criticized by both environmental and human rights organizations. Federal law 2029 eliminated the local people's guarantees to water distribution in rural areas and gave the government the right to expropriate the water and irrigation systems to Aguas del Tunari. This meant that farmers dependent on irrigation and local communities and neighborhoods on the periphery of the city suddenly lost all rights to these water sources.

While international human rights law recognizes progressive realization—the idea that governments have the right to adopt a clear plan for moving toward the achievement of certain social, cultural, economic, and political rights—many perceived the privatization of the city's water supply as a step backward, especially since Aguas del Tunari immediately increased water prices for the local poor by as much as 200 percent. Opposition became centered in La Coordinadora (The Coalition for the Defense of Water and Life), which organized widescale protests against the government and called for the water supply to be put back into Bolivian hands. Violent clashes, riots, and strikes resulted, and international attention became focused on the issue. The government finally took away Bechtel's right to control the water supply, but in November 2001 the company filed a $25 million suit against the Bolivian government.

Is the author being unduly pessimistic? Can transnational corporations also bring benefits to poor economies, such as education, training, and new technology opportunities?

Bolivia's political system is notoriously corrupt. Combine this with transnational corporations bent on maximizing profits and the result is usually a sweet deal that leaves the dealmakers happy and leaves the public the loser. Popular sentiment can be summed up as: before we sell the gas, we need a political system that will actually do it in the people's interests. To the wealthy Bolivian élite and its allies in institutions like the IMF, the gas deal looks like a cash boon to a country that could sorely use one. To average Bolivians it looks like one more raid from abroad on its natural resources. After 15 years of being the World Bank and IMF's chief South American laboratory for pro-market economic reforms, Bolivians have clearly had enough.

Marching for change

In mid-September tens of thousands of men and women—
Indians from the high altiplano and coca growers
from the lowlands of the Chapare alike—began marching
to the capital city of La Paz. The roads leading in and
out of the city were blocked with rocks, logs and whatever
else people could find. Lozada feigned dialogue but
sent in troops.

In early October, with the death toll over 30, the
Government began to crack. Vice-President Mesa publicly
broke with the president on the radio:"I cannot accept the
number of deaths this conflict is causing."

As the repression and deaths increased, demands for the
president's resignation became overwhelming. Lozada went
into hiding in his fortressed presidential residence while the
U.S. government repeatedly proclaimed its backing for him.

As the sun rose on 17 October many expected Lozada to
declare martial law. Instead he was packing his suitcases for
his flight to Miami. In a bitter resignation letter read before
the Congress and the nation, he blamed everyone but
himself, made no apologies and made no mention of the
more than 80 dead that he had left in his wake.

Carlos Mesa Gisbert (1953–) was a historian and a journalist before he entered politics. He was President Lozada's vice president but took over as president of Bolivia in October 2003.

Does the U.S. government intervene too much in the affairs of other nations? Why should it be interested in the Bolivian government's business?

Mesa's promises

Bolivia's new president has vowed to govern independent
of the nation's highly suspect political parties. He has
committed to a binding popular vote on gas exportation, a
constituent assembly to rewrite the constitution and an
aggressive anti-corruption campaign.

One of his first acts as president was to appear
unannounced before a massive crowd of protesters
in the capital, asking for time and help to address the
nation's problems. Social movement leaders have given
him a 90-day truce to begin tackling those problems. But
Mesa will find himself stuck between their demands and
pressures from the World Bank, IMF and U.S. to stay on
their ideological course.

"This is a victory in a battle, like other battles we
have won, but we haven't won the war," says water-
revolt leader Oscar Olivera. "We are trying to recover
democracy through peaceful means."

Each of Bolivia's recent such battles has ended in
victory, yet with a growing death toll. While it remains
to be seen whether a change of president will make
a real difference, a month of protest and bloodshed
did end with something many did not expect—hope.

Oscar Olivera is executive secretary of the Cochabamba Federation of Factory Workers and spokesperson for La Coordinadora. He gained international recognition for leading a grassroots protest against the privatization of water in Cochabamba.

Is this evidence that violent protest is sometimes justified?

GLOBALIZATION SHOULD NOT BE A SCAPEGOAT FOR THE EXISTENCE OF POVERTY
Maria Livanos Cattaui

Maria Livanos Cattaui is secretary general of the International Chamber of Commerce.

X Those who really want to alleviate the poverty of hundreds of millions of people in the developing world should look at practical remedies instead of making globalization a scapegoat. There is absolutely no evidence that the accelerated integration of markets around the world is increasing the sum of human misery—rather the contrary. But that was not the picture painted in Geneva at the special session of the United Nations General Assembly, called to review progress since the UN social summit in Copenhagen five years ago.

Do you think this is a useful argument? What other factors could have resulted in such widespread poverty?

Rhetoric inside the conference and the clamour of demonstrators outside gave the opposite impression. Headlines projected the sad news from the UN that since 1995 the number of people living in absolute poverty has grown from about one billion to 1.2 billion. This terrible picture is depicted as an indictment of globalization, evidence that it has somehow flunked its test.

Given the steady rise in the world population—up by almost 400 million to 6.1 billion over the five years—how much worse would the figures have been without the benefits of trade liberalization, foreign investment and the knowledge economy? If the UN's figures are right, the world economy has managed to place an extra 200 million people above the poverty line. Little useful can learned by juggling with numbers, which can be used to prove almost anything by selecting the most convenient set of figures and time frames. There is no getting around the fact that economic growth must be the point of departure for all improvements in living standards.

This shows that it is important to check the source of any statistics you use and look at how they were created.

Strangling growth
How on earth will it help the poor if governments try to strangle globalization by stemming the flow of trade, information and capital—the three components of the global economy? That disparities between rich and poor

COMMENTARY: Amartya Sen

Indian Nobel prize-winning economist Amartya Sen is a leading advocate of and defender of globalization. Born in in Santiniketan, India, in 1933, Sen received a BA in economics in 1953 from Presidency College in Calcutta, India. He received another BA in economics and a PhD in 1955 and 1959 respectively, from Trinity College in Cambridge, England, where he currently teaches. Professor Sen has taught at many universities, including the London School of Economics, London, and Oxford University, both in England, and Harvard University and the University of California at Berkeley. He has written on many development and poverty issues, and in 1998 won the Nobel Prize in economics.

Sen and globalization

Sen has lectured and written widely on globalization and its effects. He is a widely acclaimed expert. He claims that it is wrong to think of globalization as a purely western phenomenon. In a 2001 seminar he stated that "Over thousands of years globalization has contributed to the progress of the world, through travel, trade, migration, spread of cultural influences, and dissemination of knowledge and understanding (including of science and technology). To have stopped globalization would have done irreparable harm to the progress of humanity."

Sen also believes that much antiglobalization feeling lies in the association of globalization with western imperialism, but he argues that the central problem is not with globalization itself but with "the inequity in the overall balance of institutional arrangements—which produces very unequal sharing of the benefits of globalization." He believes that the poor need to have their fair share of and fair access to the rewards of globalization, but that institutional arrangements, both national and international, need to be reformed in order for this to happen.

are still too great is undeniable. But it is just not true that economic growth benefits only the rich and leaves out the poor, as the opponents of globalization and the market economy would have us believe.

A recent World Bank study entitled "Growth is good for the poor" reveals a one-for-one relationship between income of the bottom fifth of the population and per capita GDP. In other words, incomes of all sectors grow proportionately at the same rate. The study notes that openness to foreign trade benefits the poor to the same extent that it benefits the whole economy.

Globalization was never a one-size-fits-all miracle cure for poverty eradication. The economic growth that globalization

Go to http://www.iedm. org/library/kraay_en.html to read "Growth Is Good for the Poor" by David Dollar and Aart Kray. Is their argument convincing?

Nobel prize-winner Amartya Sen in 2002. Sen is a vocal advocate of globalization.

brings is certainly essential, but it is not enough. A much more complex set of policies must be brought into play, which will include multilateral technical and financial assistance from global institutions, and targeted bilateral aid, to least developed countries in particular. Improved market access for the exports of developing countries is indispensable so that they can have the chance to pay their own way. Let us hope that they will benefit more fully from trade liberalization in the next round of world trade negotiations. Above all, progress will require self-help by individual countries: the rule of law, financial probity, political stability, the absence of conflict, a legal framework that encourages investment, both domestic and foreign.

Is it the duty of the international community to help individual countries develop?

Prospering without help?

Nobody expects the poorer countries to prosper without help. Poverty reduction will be greatly assisted by external support for education, health programmes and basic social services that are taken for granted in the industrialized world. As UN Secretary General Kofi Annan said in Geneva, the case for making extra resources available can be made compellingly when those resources are to be used for social services which benefit the poor rather than for weapons or to raise the living standards of an already privileged elite.

Critics argue that rich nations, such as the United States, often support free trade but in practice adopt protectionist measures if their own domestic industries are threatened. Should countries that do this be penalized?

The World Trade Organization recently buttressed the case for globalization with a study showing that those developing countries that are the most open to trade—that is, most ready to take part in the global economy—are the most successful in catching up with rich countries. Countries that stay on the sidelines tend to languish. Cynics will say that the evidence in these and similar studies is self-serving. But leaving aside the war of figures and statistics, it is surely no more than common sense to state that the more wealth in cash and kind that is moving around the world, and the more widely it is distributed, the better for everybody.

Governments must not be stampeded into a futile attempt to stop or slow globalization when the causes of poverty and exclusion lie elsewhere.

Summary

In the first article Jim Shultz attacks globalization, using events that took place in Bolivia to support his case. A series of popular protests sparked by the government's intention to export Bolivian natural gas to California ended with the resignation and flight of President Gonzalo Sànchez de Lozada. In his critique Shultz claims that the deal would only have benefitted Bolivia's already wealthy elite, leaving the poor out of the loop. Nevertheless he ends on a note of hope and a vote of confidence for Carlos Mesa Gisbert, the new president, who has committed himself to tackling Bolivia's poverty and other problems.

Maria Livanos Cattaui, on the other hand, takes a completely different view. She argues that there is no evidence whatsoever that the integration of markets around the world has increased inequality. She dismisses conclusions that she says are wrongly extrapolated from data collected by the United Nations about the increasing number of people living in absolute poverty: She maintains that these numbers can be used to serve almost any purpose depending on the way they are presented. Backing her statement is a World Bank study, which notes that openness to foreign trade benefits the poor to the same extent that it helps the whole economy. Cattaui ends by stating that governments must not be pushed into slowing down or stopping globalization from occurring in poor nations when the causes of poverty and exclusion actually lie elsewhere.

FURTHER INFORMATION:

Books:

Marber, Peter, *Money Changes Everything: How Global Prosperity Is Shaping Our Needs, Values, and Lifestyles.* Upper Saddle River, NJ: Prentice Hall, 2003.

Useful websites:

http://globalization.about.com/cs/whatisit/a/gzgoodorbad2.htm
About globalization site with lots of links to pro and con articles.
http://www.globalpolicy.org/globaliz/define/index.htm
Global Policy subsite listing articles defining globalization.
http://www.iccwbo.org/home/menu_case_for_the_global_economy.asp
International Chamber of Commerce site listing pro and con articles on the global economy.
www.newint.org
New Internationalist site features much on globalization.

The following debates in the Pro/Con series may also be of interest:

In this volume:
Part 2: Social and economic issues

Part 3: International development

In *International Development*:
Topic 10 Are protectionist policies essential to economic growth in poor nations?

In *Commerce and Trade*:
Part 2: Globalization and its effects

HAS GLOBALIZATION INCREASED INEQUALITY?

YES: The World Bank, for example, sometimes favors policies that are not in the best interests of the local communities. Some critics believe that it has used loans and aid to advance the interests of rich nations.

YES: Some experts claim that globalization only benefits the wealthy elite and big corporations. They believe that regional associations would help development.

INTERNATIONAL ORGANIZATIONS
Have organizations such as the World Bank exacerbated the rich–poor divide?

CURSE
Are poor nations better off without globalization?

NO: The World Bank and other organizations exist to help reduce poverty. The uneven effects of globalization are due to greed and other factors.

HAS GLOBALIZATION INCREASED INEQUALITY?
KEY POINTS

NO: The IMF argues that countries that have been able to integrate with the global economy are seeing faster growth and reduced poverty

YES: Supraorganizations, such as the World Trade Organization, while meant to promote trade liberalization, often penalize poor nations while advancing the economic interests of rich nations

YES: Statistics show that while poor nations may benefit from trade liberalization, for example, rich nations are gaining more

STATISTICS
Are statistics a reliable way to judge whether globalization benefits rich nations?

TRADE
Have poor nations suffered from trade with rich nations?

NO: The measures used are too narrow; education and life expectancy, for example, should be taken into account when analyzing globalization's effects

NO: Globalization and trade liberalization have brought much-needed medical, technological, and financial assistance to some developing countries

Topic 12

SHOULD DEVELOPING NATIONS TAKE MORE RESPONSIBILITY FOR THEIR OWN POVERTY?

YES
"NOW, THINK SMALL: POOR COUNTRIES COULD HELP THEMSELVES GET RICHER BY FIXING THEIR INSTITUTIONS"
THE ECONOMIST ONLINE, SEPTEMBER 13, 2001
THE ECONOMIST

NO
FROM "CAN THE FINANCING GAP BE CLOSED?"
AFRICA RECOVERY, VOL.15, NO. 4, DECEMBER 2001
JULLYETTE UKABIALA

INTRODUCTION

In developing countries some 1.2 billion people survive on less than $1 a day. Around the world, about 30,000 people die every day from starvation or related causes. While the average income in the United States is over $40,000 per year, in Sudan it is just $63. This evidence shows that poverty remains a huge problem in the developing world—the term used to describe those countries, mainly in Africa and Asia, that are not fully integrated into the global economy. However, the causes of that poverty are the subject of much debate.

Some people believe that poverty is a natural condition: Certain nations have more fertile land, greater supplies of valuable minerals or fossil fuel, or better harbors that are more suited to trade than others. From this point of view extreme poverty-related disasters, such as the famine that struck Ethiopia in the early 1990s, are the natural consequences of too many people living in regions that do not have enough resources to support them. Poverty can therefore be seen as a natural check on overpopulation and the exhaustion of natural resources.

Other observers believe that this view of poverty is fatalistic. They argue that poverty is often created by human actions, such as poor government, economic exploitation, or warfare. There is, however, much debate about who causes these factors to happen. While some people see poor countries essentially as victims of a global economy dominated by the richer industrialized countries of the West, others believe that they often bring poverty on themselves through such factors as bad governance.

Subscribers to the first view often refer to the link between poverty and colonialism. They state that many developing nations were ruled by imperial powers, such as Great Britain, from the 16th century onward. The colonizers exploited the natural resources of their colonies but invested little in return, they claim: When the colonial powers withdrew from these nations—India and South Africa, among them—they left behind politically weak states and underdeveloped economies.

"Genuine global prosperity and progress depend on unification of the interests of all people."

—ARCHBISHOP MIGLIORE, VATICAN PERMANENT OBSERVER TO THE UNITED NATIONS (2003)

Other institutions that are often blamed for creating poverty in the developing world include transnational corporations (TNCs)—companies that have business operations in several countries. TNCs are accused of exploiting resources in poor nations and utilizing free-trade policies promoted by international economic bodies such as the World Trade Organization (WTO) and the World Bank to their advantage. The use of protectionist tariffs by the United States, for example, has also been criticized for limiting trade opportunities for poor nations.

Other observers believe that in many cases developing nations themselves are at least partly responsible for creating their own poverty. They argue that even if western aid were increased, it would not necessarily improve the situation of low-income countries. Some refer to examples of foreign aid being appropriated by governments or armed forces rather than being used to feed the poor or improve water security. Others claim that aid can actually prolong poverty by causing poor nations to become aid-dependent. Such critics argue that aid can only help in the short term, and even then only if it is backed up with a holistic approach that tackles the underlying issues causing poverty.

Some observers argue that western nations could help poor nations by canceling the nearly $3 trillion in debts owed by them. They argue that even paying the interest on such debts can cripple emerging economies. For others, however, the responsibility for such debts lies with the developing nations themselves, which often borrowed large sums of money in order to modernize their economies after decolonization. They believe that since these countries borrowed the money in good faith, they have a duty to repay their debts.

Commentators, such as Robert Guest, Africa editor of the British journal *The Economist*, also argue that the key to poverty reduction lies with poor nations themselves. The promotion of good governance, which involves among other things, establishing stable government, ending corruption, gaining adequate food and water security, promoting the rule of law, and investment in education and industry, would help end poverty, they claim.

The following articles examine the question in greater detail.

NOW, THINK SMALL: POOR COUNTRIES COULD HELP THEMSELVES GET RICHER BY FIXING THEIR INSTITUTIONS
The Economist

The Economist *is a British weekly journal that provides international news and economic analysis.*

YES

ILLEGAL money-traders bustle on the streets of Myanmar [formerly Burma], one of Asia's poorest and most authoritarian countries. Taxi-drivers and diamond-dealers tout for business and curio-sellers walk the beaches of Sierra Leone, in west Africa, despite a decade of war and general collapse. Proudly communist Vietnam thrives with young capitalist entrepreneurs. However destitute a country may be, some form of market activity seems to survive. But can the poorest find a way to turn that activity into useful growth?

Go to http:// econ.worldbank. org/wds/ to read the most recently published 2004 World Development Report.

Yes, with some help, said the World Bank this week. Its annual World Development Report, which this year looks at the way governments can encourage successful markets, suggests that when poor people are allowed access to the institutions richer people enjoy, they can thrive and help themselves. A great deal of poverty, in other words, may be easily avoidable.

Open flows

The study, which gathered existing research and added a survey of around 100 countries, found that economies that allowed open flows of information to as many people as possible (with free, competitive media), good protection for the property rights of the poor (especially over land and the efficient collection of loans) and broad access to judicial systems (even for illiterate peasants or people who cannot pay high legal fees) were most likely to be competitive, and to develop.

A "boon" is a timely benefit or favor.

Efficient formal and informal institutions, in other words, are crucial for turning subsistence farmers, petty traders and other would-be money-makers into a boon for the general economy. If it is too expensive and time-consuming, for example, to open a bank account, the poor will stuff their savings under the mattress. When it takes 19 steps, five months and more than the average person's annual income

COMMENTARY: Hernando de Soto

Hernando de Soto (1941–) is renowned internationally for his pioneering work on the causes of wealth and poverty. His theory that the lack of formal property rights is a cause of poverty in developing nations has revolutionized global understanding of poverty. It has also brought him acclaim: He was named one of the five leading Latin American innovators by *Time* magazine in 1999. In 2004 he was also awarded the Milton Friedman Prize for Advancing Liberty by the Cato Institute.

Born in Arequipa, Peru, de Soto spent his early business life in Europe. He returned to Peru in 1979 to a country plagued by poverty. He decided to devote his life to answering the question of why some countries are rich while others are poor. In 1980 he set up a research think tank, the Institute for Liberty and Democracy (ILD).

De Soto discovered that many poor Peruvians lacked the formal legal title to their property and that this held them back since they were unable to use their assets as collateral to borrow against. De Soto expanded his work to look at other economies: He calculated that the amount of "dead capital" in untitled assets held by the world's poor was at least $9.3 trillion.

De Soto's advice on poverty and wealth issues has been sought by many leaders, including Peru's former President Alberto Fujimoro (1990–2000) and Mexican President Vicente Fox (2000–). Cato Institute President Ed Crane said of de Soto, "Everyone talks about helping the world's poor. This is a man who [has] figured out how to do it."

to register a new business in Mozambique, it is no wonder that aspiring, cash-strapped entrepreneurs do not bother. In general, poorer countries charge far more, relative to income, than rich ones to register new businesses. They also demand that applicants jump through more bureaucratic hoops, and so increase the opportunities for corruption. All this stifles growth.

Good institutions lead to growth

Since the poor economies that are growing faster are the ones with good institutions, says Roumeen Islam, overseer of the report, other countries must follow suit. But which institutions are best in these conditions? Simple and accessible ones, is the answer, which do not intimidate the poor. Zambia and the Gambia both set up local stock exchanges in the early 1990s, only to find they drew almost no business. They would have done better to consider less ambitious schemes, such as the small-claims courts set up in Tanzania—where the

Roumeen Islam is a World Bank economist and director of the team behind the World Development Reports. He is a U.S. citizen of Bengali origin.

Rickshaws in Ernakulam, in the southern Indian state of Kerala. Despite progress in health care and literacy, Kerala has not achieved corresponding economic and industrial growth.

average court case has been speeded up from 22 months to three—or the micro-credit banks, lending small sums on minimal security, set up in Bangladesh, South Africa and Bolivia.

The World Bank report sees such small institutions as particularly useful in places—Vietnam, Peru and Ethiopia, among others—where farmers and the urban poor are unsure of their legal rights to their land or homes. Granting formal property titles is essential in the long run, to allow people to raise loans and trade their property. But until other institutions are developed, the poorest are unlikely to use those formal titles.

A little practical help?

Has the World Bank hit on something new? Not if you ask development economists such as Peru's Hernando de Soto. Ever since he found that his government demanded over 700 bureaucratic steps to obtain legal title to a house, Mr de Soto has argued that growth follows respect for the property rights of the poor. He may wonder why the World Bank feels the need to make the point again. But modest suggestions of this sort may be easier for some to accept than grander World Bank prescriptions. And it is heartening to find the Bank admitting that big institutions, imposed by foreign donors in the belief that one size fits all, can sometimes do more harm than good. Now, what about following the fine words with a little practical help?

"Microcredit," or microfinance, is an antipoverty strategy that concentrates on providing very small loans, often under $100, to help people expand their small businesses such as raising livestock.

For more information about Hernando de Soto, see the commentary box on page 155.

CAN THE FINANCING GAP BE CLOSED?
Jullyette Ukabiala

Jullyette Ukabiala writes for Africa Recovery, part of the United Nations Department of Public Information, which aims to produce accurate news and analysis on the economic development of Africa.

NO

As aid from rich countries slides further, a UN independent panel on development financing recently proposed new ways of raising more funds to rescue millions of people from poverty—most of them in sub-Saharan Africa. In 1999, donor countries gave just $12 bn to the region as official development assistance (ODA), $6 bn less than they gave in 1995. Such aid, even at its peak, fell far short of the continent's needs. The panel, chaired by former Mexican President Ernesto Zedillo, was set up by UN Secretary-General Kofi Annan to identify innovative methods for raising the estimated $50 bn needed yearly to implement the UN's commitments to poverty reduction and sustainable growth in developing countries....

Among the proposals are taxes on the consumption of fossil fuels and on international currency transactions. The panel urges new ways to boost aid and investment flows to poor countries, and to assist countries raise funds from within their own economies through better political and economic management, including by improving their ability to collect domestic taxes. Such efforts would be supported by the establishment of an international tax organization and the holding of a summit that would address problems arising from globalization, the panel stated. Members agreed that reversing the widening and "shameful" gap between rich and poor countries "is the pre-eminent moral and humanitarian challenge of our age."...

Do you think wealthy developed nations should be prepared to pay more taxes to help the developing world? If so, why?

A currency tax

Combating poverty, the panel argued, requires the provision of vital services which strengthen social and political stability, such as peacekeeping, health care facilities and programmes for environmental protection—described collectively as "global public goods." To secure the enormous amount of money needed yearly for that, it said a global system of taxation is necessary....

A currency transaction tax, also known as a "Tobin tax"—named after Yale University economist James Tobin, who first proposed it—would have individual countries collect a "small tax" of between 0.1 and 0.5 per cent on all foreign exchange

Is a global taxation system the fairest way of reducing world poverty? What are the other options? Go to www.google.com, and look up The Economist and the New Internationalist magazines to read some articles on this subject.

transactions in their national currencies anywhere in the world. With the total value of such transactions currently put at $1,600 bn a day, up to $400 bn yearly would be raised at a minimum tax rate of 0.1 per cent. Each country would keep part of the revenue collected and release the remainder to international agencies funding global public goods.

The panel noted that such a tax could have a side benefit of helping to curb potentially damaging speculative buying and selling of currencies—aimed at making profit later when prices change. Such "gambling" was in part blamed for the devastating capital outflows that plunged Southeast Asian countries into economic crisis in 1997–98.

The Tobin tax has been criticized on the grounds that it could be evaded, might not actually yield the expected benefits and could unwittingly hurt global economic growth by discouraging financial transactions of all kinds. However, several major industrial nations have voiced support for the tax, which is also backed by a growing coalition of non-governmental organizations (NGOs).…

Taxing fuel consumption

The Zedillo panel also proposed a tax on the consumption of fossil fuels. Support for such a "carbon tax" has been growing since the 1992 UN Earth Summit focused international attention on the damage to the environment caused by excessive use of fossil fuels worldwide.…

The main energy sources that would be affected by a carbon tax include coal, petroleum, kerosene and natural gas. The tax would be reflected in an increase in their price, at a level based on the capacity of each type of fuel to emit carbon dioxide. The higher the carbon content, the higher the minimum tax rate. The tax would [most] likely be collected by fuel vendors. Implementation would not be difficult since many countries already impose taxes on fossil fuels. An additional carbon tax … should encourage consumers to shift to lower or non carbon-emitting sources of energy, such as solar energy and wind power.

African states, like most other countries, are heavily dependent on fossil fuels for transport and industrial activities in both urban and rural areas. A carbon tax, which would make fuel more expensive for many families, would therefore also reduce the amount of money available for food and other basic necessities. Public demonstrations in countries like Nigeria and Zimbabwe following fuel price increases also indicate that a carbon tax could aggravate social discontent and political instability.

Use statistics and figures carefully to illustrate your argument, but make sure that you check the source carefully.

In the 1980s and early 1990s Southeast Asia experienced rapid economic growth. In 1997, however, the region was gripped by a serious economic crisis. Go to www.facts.com/icofli00063.htm to find out more.

For more on the question of energy sources see Volume 4, Environment, Topic 8 Can wind and solar resources meet our energy needs?

Quoting recognized experts and commentators judiciously can add strength to your argument.

Would such a tax be good or bad for poor African countries? Good, says Ms. Emira Woods, programme manager for development policy issues at InterAction, a US-based coalition of over 165 NGOs, many of which are involved in development and humanitarian activities in Africa. Besides helping to clean up the environment, it would provide them with more development funding, she notes. Similarly, the deputy director of the regional bureau for Africa of the UN Development Programme (UNDP), Mr. Jacques Loup, told *Africa Recovery* that a carbon tax in rich countries would help "boost the international resource base for aid to Africa." However, Mr. Geoffrey Mwau, an economic and social policy adviser at the UN Economic Commission for Africa (ECA), cautions that the benefits would be lost if the tax collected from rich countries is treated as a "substitute" for ODA.

An international tax organization

Do you think multinational companies should bear the heaviest burden of international taxation?

With increasing cross-border movement of goods, services and capital in the world today, states are less able to collect taxes from multinational corporations, the panel observed, bringing substantial losses in revenue. Pointing out that taxes have become a potential source of conflicts among states, it noted that "the taxes that one country can impose are often constrained by the tax rates of others." The lack of precise and established regulations for taxing the income of multinational corporations makes it difficult to determine which country is entitled to which tax....

Several international and governmental organizations already deal with international tax issues, including a UN group of experts on international cooperation in tax matters. The panel said a new international tax organization should be created to assume all functions performed by existing institutions. It would serve as a global intergovernmental forum for international cooperation on all tax issues. It would also help resolve conflicts between countries and help them to increase tax revenue by fostering information exchanges and measures that could reduce tax evasion on investment and personal income earned at home and abroad. Funds raised could be used to increase spending on public services.

Corruption is a major problem in poor countries. For a debate about this see Volume 14, International Development, Topic 2 Is corruption a major issue in preventing economic growth?

The capacity of many African states to generate income on their own is often hindered by inefficient tax collection. Mr. Loup of UNDP believes the proposed international tax organization could help African governments reform their tax policies, but it should not interfere with their authority to design their own tax systems. The real problem with the tax policies of African states has more to do with corruption,

Mr. Mwau of ECA believes. Most Africans are poor and the small number of the rich from whom substantial taxes could be collected "are able to avoid taxes through corruption." For as long as that remains the case, he argues, tax reforms alone would not help Africa.

Globalizing decision-making

Existing international bodies … are no longer equipped to address problems arising from the growing interdependence of nations, the panel stated. There are no satisfactory means of dealing with global economic "shocks" and no effective way to ensure that all voices are heard. "Global economic decision-making has become increasingly concentrated in a few countries." The panel called for the creation of a global council to lead the international community … in managing today's global issues. The council would be more broadly based than the Group of Seven industrialized countries or international financial institutions such as the World Bank and International Monetary Fund. Its decisions would not be legally binding, but it should have the political clout to promote development, encourage international economic organizations to improve their policies and build consensus for resolving global economic and social problems.…

African leaders and advocacy groups have been complaining about the continent's increasing marginalization and impoverishment as a result of globalization and are not sure how the proposed global council and summit could benefit them. They "would be worthwhile," Mr. Loup said, so long as they devote adequate attention to issues that seriously affect Africa—crippling debt, aid flows, information and communication technology, market access and the environment. Mr. Lamin Manneh, UNDP's strategic and regional programme adviser for Africa, said more needs to be known about how a global council would help resolve "the problems we face today." A special forum or channel, he argued, should be created to enable African countries to express their concerns forcefully within the new institutions.

The ECA's Mr. Mwau notes that "attempts to deal with global issues through the existing mechanisms have failed not just because the institutional arrangements for dealing with them are inadequate, but more fundamentally because there is no political will." The creation of a new global council by itself would not help unless the international community commits to enforcing the council's decisions. African states, he argues, would benefit only if they are not excluded from making those decisions.

For a debate about the effectiveness of the World Trade Organization see Volume 3, Economics, Topic 11 Is the World Trade Organization fair to poor countries?

Do you think that globalization is a good or bad thing? Go to Volume 3, Economics, Topic 9 Is globalization inevitable? for further information.

The author concludes her argument on a forceful point: At the end of the day no amount of aid or network of good institutions can solve Africa's poverty unless the political will of the world community is there to see that it works.

Summary

The preceding articles by *The Economist* and Jullyette Ukabiala agree that poverty is a problem, but they disagree about the best way to tackle it.

The Economist asserts that a great deal of poverty could be avoided if the poor were able to access the same institutions as the rich. It points out that even in the poorest countries some level of market activity always survives, and the key to ensuring that it grows is for government to provide the means to facilitate it. By reducing bureaucracy, providing meaningful access to information, and protecting the rights of the poor, a government can empower its own people. *The Economist* suggests that developing nations should think small at first: Trying to replicate the institutions of rich countries, like a stock market, could be too ambitious. Tailoring small-scale initiatives that encourage the poor to take part in the regeneration of their own economy would help lay the real foundations of a sustainable economy, concludes *The Economist*.

Jullyette Ukabiala, on the other hand, says that such initiatives will always be frustrated while richer countries pursue policies that protect their own interests at the expense of developing nations. She reports on the meeting of a panel set up by the United Nations to reduce poverty. The panel argued for the provision of services to strengthen social and political stability, or "global public goods." The panel suggested that this could be funded by new taxes on either currency transactions or fossil fuels. Ukabiala points out that global decision-making has been concentrated in a few rich countries, which means that decisions will always lean toward their interests. One proposal is for an inclusive global council to address the needs of developing nations.

FURTHER INFORMATION:

Books:

De Soto, Hernando, *The Other Path: The Invisible Revolution in the Third World*. NY: HarperCollins, 1986.
Landes, David S., *The Wealth and Poverty of Nations: Why Some Countries Are So Rich and Some So Poor*. NY: W.W. Norton & Company, 1999.

Useful websites:

http://www.globalpolicy.org/socecon/inequal/
2003/0709rich.htm
New York Times 2003 article on Bush's trip to Africa.
http://japan.usembassy.gov/e/p/tp-ec0399.html
International Monetary Fund managing director's remarks in 2002 on poor countries needing good governance.
http://news.bbc.co.uk/1/hi/business/3136176.stm
Article on "Growing Gulf between Rich and Poor."

The following debates in the Pro/Con series may also be of interest:

In this volume:

Topic 10 Should people have to pay for natural resources?

Part 3: International Development

In *Economics*:

Topic 12 Should rich countries cancel "Third World debt"?

SHOULD DEVELOPING NATIONS TAKE MORE RESPONSIBILITY FOR THEIR OWN POVERTY?

YES: Aid encourages poor countries to become dependent on rich nations. This prevents them from dealing with the real causes of poverty, such as corruption, conflict, and food and water security.

YES: Good governance is key to tackling poverty. It provides developing nations with the tools necessary to rise above poverty.

AID
Does financial aid mask the real causes of poverty in poor nations?

SELF-EMPOWERMENT
Should developing countries take responsibility for increasing their own prosperity?

NO: Poor countries do not have the capital to help themselves, and aid can give much-needed help to those who require it most

SHOULD DEVELOPING NATIONS TAKE MORE RESPONSIBILITY FOR THEIR OWN POVERTY?
KEY POINTS

NO: Developing countries are hampered by huge debts and unfair policies that favor rich nations. Until this changes, developing nations will never be able recover financially.

YES: Former colonial powers cannot be held financially or economically to ransom by poor nations for past deeds

YES: Small-scale initiatives at a local level will facilitate the empowerment of the poor and be more effective at reducing poverty

HISTORY
Is it wrong to put the burden of blame for poverty on former colonial powers?

GLOBAL VS. LOCAL
Do developing countries need to concentrate on local initiatives?

NO: Poverty in many developing nations can be traced back to the exploitation of their natural resources and people by colonists. These nations owe a debt to poor nations, and aid is a way of helping them reduce poverty.

NO: The inclusion of developing countries in global decision-making will promote economic growth for all

Topic 13

SHOULD RICH NATIONS COMPENSATE COUNTRIES WHOSE ECONOMIC RESOURCES THEY HAVE EXPLOITED?

YES

FROM "WHAT IS 'ECOLOGICAL DEBT'?"
HTTP://WWW.FOEI.ORG/PUBLICATIONS/ECODEBT/STATEMENT.HTML
FRIENDS OF THE EARTH

NO

"ECOLOGICAL DEBT: A RESPONSE"
MARILYN FREEMAN

INTRODUCTION

Throughout history peoples have exploited each other's resources. Among early peoples such exploitation often took the form of raids to seize crops, livestock, or people to take into slavery. Cultures also began to establish permanent dominion over other peoples. The Roman Empire, for example, included much of Europe and the Mediterranean region between 27 B.C. and the fifth century A.D.; in the 13th and 14th centuries Mongol dominion stretched from eastern Europe to China. Behind the creation of such empires lay the attraction of natural resources—grain, timber, or gold and iron, for example—and of income generated either by trade or by systems of tribute and taxation.

The dawn of Europe's age of discovery in the 15th century signaled a new age of exploitation. It often took the form of trade with indigenous peoples. French pioneers set up trading posts in what is now Canada, for example, to trade for furs with Native Americans. Likewise, in Africa European traders depended on local middlemen to provide slaves for shipment to Europe or, later, to the Americas. Increasingly, however, exploitation took the form of colonization, or permanent settlement. Europeans took over much of North and South America from the 16th century onward, India from the 17th century, and Africa in the second half of the 19th century.

The economic relationship between the home country and its colonies was complex. On the one hand, European nations were eager to exploit natural resources, such as gold and silver from South America, sugar and tobacco from the Caribbean, palm oil from Africa, or tea from Asia. People were another resource: The colonies provided a valuable source of cheap labor. On the other hand, these countries were often most valuable not as providers of resources but as a market for goods produced in the home country itself. They were also expensive to establish and maintain, due largely to the costs of government and military protection.

Through the first half of the 20th century the colonial system came under increasing criticism both from nationalist movements within the colonies, objecting to the exploitation of their nations by foreign countries and demanding independence, and also from protesters objecting to the cost of the colonies to their home countries. After two expensive world wars most European countries could simply no longer afford to maintain their empires.

"A state in the grip of neocolonialism is not master of its own destiny."

—KWAME NKRUMAH (1909–1972), FORMER PRESIDENT OF GHANA

The decolonization that took place in many African and Asian states after 1945 when World War II ended did not mark the end of exploitation by richer nations, observers claim. Economists use the term "neocolonialism" to describe a situation in which a former colonial power maintains effective economic control over a nominally independent country by, say, taking control of mining or agricultural enterprises, sometimes through private companies.

Decolonialism generally left former colonies poor and their former rulers rich. The loans that former colonies took out to fund their own industrial development often plunged them deep into debt. Some experts now argue that former colonial powers should compensate their former colonies—in the form of aid, loans, or technical assistance, for example—for centuries of exploitation of economic resources.

Advocates of this view argue that it is a straightforward question of morality: Colonialism was wrong, and nations should be compensated for the damage that it caused. However, this raises a number of issues. Critics question how it would be possible to assess the monetary value of exploited resources. Others state that it is not fair that people should have to pay for the actions that their ancestors took hundreds of years ago, particularly when many of them agree that colonialism was wrong.

Critics claim that colonial powers often invested just as much in the colonies as they earned from them. They built essential infrastructure—including railroads—established education systems, and set up the apparatus of government in many nations. Many Europeans, for example, also encouraged economic development in other ways. They introduced coffee and rubber from Latin America to Southeast Asia, for example, where they remain highly lucrative exports. It would be difficult, critics state, to take the benefits of colonialism into account when setting any rates of compensation to award to former colonies.

The following articles by Friends of the Earth and Marilyn Freeman look at the issue further.

WHAT IS "ECOLOGICAL DEBT"?
Friends of the Earth

Friends of the Earth is an international pressure group that campaigns "on the most urgent environmental and social issues of our day." This article was written by a member from Argentina, which is why a lot of the examples cited are South American.

✓ Ecological Debt is the liability that industrialized countries have for the damage they have caused to the livelihood of humans and to life on the planet. Such destruction is the direct effect of their production and consumption, which constitute an unsustainable model of development, strengthened by globalization, and a threat to the sovereignty of nations.

Ecological Debt is the obligation and responsibility that industrialized countries of the North have with the Third World, for the exploitation of their natural goods such as oil, minerals, forests, biodiversity, indigenous and peasant knowledge, marine goods, and for the disproportionate and illegitimate use of the atmosphere and of the oceans to dump waste, including greenhouse gases.

Damage without accountability

Raw materials, fossil fuels and other goods are exported from the South to the North without taking into consideration the environmental damage that they cause, as well as the cheap price of human health and livelihood of the local populations. Transnational corporations exploit such resources. Court cases against transnationals claiming damages for environmental destruction very often fail. There is no corporate accountability. There is therefore an ecological unequal exchange, because the South exports much energy and materials at a cheap price. In addition to this, the Third World is home to the production of chemical and nuclear arms, toxic products are manufactured (as in Bhopal) or toxic waste is deposited in their soil.

Ecological Debt was generated in the colonial era and has been increasing ever since.

This social and environmental, local and global destruction benefits economically a small, powerful group that maintain a model of development based on exaggerated consumption and waste. According to United Nations figures, 20% of the population of the world, the majority [of whom] live in the North, consume 80% of the planet's natural resources.

The way of life that Northern industrialized countries enjoy is due to the flow of natural goods, financial resources and

The Union Carbide pesticide factory in Bhopal, India, was the site of an accident in 1984 in which toxic gas escaped from a storage container. About 3,800 people were killed. See Volume 4, Environment, Topic 10 Do corporations have a moral responsibility to nature?

the poorly paid work of the Third World, without taking into account the social and environmental damage that the extraction of these goods generates.

The impoverished countries of the South subsidize this industrialized model. This has to stop.

Currently, the mechanisms of exploitation and destruction are contributing to increasing the ecological debt, aided by new strategies applied by transnational corporations, as well as structural adjustment programs, various forms of credit for mining and fossil fuel extraction, or free trade agreements.

Foreign investment for development, the deregulation of states, the privatization programs for services and natural goods, intellectual property rights agreements and technology transfers … are some of the new forms of domination and generation of the ecological debt….

"Structural adjustment programs" usually include the privatization of publicly owned resources, the introduction of user fees for health services and education, and the raising of interest rates. The World Bank imposes them as a condition of making loans to developing nations.

Arguments in favor of … the Ecological Debt: …

• An historical debt Ecological Debt means to claim the historical debt that industrialized countries of the North have with the Third World for the exploitation, destruction and devastation that they generated during colonization.

The colonial era was marked by European countries mining gold, silver, precious stones, fine wood, and exploiting other biological resources from the colonies. Added to this was the forced payment by local populations to the European conquerors. Models of extraction and production were imposed that responded to the necessities of the European economy and later aided the industrial revolution.

All of this occurred at a great cost: the death and enslavement of native populations. With the arrival of the Spanish conquerors, the population of America was around 70 million. Only a century and a half later it was reduced to 3 and a half million. [There is] a long history of ecological degradation in South America. Well-known examples are: mercury contamination from silver mining in Bolivia and from the exportation of gold in the Minas Gerais in Brazil, rubber production in the Amazon … quebracho from Argentina, cutting quinine trees in the Andes, and later the pollution of water and the air by copper smelting in Peru or Chile, among others. These are the open wounds of Latin America, which are still increasing.

Quebrachos are a type of hardwood tree harvested for their timber and also for red dye. Quinine is a South American tree whose bark is used to treat malaria.

• Intellectual appropriation of ancestral knowledge

… [It] means to claim the debt that industrialized countries of the North have with the South for the intellectual, historical and present appropriation of ancestral knowledge.

The main knowledge that is being appropriated illegally and illegitimately is [of] the improvement of seeds and medicinal plants, nowadays used to sustain the modern biotechnology and agricultural industries, for whose products we must pay royalties....

The former secretary of state of the United States, Warren Christopher, valued at $7 billion the annual contribution of foreign corn germplasm to the benefit of the economy of the United States. The United States never paid for this. However, since corn is now part of the commercial trade agreement within NAFTA, since 1994, millions of poor farmers in Mexico, have been affected because of the imports of corn from the United States (including transgenic corn, a new form of "pollution").

It has been calculated that the value of germplasm from the Third World that is being used by the pharmaceutical industry is more than $47 billion every year. Information with respect to the use and knowledge of plants that local communities possess, especially shamans and other traditional healers, has been given freely, and now often leads to patents in the North. This is biopiracy....

• Use of natural goods and services such as soil, water and air

Ecological Debt means to claim the debt that industrialized countries of the North have with the South for the use and degradation of our best land, water, air and human energy.

The countries of the South, in order to take care of basic needs under the heavy burdens of external debt, are forced to produce goods for export. The current model of development is based on increasing exports of primary materials and fossil fuels, of agricultural products such as food, flowers, wood and shrimp.

These monocultures use the best soil, water and low-paid labor in order to ensure exports. These crops use technological packages based on "improved" seeds or transgenic seeds, as well as agrochemicals, contributing to the pollution of the soil, water and air, and affecting the health of the workers and local communities, while using great amounts of energy.

Monocultures put at risk the food and cultural sovereignty of local communities since they affect the traditional forms of production and provision for local and national markets, affecting the dynamics of the lives of these producers, as well as causing loss in soil fertility, desertification and contamination.

"Germplasm" is the total set of genes that make up all the varieties of a single species, such as all the different types of maize (corn).

Patents on life forms, such as plants, were not allowed (since they are discoveries, not inventions) until the Supreme Court's decision in Diamond v. Chakrabarty (1980). See http://resurgence.gn.apc.org/articles/kimbrel.htm for further details.

A "monoculture" is one in which a single crop is produced over a large area. The risks are that if the plant or animal is attacked by a disease, everyone in the area is affected because there is no other crop to fall back on; and if the world price for the crop falls due to global oversupply, the country that produces it can become destitute.

The paradox is that agricultural countries in South America suffer from malnutrition; in some parts as much as 50% of the population is malnourished. Meanwhile, the export products contain high amounts of proteins, vitamins and minerals.

The immense forest plantations of eucalyptus and pine feed the paper industry and have displaced large areas of natural forests, other natural ecosystems and agricultural land in Argentina, Chile, Uruguay as well as other parts of the world. It is estimated that industrial plantations occupy almost 100 million hectares of tropical and non-tropical regions. Peasants in many countries, such as Thailand, have resisted these trends.

In Argentina, small agricultural production units have been replaced by large units of transgenic soybeans for export, displacing the livestock and wheat crops, which constitute the base for food security....

In northeast Thailand in the late 1990s many villages refused to allow their land to be cleared for tree plantations and persuaded the provincial governor to reverse his tree-planting drive.

• Carbon debt

Ecological Debt means also to claiming the debt that industrialized countries of the North have with the South for the disproportionate appropriation of the atmosphere and the capacity of oceans, soils and new vegetation to absorb carbon dioxide.

The countries of the North act as if they were the de facto owners of all carbon sinks and reservoirs. They are for the most part responsible for climate change, due to their production of carbon dioxide, emitted by their industries, the burning of fossil fuels as a source of energy and for a way of living that is not sustainable. Their per capita emissions, historically and at present, are much larger than those of other countries. Rich countries import fossils fuels from the South, causing great local damage, then they burn them and produce excessive amounts of carbon dioxide. They should pay back their ecological debts.

The impacts of climate change at a local and global level can be seen by the decrease in rain in deforested areas, floods in coastal areas, more frequent desertification, intensification of climatic events such as hurricanes, El Niño, storms, the melting of the polar ice caps and the elevation of sea levels.

These impacts translate into the loss of human lives and of agricultural crops, as well as the destruction of roads and houses. For instance, Bangladesh will be heavily affected, while it contributed little to climate change. An ecological debt is due....

A carbon "sink" or "reservoir" is something such as a large area of woodland that stores more carbon than it emits into the atmosphere. Since the increase in carbon dioxide in the atmosphere is a major cause of global warming, the size of these sinks is crucially important.

Bangladesh is a low-lying country on the Indian Ocean that is highly vulnerable to any rise in sea levels due to climate change. Go to http://news.bbc.co.uk/1/hi/world/south_asia/2116055.stm to read about the floods that devastated the country in July 2004.

ECOLOGICAL DEBT: A RESPONSE
Marilyn Freeman

Marilyn Freeman is an environmental activist and writer.

X The tenth commandment states "Thou shalt not covet thy neighbor's house, thou shalt not covet thy neighbor's wife, nor his manservant, nor his maidservant, nor his ox, nor his ass, nor anything that is thy neighbor's." Jealousy may seem relatively insignificant compared to "Thou shalt not kill," but consider how important such a tenet is to the well-being of a community: if a person wants a meal, or a spouse, or somewhere to live he or she must earn it for him- or herself. The latest leftist notion for wealth redistribution, ecological debt, is not just bad economics therefore: it is down right immoral. People cannot expect or hope to improve themselves by coveting—or indeed stealing—what others have; people can prosper only through their own efforts, through hard work, entrepreneurship, and ingenuity.

Do you think people earn a right to the things that they covet or possess? Is this fair when some people have either no or low incomes?

Domestic versus international economics

With domestic economics it is often assumed—wrongly, needless to say—that the prosperity of wealthy individuals depends directly on the poverty of society's poorer members. In most industrialized countries, therefore, governments seek to "right" such inequality through so-called "progressive" taxes and welfare handouts to the poor.

"Progressive" taxation rises in proportion as income increases.

Similarly, in international economics there is an increasingly influential lobby that argues the prosperity of the developed world is directly dependent on the poverty of the less-developed world. Unlike in the domestic arena, however, there is no world government to take from the relatively wealthy and give to the poor. It is for this reason that many liberals, socialists, environmentalists, and antiglobalization campaigners have devised the idea of "ecological debt"—that industrialized nations should be obliged to make payments to poorer nations to "compensate" them for environmental damage, exploitation of natural resources, and for harming the livelihoods of the poor in some way.

If the international community is concerned about conserving natural resources and making sure that companies employ policies for sustainable development, is an ecological debt still necessary?

Thus it is that we find ourselves increasingly subject to claims that "excessive" consumption in the developed world is causing people in developing countries to starve. Or that "excessive" production is contributing disproportionate

Should rich nations compensate countries whose economic resources they have exploited?

An oil flare in the desert symbolizes two key aspects of the ecological debt: The extraction of mineral resources from poor countries by rich ones without adequate compensation, and the creation by the activities of rich countries of more greenhouse gases than the planet can absorb at a sustainable level.

See http://www. foeeurope.org/ publications/from_ environmental_ %20space_to_ ecolog_debt_ english_version %20final.pdf for a paper detailing the proportions of greenhouse gases that different parts of the world are responsible for emitting.

quantities of greenhouse gases and waste to the Earth's atmosphere and oceans. Or that the rich have somehow exploited (and continue to exploit) without adequate payment the oil, minerals, forests, biodiversity, knowledge, and labor resources of poorest nations. Such arguments—which are really about closing the "wealth gap" or the redistribution of international wealth—ignore some fundamental truths: that productivity (and hence wealth) is expandable; that free trade benefits the poor as well as the rich; and that giving people something for nothing does not reduce poverty, nor does it contribute to economic or social development.

The fallacy of fixed wealth

Production and consumption in the West, and the economic model on which they are based, are charged by political liberals and greens as being "unsustainable." This, and the notion of economic equality, is based on flawed economics: that there is a fixed amount of wealth. However, wealth is based on productivity—the effectiveness and efficiency of the production process—and since the industrial revolution human productivity has proved to be amazingly expandable. Economist Angus Maddison found that the Earth had fewer natural resources and no more farm land in 1992 than it did in 1820, yet the value of everything produced in the world grew from $695 billion (measured in 1990 U.S. dollars) in 1820 to almost $28 trillion in 1992. With the world's population multiplied by five in that period, this meant that the amount produced per person went from $651 to $5,145.

Other measures of human well-being—infant mortality and life expectancy—are similarly impressive. In the early 1950s rich nations had an average of 58 deaths per 1000 live births; today that average has fallen to 11. Over the same period the poorest countries in the world (Chad, Mali, and Laos, for example) went from 194 deaths per 1000 live births to 109. In the early 1950s people in the developed world had a life expectancy of 66.5 years; today people can expect to live to 74.2 years on average. In the poorest nations, meanwhile, lifespans have increased from 35.5 years to 49.7 years.

According to some sources, between 1980 and 2000 the income of the poorest 5 percent of the world's population grew by 0.11 percent per year in real terms, against 1.95 percent per year for the richest 5 percent.

The message is clear: yes, the rich are becoming richer, healthier, and older, but then so are the poor! Wealth is not theft—whatever it is that makes people in the developed world rich, it does not make people in poor countries poor.

Benefits of trade and exchange

The ecological debt argument is based on yet more bad economics—in particular that by opening up its economy to foreign investment and free trade with the West, a poor or developing country is somehow leaving itself open to exploitation. International trade is about an economy specializing in and exporting those goods and services where it has a comparative advantage in exchange for products where it has a comparative disadvantage vis-a-vis its trading partner. Classical economic theory holds that such trade is in the long-term interests of both trading partners. A country such as Nigeria may choose to export its abundant oil reserves in exchange for much-needed foreign exchange; it can then use this money to purchase products that it is not as successful at producing, such as those that use sophisticated technologies. Similarly, Peru has the perfect climate for growing coffee, so it is in its interests to specialize in coffee production and export this cash crop in exchange for goods it is less able to produce.

This is not exploitation. That everyone benefits from such interactions is exemplified by the figures above: it is more (and more liberalized) trade that will continue to make the poor better off in all respects.

Do you think specialization in specific industries is a good idea? Have trade liberalization and globalization exacerbated the rich–poor divide? Go to Volume 14, International Development, Topic 10 Are protectionist policies essential to economic growth in poor nations?

The true path out of poverty
Even those parts of the ecological debt argument that have some validity—the historical misappropriation of labor resources in the form of slavery or the past excesses of colonialism—are beside the point. Surely the issue here is how poor countries can better achieve economic growth and development today. Handouts (for this is what "compensation" would amount to) such as the open-ended foreign aid programs that continue to be targeted at the less-developed world have proved to be an unequivocal disaster. Indeed, in Africa there has actually emerged an inverse relationship between foreign aid and development. For decades aid has served only to postpone economic reform and to preserve many of the continent's most ruthless dictators in power.

Nations are poor not because of global economic inequality, but because of the lack of rule of law, lack of respect for private property, liberal attempts to redistribute wealth, corruption, and war. The answer to poverty and underdevelopment lies, therefore, not with spurious attempts to excuse more handouts by rich nations to the poor, but with the encouragement of greater democracy, trade liberalization, and free markets and free enterprise.

Do you think former colonial powers should compensate the descendants of slaves? Go to www.google.com, and search for articles on this subject.

If this is true, should aid be given only to those countries that can account for its use? Is is it fair to give conditional aid?

Summary

Both articles address the question of ecological debt—"the liability that industrialized countries have for the damage they have caused to the livelihood of humans and to life on the planet." In the first article Friends of the Earth (FOE) summarizes the key arguments in favor of rich nations compensating the poor for their "exploitation" of resources, biodiversity, and indigenous knowledge, and for "disproportionate and illegitimate" dumping of waste and greenhouse gases in the atmosphere and oceans. Compensation (such as in the form of writing-off of loans) must therefore address an "ecological unequal exchange" from the poor South to the industrialized North, taking account of such factors as past colonialism and slavery and present-day neocolonialism, biopiracy, overuse of the environment and natural resources, carbon debt, and the production of toxic waste.

Marilyn Freeman, by contrast, argues that the idea of ecological debt is based on immoral reasoning, flawed economics, and a disregard for the past failure of foreign aid to address poverty and advance development. In particular, she argues that because productivity and wealth are expandable, the poor are not made worse off if the rich become richer. Instead, she claims that rich and poor alike are becoming "richer, healthier, and older" than ever before. In addition, trade liberalization is not about wealthy nations exploiting the resources of the developing world; rather, it promotes economic growth and development for all. Finally, Freeman asserts that if ecological debt arguments do succeed in "extorting" compensation from rich nations, such payments would serve only to postpone economic and political reform in poor countries.

FURTHER INFORMATION:

Books:

Agyeman, Julian, Robert D. Bullard, and Bob Evans, *Just Sustainabilities: Development in an Unequal World*. Cambridge, MA: MIT Press, 2003.
Hollander, Jack M., *The Real Environmental Crisis: Why Poverty, Not Affluence, Is the Environment's Number One Enemy*. Berkeley: University of California Press, 2003.
Shrader-Frechette, Kristin, *Environmental Justice: Creating Equality, Reclaiming Democracy*. New York: Oxford University Press, 2002.

Useful websites:

http://www.christian-aid.org.uk/indepth/9909whoo/whoo1.htm
Christian Aid report "Who Owes Who?"

The following debates in the Pro/Con series may also be of interest:

In this volume:
Topic 1 Do wealthy members of society have a duty to help the poor?

Topic 9 Does welfare perpetuate poverty?

Topic 10 Should people have to pay for natural resources?

SHOULD RICH NATIONS COMPENSATE COUNTRIES WHOSE ECONOMIC RESOURCES THEY HAVE EXPLOITED?

YES: Victims of personal injury or property damage are awarded compensation in the United States as their right in law, not as charity: Paying ecological debt is no different

YES: Rich nations do not own the atmosphere or the oceans, but they make disproportionate use of (and cause disproportionate harm to) these global resources

JUSTICE
Is paying compensation a matter of justice rather than charity?

DAMAGE
Should rich nations compensate others whose environment they damage?

NO: It is not possible to assign responsibility for past ecological debt clearly enough to avoid creating further injustice. Any help to poor countries should be prompted by conscience.

NO: The kind of exploitation and misuse of resources that used to occur would not happen today. There are many international laws and bodies around to prevent such damage.

YES: Colonialism, slavery, and neocolonialism have allowed rich nations to accumulate wealth; the colonial legacy has prevented poor nations from being able to develop and grow

SHOULD RICH NATIONS COMPENSATE COUNTRIES WHOSE ECONOMIC RESOURCES THEY HAVE EXPLOITED?

KEY POINTS

YES: Full and proper payment should be made for resources used, extracted, or traded now and in the past

POVERTY AND WEALTH
Do the rich become richer at the expense of the poor?

BAD ECONOMICS
Does compensation make economic sense?

NO: This is just an excuse used by poor nations to justify their lack of economic success. They need to help themselves.

NO: Handouts from rich to poor are inefficient and act to the detriment of all, including the recipients, who just become dependent

LIBERIA AND
THE UNITED STATES

*"I'm pleased with the progress we've made in Liberia.... We've
done everything we said we would do."*
—GEORGE W. BUSH ON U.S. INVOLVEMENT IN LIBERIA (2003)

The Republic of Liberia—the name means "land of freedom"—is situated in
western Africa. Settled by freed U.S. slaves in 1822, Liberia's history has been
extremely turbulent. Some scholars believe that exploitative relations with the
United States in particular have exacerbated many of its problems. This article
examines Liberia's tumultuous history and its relationship with the United States.

The American Colonization Society and the colony

In 1816 the American Colonization Society (ACS) was founded to facilitate the
return of freed slaves to Africa (Britain had founded the neighboring colony of
Sierra Leone for the same purpose in 1787). In 1822 the first 86 former slaves
landed at Cape Mesurado (Montserrado) on what was then called the Grain Coast.
Their settlement became known as Monrovia, named for President James Monroe
(1817–1825). Other colonists followed, either buying land or obtaining it by force
from indigenous chiefs. The ACS initially employed white agents to govern the
colony, but in 1842 Joseph Jenkins Roberts (1809–1876) was named as the first
nonwhite governor. In 1847 Liberia declared independence, becoming the first
black republic in Africa. Roberts was elected president.

During his time in power Roberts expanded Liberia's boundaries to include a
600-mile coastline and established a university. He struggled to obtain international
recognition for Liberia: Britain became the first country to recognize the republic
in 1848; Norway, Denmark, and Portugal followed the next year, and France in
1852. But the United States did not recognize Liberia until 1862, during the Civil
War, when the southern states were no longer in a position to object to a black
ambassador in Washington, D.C. Mindful of the country's U.S. origins, however, the
United States at times played a quasi-colonial role, sponsoring agreements with
European powers between 1892 and 1911 for the recognition of Liberia's claim
to further territory. For its part, Liberia took the U.S. Constitution as the model
for its own. However, since Liberia had originally been set up by private citizens,
not the U.S. government, this relationship was never given formal expression or
institutional form, allowing the United States to ignore Liberia's problems when it
chose to do so. In effect, the relationship depended on the degree of responsibility
that each U.S. president personally felt the country owed Liberia. Some observers
believe that many presidents considered that their main obligation was to facilitate
opportunities for U.S. business there.

Internal tensions

As Liberia developed, a small group of Americo-Liberians located mostly on the coast tried to dominate the larger local communities in the interior. The Americo-Liberians emulated Americans: They built churches and schools, spoke only English, and established trade relations with other nations, exporting coffee, rice, and timber. Even so, their import costs exceeded export revenues, and Liberia was obliged to take out loans on unfavorable terms; it declared bankruptcy in 1909.

To bring in more revenue, the government leased large areas of land to American companies. In 1926 Firestone Tire and Rubber signed a 99-year lease on one million acres of land for use as a rubber plantation in exchange for a $5 million loan. While Firestone created employment, it also arguably exacerbated the divisions between ethnic groups in the country. However, many scholars believe that the loan was essential to Liberia's economy, so much so that even after Britain accused Liberia of using forced labor and asked the League of Nations to take over the country as a mandate, the influence of Firestone and the U.S. government prevented the loss of Liberia's independence.

Descent into chaos

In 1971 William Tolbert (1913-1980) succeeded William Tubman (1895-1971) as president. Many people hoped that Tolbert would build on reforms introduced by Tubman, who had held office since 1944, and improve the situation of indigenous Africans. However, they were largely disappointed. In 1980 Tolbert was killed in a coup led by Samuel Doe (1950-1990). Doe presented himself as the liberator of Liberia's indigenous people, but, historians contend, he soon proved as corrupt as his predecessors. He also had U.S. support: President Ronald Reagan's administration (1981-1988) contributed half a billion dollars in economic and military aid in the first five years of Doe's regime. Critics argue that the United States saw Liberia as a vital Cold War ally and ignored Doe's excesses—such as a fraudulent election in 1985 and persecution of the indigenous Gio and Mano peoples—in exchange for being allowed to establish air and sea bases there.

In late 1989 Charles Taylor (1948-), a former minister in Doe's government, crossed the border from exile in the Ivory Coast with a hundred rebels. Thousands of Gio and Mano joined them, and civil war broke out. In September 1990 Doe was captured and killed, but the conflict did not end. Soldiers, some of them children, committed terrible atrocities. The international community attempted to intervene, organizing a ceasefire in 1995 that led to Taylor's formal election as president in 1997. Many people felt, however, that the United States did not do enough to stop the continuing violence. In 2003, after much pressure, President George W. Bush (2001-) sent 200 marines to Liberia to assist a West African peacekeeping force. In August Taylor was persuaded to step down. However, sporadic violence continued after the United Nations assumed peacekeeping duties in October.

Around 200,000 people have been killed in the conflict and another 1.5 million made homeless or refugees. Many Liberians feel that the United States bears some responsibility for their country's decades of conflict not just in its support of exploitative businesses but also its backing of oppressive regimes.

Topic 14

WILL BRIDGING THE DIGITAL DIVIDE HELP LESSEN THE GAP BETWEEN RICH AND POOR COMMUNITIES?

YES

FROM "GLOBAL DIGITAL DIVIDE: TARGETING RURAL AND
ECONOMICALLY CHALLENGED COMMUNITIES"
BENTON FOUNDATION, 2004
MUGO MACHARIA

NO

"NATIONAL 'IT SECTOR OVERRATED'"
MARCH 4, 2004
THE HINDU

INTRODUCTION

The growth of new technology and communications, such as computers and the Internet, is revolutionizing trade and the exchange of knowledge around the world. Some commentators are concerned, however, that there is a growing gap between those who can make effective use of information technology (IT), such as the Internet, and those who cannot. This, they say, may exacerbate existing inequalities between rich and poor communities.

In 2001 an estimated one-sixth of the world's population, or 429 million people around the world, had access to the Internet. Of that total 41 percent were located in North America, 27 percent were in Europe, the Middle East, and Africa, 20 percent were online in Asia and the Pacific, and 4 percent were located in South America. Some critics believe that such figures are evidence of a "digital divide"—so named because computers rely on digital technology—between rich and poor nations. They believe that the unequal rates of adoption of computer technology around the world exclude many people from reaping the fruits of the new economy. They argue that aid and education programs to poorer nations are essential to closing the gap and ensuring that poorer countries do not get left behind.

Among those who emphasize the importance of new technology to growth and development is United Nations Secretary-General Kofi Annan. He argues that: "Knowledge has long been synonymous with power, but with the advent of the Internet, access to knowledge is quickly becoming a requirement for power, whether social, political, or economic. In our increasingly interconnected world, we must work together to see that all people have access to the knowledge the Internet has to offer."

"[P]overty is not a technology-deployment issue.... It is an issue of wealth and asset creation. Technology can help...."
—KENAN P. JARBOE, ECONOMIST (2002)

Annan, among others, asserts that economic development and digital capability go hand in hand: Those people with the skills and tools to compete in the new economy are at a distinct advantage over those that do not have them. They are empowered since they will be able to operate easily in the global community. IT is also essential, many argue, for groups to remain competitive in attracting and retaining business. Governments must therefore make it a priority to ensure that they both create a well-trained and computer-literate workforce, and also develop communications facilities. Some experts also argue that the rise of transnational corporations (TNCs)— companies with operations in many countries, including developing nations—makes it even more important for people in these nations to be able to use new technology.

Critics of such a view argue that this is putting the cart before the horse. In their opinion the importance of new technology for economic growth and poverty reduction is often overstated. It generally benefits members of a nation's educated elite, and in any case, TNCs and other firms that operate in poorer nations often provide IT training if it is necessary, they claim. Such critics believe that real economic growth depends on the solution of far more fundamental problems. They include, for example, access to decent amounts of food and clean water sources, education and literacy, an increase in good governance, and a reduction in corruption. The priority of international organizations should be to apply pressure for such basic reforms.

In the view of such observers an advanced communications system is of little use to the millions of people in the world who live hand-to-mouth existences. Their real concern is where their next meal is coming from. To them, bridging the digital divide is as irrelevant as flying to the moon.

The Digital Divide Network, an online forum for digital access issues, also argues that IT alone is of little use without high levels of literacy. It believes that "unless all citizens are able to learn and apply a wide set of literacy skills, mere access to technology will mean very little to them."

Many observers think that investment in fundamental areas such as education is key to helping poor nations and communities to participate properly in the world arena. Others argue that although IT may not be a magic wand that eliminates the need for sound developmental investment, it can still have a crucial role to play in helping improve the quality of life of disadvantaged communities whether at home or abroad.

The following two articles look at this question further.

GLOBAL DIGITAL DIVIDE...
Mugo Macharia

Mugo Macharia is a Kenyan journalist now based in Washington, D.C. This article was written for the Digital Divide Network, a research forum of the Benton Foundation.

See www. geponline.org for more information about the GEP's programs and aims.

YES

✓ Bridging the Global Digital Divide is a tall order even for giant development agents like the United Nations Development Program's Sustainable Development Networking Program and the World Bank's InfoDev Project. But while the likes of UNDP and the InfoDev may have millions of dollars at their disposal to carry out their projects, an Oakland-based NGO is slightly ahead in addressing issues of closing the digital divide locally and internationally.

The Global Education Partnership (GEP) is approaching the digital divide challenge holistically, offering not just computer skills to the more than 800 youth who enter and leave its programs every year, but also entrepreneurship skills, work readiness skills, and skills for the global marketplace, all on a shoestring budget. This approach fits well with its mission: to provide access to educational resources that increase the capacity of young people to become employable and self-reliant in today's global marketplace. Its School-to-Career model is implemented through its flagship program, the Entrepreneurship and Employment Training Program (EETP).

Empowering through technology

EETP offers skills in job readiness, cross-cultural and international programs and entrepreneurship and computer training. It is offered after school in four divisions spread out in three continents. Each GEP division has a 25-computer facility—with donated computers—that provides the medium for the EETP....

How much can be achieved by courses taught in computer labs if students do not have access to computers outside class? Is practice important when learning a new skill?

The idea of starting this global initiative was presented by an African American Studies Professor to his students at the University of California at Berkeley. It was started with $20,000 collected from UC Berkeley students and has now grown into a $1.5 million dollar a year budget. What is unique about GEP is that it targets the rural areas in the Third World, and economically challenged communities in the San Francisco Bay Area. GEP treads where few, including various governments and private telecom investors, dare put their money. Not only has GEP ventured into the last frontier of the digital divide, it boasts the highest number of computers in its rural facilities, outside of the cities.

According to Professor Percy Hintzen of the African American Studies Department at the University of California, Berkeley, and a co-founder of GEP with his former student Tony Silard, global access to information technology is the hallmark of GEP. Dr. Hintzen envisions that, by giving the youth the knowledge and skills they need to succeed right in their locales, his organization will not only give them the required tools, but also stem the brain drain. He points out that youth are apt to leave the rural areas and move to the city in search of work....

While this means that people in rural areas do not have to move to the city to get computer training, will it necessarily make them more likely to stay in their home villages afterward? Is investment in businesses that use new technology also important?

Start-up success story

GEP has its Headquarters in Oakland, California, where it targets economically marginalized communities of the San Francisco Bay Area. Ismael Cardenas grew up in a little city [East Palo Alto] in San Francisco Bay Area that had high crime rates since the 1950s.... But 17 year-old Ismael, otherwise known as "thegaragegeek" in the business world, runs his own web development start-up, thanks to skills he acquired from Global Education Partnership.

Ismael signed up for the Entrepreneurship and Employment Training Program (EETP) in search of extra credit for high school. In addition to the extra credits, he learned how to put a portfolio together, salesmanship, and earned a $500 scholarship grant that allowed him to start his web development start-up. "GEP gave me the motivation to start my own business.... I decided to build a website after attending the EETP," Ismael said. For the last six months, Ismael says he has had the happiest job in the world. As a web designer, he currently has five customers, and more are coming....

Ismael is among 800 low-income youth who benefit from EETP's 12–14 week program offered after school 2 days per week, in the San Francisco Bay Area, Kenya, Tanzania, Guatemala, and Indonesia. According to Anita Akerkar, Director of Bay Area Division, GEP targets economically challenged pockets of the Bay Area. They work with selected partners to provide computer-based employment training for high school youth. They teach the youth how to use technology on a basic level, and important life skills, instilling a greater sense of self. Some of the recipients of GEP services have never seen successful role models, according to Ms. Akerkar. The EETP focuses on 4 core skill areas:

Do you think instilling confidence in young people in poor communities is an important factor in education programs? Does it make them more likely to use their new skills properly?

- Entrepreneurship skills
- Work readiness skills

Do you agree with the emphasis placed on career development? Or do you think that the emphasis should be more on using computers for communication, study, and creative work?

- Computer skills
- Skills for the global marketplace

"Everything they do is hands on. They do market surveys, write business plans on their computers," she says. In the Bay Area, students are recruited from community-based organizations, especially those that deal with foster children and teen mothers, and schools. The organizations GEP partners with have to have:

- A base of students to recruit
- A computer facility with at least 15 computers
- A monetary contribution

What do you think are the most important computer skills to have? What should be learned first? Think about things such as typing skills, e-mail, word processing, attachments, and spreadsheets.

GEP not only offers its students computer skills, it also gives them work readiness skills, and help match students with employers. "Before they get out of EETP, we make sure they have a business plan in hand," says Akerkar. She adds that computer skills are the major component of their programs. "If you don't have technical skills before you leave us, we haven't done our job completely." GEP recently authored a tech-focused curriculum for teachers called *From Vision to Action*, to be available nationwide. One of the chapters in this curriculum is called "Global Connection: Understanding how people interview in South Korea." It is meant to teach about cross-cultural communication, to prepare the global workforce of tomorrow. "They begin to realize there is a vast variety of people out there," says Akerkar. The program also emphasizes community service by having the students use part of their business profits to set up a foundation to help the needy. After completing the Skills for the Global Marketplace component of the EETP, students in all five of GEP's divisions will have:

The Internet allows people located across the globe to work together, so online communities are not limited by geography. This is why it is important to be able to communicate with people in other parts of the world and understand cultural differences. This is part of what is meant by the idea of a "global village."

- Communicated via the Internet and video-conferencing with their partner students in Kenya, Guatemala or the U.S.
- Researched economic, political and cultural information on other countries using the World Wide Web
- Discussed global business and cross-cultural interaction with guest speakers from over 5 foreign countries

Addressing the global digital divide

With its unique model of sustainable development, GEP has grown from an idea hatched in a college classroom between a student and his professor, to become an international organization focussed on empowering low-income communities in the U.S. and in developing countries. It is not just bridging the digital divide in economically marginalized communities in the San Francisco Bay Area, it is a pioneer in bringing computer centers to neglected rural hamlets in four developing countries in three continents. GEP is steered by the vision and belief that development is only possible if the people that ultimately benefit from a program are viewed not as recipients of the program, but as participants in designing and implementing a program to suit their needs.

Do you think investment in water security or local infrastructure should take precedence over investment in IT?

GEP was started in 1994 in Oakland, California. In 1995, GEP divisions were established in Kenya and San Francisco Bay Area, and in 1996 GEP established its third division in Guatemala. Divisions in Tanzania and Indonesia were formed in 1998 and 1999, respectively. As a Community Development Worker in Kenya with the Ministry of Education, Silard listened to community voices and saw the dire need for textbooks and basic school supplies that developed countries take for granted. Working with a local education specialists, Silard provided Kenyan parents with an incentive to raise funds for textbooks for their children by matching the amount they raised with funds from U.S. donors. Within two years, "the matching-funds textbook project" provided over $120,000 in textbooks to over 40,000 students in 58 schools....

The African Virtual University (www. avu.org), founded in 1997 and run by the World Bank, enables students in 16 African countries to take courses from professors in western countries, particularly on subjects for which local staff are in short supply, such as science and engineering.

Future goals

GEP plans to provide long-distance learning to its divisions around the world by piggybacking on those who have the infrastructure like the World Bank's Virtual University. One of the problems the organization is facing is lack of infrastructure on the ground, in the remote areas they serve in developing countries. Lack of trained maintenance workers for their computer hardware is another challenge they face, but plans are underway to train local people how to repair the hardware. GEP receives funding from Hewlett Packard to the Governments of Finland and Japan. It plans to expand services in the countries it serves by opening facilities in other remote villages in the future.

According to Professor Hintzen, who is also the Board President of GEP, he and Tony disapproved of the way development was being carried out in developing countries. "We felt there should be a partnership between the donors and the community being served," says Prof. Hintzen. So, the two embarked on the mission of providing marginalized communities with the resources they need to develop, by empowering the youth.

NATIONAL "IT SECTOR OVERRATED"
The Hindu

This report is of a meeting held on March 3, 2004. It appeared in The Hindu, one of India's leading English-language newspapers. Manabendra Mukherjee, a management studies graduate of Calcutta University, was West Bengal's tourism minister until June 2001, when he was given the newly created post of minister for information technology.

NO

X The West Bengal Information Technology Minister, Manab Mukherjee, today said the IT sector was somewhat overrated in terms of its contribution to the economy. His remarks came in the presence of Kiran Karnik, president of the National Association of Software and Service Companies (NASSCOM).

Mr. Mukherjee reiterated the State Government's commitment to help promote need-based use of IT to remove the digital divide and create employment.

Contribution to economy

Addressing a seminar on "Use of IT in open and distance learning systems of higher education: Mapping in the new millennium," organised by the Netaji Subhas Open University here [Calcutta], he said that irrespective of the hulla balloo, IT contributed merely six per cent of the GDP and 16 per cent of the country's export revenue.

Emphasising that the IT sector, including the Business Process Outsourcing (BPO) operations, were no match to the manufacturing and other service sectors in terms of job creation, he said that in Bangalore, the IT capital of the country, the sector had created 1.8 lakh jobs while three lakh jobs were lost in the manufacturing sector during last few years [a lakh is one-hundred thousand].

"I have no hesitation to say that the West Bengal Government does not look at IT as a means to create urban employment in plush office buildings. We pursue a completely different policy in this regard compared to other states and are looking forward to use it for the benefit of the commoners," he said.

Two months after this meeting, Mukherjee announced that the state government was introducing basic computer literacy in 1,000 schools and was in negotiations with IBM to expand the program to a further 2,500 schools. Go to www. google.com, and look up poverty and wealth statistics for West Bengal. Do you think that this was a good use of government funds?

Loopholes

Finding loopholes in the generally followed practices of digitalisation of government services and making them available on the Net, he said "the minimum infrastructural requirement to take advantage of such services is a PC. Given that the price of a PC is equivalent to 45 months' wages and salaries of an average Indian (in terms of per capita income) as against 13 months' wages in China, the chances of mass

Will bridging the digital divide help lessen the gap between rich and poor communities?

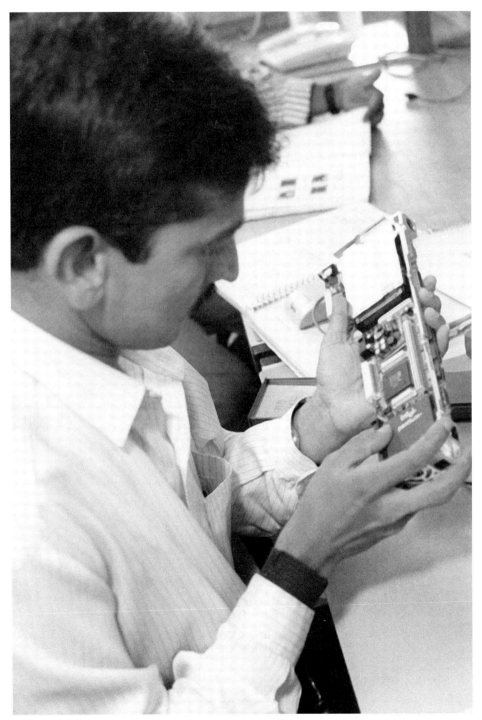

An engineer inspects a component from a computer at a factory in Bangalore, India.
Bangalore has become India's main center of both the software and hardware industries.

COMMENTARY: IT and Bangalore

Historically India has always had huge problems with poverty and below-average incomes. However, its 1.05 billion population means that these averages hide a substantial middle class, originally of merchants but now of business people and professionals, some 200 million strong. This has resulted in a large pool of highly educated labor—around three million graduates a year, two-thirds of them English-speaking. While many Indian scientists, academics, and economists, among others, work in western nations, many have chosen to stay in India and are helping its economy develop. India's information technology (IT) industry is very important, and Bangalore, a city of six million people (including 40,000 holders of PhDs) in the southern state of Karnataka, is the center of that industry. Bangalore has had the lion's share of IT investment among India's cities: Its IT companies had software exports of $3.8 billion in 2003–2004, around 31 percent of India's total software sales abroad. Karnataka's total IT exports are $4.3 billion—42 percent higher than that of Tamil Nadu, the next-highest earning IT state.

The Bangalore IT industry, which in 2004 employed some 110,000 people (20 percent of India's total IT workforce), runs the gamut from hardware manufacturing (U.S. chip manufacturer Intel makes microprocessors there) to software development. Businesses based there include indigenous Indian firms such as Wipro, MphasiS, and Infosys—which are building work campuses that rival the size of U.S. transnational Microsoft's facility in Redmond, Washington—to business process outsourcing (BPO) companies such as call centers and back-office banking operations.

The concentration of the Indian IT industry in Bangalore is an example of clustering. Businesses working in the same sector find it advantageous to set up near each other often because of the availability of raw materials or good transportation links. Workers are then attracted to move there, enabling new businesses to recruit staff and expand. In Bangalore's case the clustering is fed by the large supply of well-educated workers, highly paid in Indian terms ($9,000 per year, compared to the Indian average of $1,500), and thus highly motivated, but available for a fraction of the cost of similarly qualified labor in the West. Higher-than-average salaries have had the carryover effect of developing the service industries of Bangalore, such as restaurants, cellphone providers, and car dealerships (one-third of all new cars in India are bought by IT workers). Bangalore's IT workers, most in their early 20s, are among the first generation in Indian history to experience such affluence in significant numbers at a young age, often buying homes that their parents would not have expected to own. This also means, observers say, that as the divide closes between Indian IT workers and their counterparts in the West, another is opening between Bangalore's young wealthy elite and India's still rural, unskilled population.

use of such practices are remote in the Indian environment. Moreover, 67 per cent of the web content is in English, a language known to only five per cent of Indians."

To overcome this problem and make IT really useful to the public at large, "we are looking forward to providing one networked PC in every gram panchayat providing the most sought after information on agriculture, weather, crop prices and so on in the local language (Bengali)."

Referring to the State Government's recent initiative on tele-medicine, Mr. Mukherjee said that the effort proved extremely fruitful in networking the rural public health centres with the centres for excellence in Kolkata [Calcutta]. The project was being carried out in technical collaboration with the IIT, Kharagpur. "In fact, we have proved that two-way data, voice and video transmission facilities could be provided."

A "gram panchayat" is a village or group of villages under a single municipal government. Each computer would therefore be shared by hundreds of different users.

Telemedicine is the real-time linking of a physician in one place with a patient in another through the Internet. The connection might be voice and video for a simple consultation or linked to an instrument such as a medical scanner sending data direct to the doctor's computer.

Summary

Will bridging the digital divide help lessen the gap between rich and poor? Mugo Macharia describes how the GEP thinks this is possible by essentially enabling people to help themselves. GEP realizes that providing handouts and infrastructure is not enough: Communities have to be encouraged to become self-sufficient and see the program as a partnership rather than as charity. By providing a holistic approach, in which the Entrepreneurship and Employment Training Program teaches students not only how to use computers but also other vital skills, the program ensures that they are employable in a global marketplace. While GEP's projects are sometimes hampered by poor telecommunications infrastructure, that has been partly overcome by borrowing the facilities of existing networks; and the whole operation is streamlined to thrive on a shoestring budget. By focusing on rural and low-income communities, the GEP aims to show that sustainable development is achievable by providing the right tools so that students will stay and use their skills to enrich those communities rather than move away.

West Bengal IT Minister Manab Mukherjee, however, does not realistically expect the newly emerging IT sector to lessen the gap between rich and poor. Although IT provides jobs in Bangalore, such employment makes up a much smaller percentage than that found in other traditional work sectors. The growth in the IT sector has also not been enough to replace jobs lost in other sectors. While the GEP's approach may work in small communities, Mukherjee claims that buying a PC is beyond the reach of most Indians. He also points out that many Indians are immediately disadvantaged by the fact that most of the content on the web is in English. Although the state government does not see IT as bringing financial benefits to poorer communities, it does believe that infrastructure can enhance their existing livelihoods by providing networked health care and other key services.

FURTHER INFORMATION:

Books:

Norris, Pippa: *Digital Divide: Civic Engagement, Information Poverty, and the Internet Worldwide.* New York: Cambridge University Press, 2001.

Solomon, Gwen, Nancy Allen and Paul Resta, *Toward Digital Equity: Bridging the Divide in Education.* Boston, MA: Allyn and Bacon, 2003.

Useful websites:

http://www.digitaldividenetwork.org/content/sections/index.cfm?key=20
The Digital Divide Network.
http://www.firstmonday.dk/issues/issue7_7/warschauer/

Article on reconceptualizing the digital divide.
http://news.bbc.co.uk/1/hi/special_report/1999/10/99/information_rich_information_poor/466651.stm
BBC report on digital divide; case studies of four countries.

The following debates in the Pro/Con series may also be of interest:

In this volume:

Topic 11 Has globalization increased inequality?

WILL BRIDGING THE DIGITAL DIVIDE HELP LESSEN THE GAP BETWEEN RICH AND POOR COMMUNITIES?

YES: Access to information technology for all is the bedrock of equality in the new economy

YES: More than 429 million people have access to the Internet, and most businesses use new technology

INFRASTRUCTURE
Is access to the global network enough to promote material equality?

KNOWLEDGE
Is knowledge of new technology essential in today's economy?

NO: Development agencies like the GEP can only help a small percentage of people take advantage of the global network compared to the world's many millions of poor who will never be able to afford to

NO: Poor literacy and lack of suitable web content will limit the usefulness of information technology for many poor communities

WILL BRIDGING THE DIGITAL DIVIDE HELP LESSEN THE GAP BETWEEN RICH AND POOR COMMUNITIES?
KEY POINTS

YES: Access to the global network provides the opportunity for everyone to take advantage of the IT boom

YES: It will provide the infrastructure and support to enable the poor to help both themselves and their communities

PROSPERITY
Will bridging the digital divide make the poor wealthier?

NO: There are simply not enough IT jobs to have any real effect, and in many developing countries the fact that English is not the first language also creates problems in accessing the Net

NO: The digital revolution will make no financial difference to either low-paid workers in traditional jobs or the poor

189

Topic 15

HAVE TRANSNATIONAL CORPORATIONS HELPED ERADICATE POVERTY?

YES

"THE LIFECYLE OF CORPORATION'S SOCIALLY RESPONSIBLE INITIATIVE PROGRAM:
INTI RAYMI GOLDMINE"
INTER-AMERICAN FOUNDATION
KELLEE JAMES

NO

FROM "MAPUCHE LANDS IN PATAGONIA TAKEN OVER BY BENETTON WOOL FARMS"
CORPWATCH, NOVEMBER 25, 2003
SEBASTIAN HACHER AND PAULINE BARTOLONE

INTRODUCTION

A transnational corporation (TNC) is a company that has business operations in several countries. There are more than 40,000 TNCs, and they have great influence on the global economy. According to the Institute for Policy Studies, 51 of the 100 largest economies in the world are TNCs.

Any discussion of how TNCs affect the lives of poor people leads to heated debate. Supporters of TNCs maintain that developing countries benefit from the establishment of transnational operating units. They claim that TNCs not only provide job opportunities but also boost local economies by funding infrastructure and creating the conditions necessary for offshoot industries to develop. However, other people argue that TNCs make existing economic inequalities worse. They say that trade liberalization has made it much easier for TNCs to operate in and

exploit poor nations that have low production costs and inadequate regulation in areas such as workers' rights. Profit maximization, critics assert, is all that interests TNCs; helping poor people is not a concern of theirs.

In 2002 the international charity Oxfam published a report on human rights and TNCs. It claimed that in 1990 the private sector accounted for 25 percent of investment in the developing world, while 75 percent came from international aid. By 1996 the position was reversed, and 75 percent of investment came from the private sector. Some commentators believe that private-sector investment drives economic growth and poverty reduction in poor nations. They point out that TNCs provide many new jobs, often in areas of high unemployment. Indigenous workers employed by TNCs receive better educational opportunities and training in new technologies. Moreover, local producers benefit from technology and knowledge transfer: That is, they learn from and can imitate the advanced technologies and efficient production techniques of TNCs.

"[T]here seems to be nothing to prevent the transnational corporations ... subjecting humanity to the dictatorship of capital...."

—CHRISTINE LABRIE, *LE MONDE DIPLOMATIQUE*, PARIS

Supporters also claim that TNCs help poor communities develop by building public works and providing health and transport services that are available to all, not just workers. They insist that many TNCs show a commitment to corporate social responsibility by, for example, setting up foundations to fund small businesses and by seeking to involve community members in project planning. In addition, TNCs provide tax revenue that governments can use to redistribute wealth more equitably.

However, some observers express concern that TNCs have become so dominant in the world economy. They question whether such companies have made any practical contribution to poverty reduction. They say that people who directly obtain jobs from TNCs are usually those who are educated and skilled rather than the poorest members of society. Even when TNCs do create jobs for local workers, critics claim that companies often exploit employees by

paying low wages and offering poor conditions with no guarantee of rights. For example, in Colombia Coca-Cola bottling plant managers intimidated the workforce by allegedly encouraging paramilitary groups to kidnap, torture, and murder labor union members.

Critics also assert that TNCs have a detrimental effect on a local economy. Producers often cannot compete with TNCs and are forced out of business. Communities become dependent on the public works provided by foreign companies, and they face problems maintaining facilities once a TNC shuts or moves its operation. The ability of TNCs to shift production from one place to another gives them bargaining power, and they can threaten to move a plant in order to win concessions from the local government.

Some people also accuse TNCs of seeking to minimize costs by investing in countries that have few regulations in areas such as environmental protection. For example, in 2004 the Centre for the Environment and Development (CED), an affiliate of Friends of the Earth, investigated how the local population had been affected by the construction of the Exxon Mobil oil pipeline in Chad and Cameroon, West Africa. It found that people were still awaiting full compensation for loss of land, while drinking-water sources had been polluted, and the building of a sea terminal for the pipeline had deprived local fishermen of their livelihood. Critics such as CED contend that even though TNCs claim to take social responsibility seriously, in reality their efforts to alleviate poverty are always dictated by the need to cut costs and maximize profits.

The following articles consider these issues in greater depth.

... INTI RAYMI GOLDMINE
Kellee James

Kellee James is an intern at the Inter-American Foundation and an MBA/MA International Development candidate at American University, Washington, D.C..

YES

☑ Just as corporations have an organizational life cycle, so too do the socially responsible programs that corporations create. Perhaps no operation better knows that projects have a beginning, middle and end than a mining company.

Inti Raymi gold mine

The Inti Raymi gold mine is Bolivia's most important and is responsible for over 60% of the gold production in the country. It has created 700 jobs filled by Bolivian citizens that combined represent USD $8.2 million per year in salaries and benefits. The mine also spends USD $18 million annually on local goods and services and pays USD $4 million in taxes. The Newmont Mining Corporation, a company that became the world's largest gold producer in early 2002, is the majority owner of the Inti Raymi mine. As is characteristic of extractive companies, Inti Raymi is in constant interaction with the local community.

Company commitment to social responsibility through community engagement is a major determining factor as to whether that relationship will be mutually beneficial or antagonistic. With respect to business operations, the Inti Raymi mine has one of the best reputations in Bolivia, evidenced by its strong safety and health record and good relations with the union representing the mine workers. In the area of community engagement, the mining company created a Foundation to achieve its external social responsibility objectives.

Newmont Mining Corporation has significant assets or operations in North and South America, Central Asia, Australasia, Europe, and West Africa. Go to http://www.newmont.com/en/social/index.asp.to find out more about its social responsibility program.

Inti Raymi Foundation

The Inti Raymi Foundation was formed in 1991 in order to promote sustainable development by creating an alliance between the public, private and civil sectors.

Today, grassroots development is one of the Foundation's key objectives and the organization works with the communities surrounding the mine in two main thematic areas. The first, called "productive investment" by the Foundation, centers on small business and income-generating opportunities and includes projects such as a micro-business

"Grassroots development" involves empowering local communities to meet their own basic needs. In what ways do you think this might be a better alternative to direct handouts from development agencies?

incubator and a micro-credit program. The second, called "social or quality-of-life investment," focuses on community empowerment through projects that build leadership capacity as well as responding to infrastructure priorities identified by the local population.

See the sidebar on page 157 for an explanation of the term "microcredit."

Early years

Early in its timeline of community involvement, the Inti Raymi Foundation carried out a number of beneficial programs. Examples include health initiatives such as the construction of a hospital and economic development initiatives including a sheep production project. Some of the projects were primarily intended for the mineworkers, but were made available to the wider community as well. Others, such as the sheep-raising and marketing projects, did not include miners at all and were targeted toward other segments of the population. Though the programs were described as successful and well received overall, the Foundation managed a top-down model of program funding, with ideas and implementation of projects being generated by Inti Raymi and communities not included as part of the planning process. To capitalize on corporate-sponsored social programs, communities must be able to participate fully and equally in this and other aspects of the mine's operations. When local people are equal stakeholders, sensitive issues such as land tenure and usage rights can be resolved in a transparent manner. Inti Raymi has discovered that if communities are part of the negotiations process, agreements necessary for the mine's existence are resolved much more quickly, which in turn increases profitability. Those agreements that have a certain legitimacy in the eyes of the people and the mine's daily operations are less likely to be interrupted by civil unrest.

What does the writer mean by a "top-down model of program funding"? Would a "bottom-up" model have been more effective?

The role of the IAF

The IAF's [Inter-American Foundation] methodology promotes the organizational motto "they know how." In practice this means that communities have their own ideas for development projects they would like to design and implement given access to the necessary funding. This type of "responsive funding" concerns itself with the process of community development as much as the actual results of the project. Beyond the physical benefit of a new well or schoolhouse is the community's ability to participate as a full partner and to hone skills necessary to manage its own destiny. More than donating funds to Inti Raymi's programs,

The Inter-American Foundation is an independent agency of the U.S. government that provides grants for self-help programs to nongovernmental and community-based organizations in Latin America and the Caribbean. Go to the foundation's website at www.iaf.gov to find out more.

The IAF's website provides greater detail on the Grassroots Development Framework. Go to http://207.154.15.254/grants/grassroots_dev_framework_en.asp for details.

the IAF transferred its method of funding. Included in this transfer was the IAF system of project results measurement, the Grassroots Development Framework.

The result was a decentralized fund that would respond to community project proposals, capitalized jointly by the IAF and Inti Raymi. Both organizations shared the mutual goal of community development. The IAF helped Inti Raymi to implement a more efficient way of accomplishing this.

The future of the mine and foundation

Whenever a large corporation has a physical presence in a specific location, expectations are raised within the surrounding community. This is particularly true in regions where residents have little or no other means of economic security available outside of the company's activities.

"Extractivists" are operators, such as mining companies, that extract and exploit natural resources such as minerals.

Inevitably, extractivists are in the commodity business. They, like the local community, depend on the supply of natural resources available. There is one significant distinction, however, in that the mining corporation will eventually close operations and move on, while the community cannot. In the case of Inti Raymi knowing that the life of the mine is finite, community, corporation and Foundation have worked together to develop a strategic plan to assure a smooth transition once their concession is over. Their overarching goal is to achieve continuity in the design, funding and implementation of social programs, so that even after the mine shuts down the Foundation can continue.

Why do you think U.S. foundations have had problems raising funds since the events of September 11, 2001?

To that end, the Foundation is exploring an endowment fund with seed capital from the company. As a first step, Inti Raymi created a U.S.-based foundation for the purpose of fundraising. However, like many foundations since September 11th, this U.S Foundation has had limited success in raising funds. Other sources of funding, such as the Bolivian expatriate community, are also being explored. Beyond organizational self-sufficiency, Inti Raymi is considering project-specific sustainability for certain activities like its micro-credit program. Another important factor in long-term planning is the development of sustainable leadership.

If Inti Raymi has the interests of the local community at heart, should it have allowed community members to join the board of directors while the mine was a going concern?

Attracting visionary leaders to run the Foundation could become more difficult once the business interest is no longer behind the organization. In response, Inti Raymi expects to open its Board of Directors to both community members as well as nationally known leaders, thereby increasing both the talent pool and the visibility of the foundation's management. Finally, certain procedural issues have already been planned in conjunction with community input, such as ownership of land and payment/compensation for land use. Due to the presence of the mine for so many years, the region enjoys good infrastructure such as roads, electricity, and airport, etc. This could open the door for new productive land use. Possible replacement institutions once the mine shuts down are an industrial park, a university, or a wildlife habitat. Whichever option is pursued will have the strength of community consensus behind it.

> *Do you think employers have a responsibility to facilities once they cease operations?*

Lessons learned:
- For corporations involved in socially responsible programs, there is a learning curve which can be accelerated by partnerships with institutions that have experience in community engagement;
- Though obvious for a mining company, a well-planned exit strategy should be a part of every company's efforts in community engagement;
- Individual social projects are part of a strategic plan to build capacity and leadership within the community.

MAPUCHE LANDS IN PATAGONIA TAKEN OVER BY BENETTON WOOL FARMS
Sebastian Hacher and Pauline Bartolone

Sebastian Hacher is an Argentine journalist and photographer. Pauline Bartolone is a reporter for Free Speech Radio News. This article appeared on the CorpWatch website—www.corpwatch.org—in November 2003.

The Mapuche are an indigenous people of southern Chile and Argentina. In their language "Mapuche" means "People of the Land." Of the 200,000 Mapuche who live in Argentina, 94 percent do not own the title deeds to their land.

The Benetton Group today has 5,000 clothing stores in 120 countries around the world. Its average annual revenue is 2 billion euros (about $2.5 billion).

NO

In Patagonia, turquoise rivers divided by wire fences are a common sight. The snow capped mountain range in the southern Andes that runs along the border of Argentina and Chile, or the Cordillera as the locals call it, is one of the most pristine in the world. Under the mountains lies flat earth filled with bushes and vegetation that sheep and cattle graze on. The gold and quartz inside the mountains of Argentina's southern province of Chubut have recently brought in mining companies such as Meridian Gold, and now Benetton, for its exploitable and vast plains—perfect for the mass production of wool.

Largest landholder in Argentina

To the Mapuche Indians in southern Argentina, the Italian clothing manufacturer Benetton is the newest conquistador in 10,000 years of land struggles in Patagonia. Today Benetton is the largest landholder in Argentina, owning 900,000 hectares (2.2 million acres) in the resource-rich region of Patagonia. With 9% of Patagonia's most cultivable land, their holdings amount to 40 times the size of the capital city of Buenos Aires, the second largest city in Latin America.

"Here they fenced off all that they wanted. If it was a pretty valley, for that reason they appropriated it, if it was beautiful pampas, they closed it out. They left us among the stones, among the worst fields," says a Mapuche farmer Rogelio Fermín.

New colonization of Patagonia

"Patagonia gives me an amazing sense of freedom," said Carlo Benetton when assuming ownership of the Argentinean territory. In 1991 Benetton bought out the British-owned Compañia Tierras del Sud Argentina S.A. (CORP) for a total of $50 million. The records of CORP acknowledge the presence of indigenous people in the area. In return for the land that has been occupied by Mapuches for 13,000 years, Benetton constructed the Leleque museum, located in front of the Benetton estate in Chubut, to "narrate the history and culture of a mythical land."

But Benetton's occupation of Argentina land reaps more than just a personal sense of freedom and museums of the past: Benetton's 280,000 sheep produce 6,000 tons of wool a year, 10% of the production needs of the world's biggest consumer of virgin wool.

The Curiñancos, Santa Rosa, and Benetton

Two hundred meters [660 feet] away from the Leleque Museum live a Mapuche family called the Curiñancos. Atilio Curiñanco was born and raised in Leleque, but later moved to neighboring Esquel. After suffering from Argentina's economic crisis in December 2001, Atilio and his wife Rosa decided to return to the fields, and attempt to grow their own food, raise animals, and establish a micro-enterprise. "It all started when we proposed to start a family enterprise in Santa Rosa," says Atilio Curiñanco, age 52. "I have known that land since I was born, and I saw that nobody occupied it, so we thought it would be a good opportunity."

The Curiñancos contacted the Instituto Autárquico de Colonizacion (IAC), a government-managed real estate agency, to request permission to occupy an estate called Santa Rosa, situated in front of one of Benetton's properties. The land is well known to the Mapuches as unoccupied indigenous territory and was verbally confirmed as such by IAC. After waiting 8 months, the Curiñancos hadn't received a response about the Santa Rosa property. Finally IAC presented a note to the family saying "information has been obtained that leads us to believe that the property is zoned commercial" and that "our interest is to reserve it for a micro-enterprise."

The Curiñancos showed up at the Esquel Police station in Chubut to make it known that they would occupy Santa Rosa. In the same afternoon, a group of campesinos began to work the land with the little resources they had—plowing, sowing vegetables, and bringing in farm animals. "We went to [the] land without harming anyone," says Atilio Curiñanco. "We didn't cut a fence, we didn't go at night, we didn't hide ourselves. We waited for someone to come to let us know if it bothered them, to present us with a document that the land belonged to someone, and no one ever showed up."

The local Benetton office maintained that the Santa Rosa estate was company property. Benetton issued a report claiming that the estate "is not to be used for cattle raising" and stated their intentions to take control of the property. After two months of land occupation, the police dismantled and seized the belongings of the Curiñanco family.

The Argentinean constitution states that the Mapuche are "guaranteed possession and ownership of the lands which they traditionally occupied," and that the lands are not transferable.

"Campesino" is Spanish for peasant or farm worker.

Benetton took the Curiñancos to court over the disputed land. Many people saw the case as a test of the rights of indigenous people to their traditional lands, but on May 31, 2004, the court ruled in Benetton's favor.

When questioned about the eviction, Benetton lawyer Martin Iturburo Moneff says that the land takeover by the Mapuche family was simply a problem of "common delinquency."

The Benetton land surrounding the Santa Rosa property continues to be unoccupied. The Curiñancos say that they will return to the land that was taken away from them, and refuse to let Benetton redraw the lines of their history. "As indigenous people, we are going to fight until the end until this land is ours," says Atilio.

Eviction threats in Leleque

Across the dusty highway from the Santa Rosa property, Atilio's mother, 85 year-old Doña Calendaria, has to jump the fence of the Benetton property to access water from the area's only stream. "The way to the Chubut River is a local road. That shouldn't be closed," says Laura, a resident of the region for 40 years....

Leleque is a village made up of eight families who worked for the Argentinean railroad company loading wool, leather and other goods for transport to the capital city. In 1992, a year after Benetton bought the surrounding property, the loading station in Leleque was closed....

Why might the government be trying to force Leleque residents off the land?

When the loading station was shut down, running water for the families was cut off and police stopped serving the area. The local cemetery is now part of the Benetton estate.... Without work, potable water or land to grow food, the Leleque residents only had their animals to help them survive. At the end of September 2003, the state passed a resolution prohibiting the Leleque residents to have animals.

In September of this year, the 50 Leleque residents, the majority of whom are Mapuche women and children, were told by the state-owned railroad company that they had three months to abandon their houses to make way for a tourist attraction, which would use the very houses that they occupy.

Is economic investment in Patagonia more important than the livelihood of a handful of Mapuche? See Volume 14, International Development, Topic 14 Is the protection of indigenous people more important than economic growth?

The tourist project, supported by the county of Chubut, involves reactivating the railway for a guided train tour of Patagonia. Although provincial officials deny that the project has any relationship with the Italian company, one of the central offers of the tour is to visit the Benetton property....

Upon the eviction of the Leleque residents, a school house for 18 students will also be shut down. Although the state promises housing for the evicted residents, it is not guaranteed. "I don't like to use the word eviction," says Miguel Mateo, spokesperson for the Ferrocarril Provincial del Chubut (Provincial Railroad Company of Chubut). "It implies that the people are being thrown out into the street."

In the face of eviction, the residents of Leleque have begun to organize. They point out that the local communities have been integrated into other tourist enterprises at other train stations in the area, such as in Nehuelpan. The difference, they say, is that those stations are not surrounded by Benetton lands.

"Little by little, they have been closing the door on the Leleque community. It's a very strategic plan," says Mauro Millan, spokesperson for Mapuche organization 11 de Octubre. "Up until now, we have been defenseless but now we are in the era where the Mapuches are on the offensive. We have decided that there won't be any more evictions— from the state or from Benetton."

Benetton around the world

The Benetton Group was founded in 1965 by the Northern Italian Benetton family, which maintains a majority stake in the company.... The company is famous for its controversial advertisements, depicting AIDS victims and death row inmates among other gripping images, which promote social responsibility and multiculturalism. Yet, Benetton's labor and political practices provide a stark contrast to its PR message.

Benetton was the center of a child labor scandal in Turkey in 1998, when several children ages 11–13 were photographed working at the Bermuda Tekstil factory in Istanbul, a textile plant that produces Benetton line clothing. Turkish law and the international labor convention forbid the work of children younger than 14. Benetton suspended its dealings with the subcontractor after the violations were revealed by a Turkish trade union.

Benetton found itself again in a storm of controversy when the Kappa Company, partially owned by Benetton, proposed a clothing-manufacturing center in the Occupied Palestinian Territories [OPT] in the late 1990's. After a human rights groups campaigned against the plan, warning of its violation of international agreements set up by the Fourth Geneva Convention regarding enterprises in the OPT, Kappa finally rescinded its plan.

Just last year, the Consumers Against Supermarket Privacy Invasion and Numbering launched a boycott campaign against Benetton, for its plan to use one million Radio Frequency Identification Chips, or RFIDs, for inventory purposes in its clothing. Benetton dropped the plan after critics voiced concern that the devices placed within clothing items could potentially allow the manufacturer to track the movements of its customers.

Mapuche International Link is an organization dedicated to promoting the cause of the Mapuche. Visit http://www.mapuche-nation.org/english/main/benetton/main/info.htm to read more about the Mapuche fight against Benetton to regain their ancestral land.

Go to www.benetton.com to view some of these controversial advertisements.

For more on this issue see Volume 18, Trade and Commerce, Child labor, pages 126–127.

The Fourth Geneva Convention governs the treatment of civilians during wartime or occupation by a foreign power. It prohibits population transfers in occupied territories. Critics argue that by trading with enterprises based in Israeli settlements in the West Bank, Gaza Strip, and East Jerusalem, nations are implicitly accepting the legitimacy of those settlements.

Summary

The question of what role transnational corporations (TNCs) play in the alleviation of poverty in the modern world is one that often leads to heated discussion. The preceding articles examine different aspects of whether TNCs have helped eradicate poverty. In the first article Kellee James focuses on the case of the Inti Raymi gold mine, the major gold-producing mine in Bolivia. The Newmont Mining Corporation is the major shareholder in the mine, and James argues that the company is in constant dialogue with the local community. She says that Inti Raymi has proved to be socially responsible and concerned with sustainable development. It set up a foundation to encourage community empowerment through, for example, helping establish small businesses in the area. James claims that Inti Rami is also concerned that its social programs will continue to have a long-lasting beneficial effect on the community even after the mine has shut down.

In the second article journalists Sebastian Hacher and Pauline Bartolone focus on the multinational clothing company Benetton, which has become the largest landowner in Argentina through its purchase of cultivable land in the Patagonia region. Benetton is accused of occupying land that traditionally belonged to the indigenous people, the Mapuche. Local people who tried to farm the land had their property seized and were evicted. The authors quote residents who claim that since Benetton bought land, they have had access and water rights denied. There are also plans for a tourist project that, Hacher and Bartolone suggest, is linked to Benetton. They conclude by accusing the company of poor labor and political practices.

FURTHER INFORMATION:

Books:

Fatemi, Khosrow (ed.), *The New World Order: Internationalism, Regionalism, and the Multinational Corporations*. New York: Pergamon, 2000.

Montgomery, John D., and Nathan Glazer (eds.), *Sovereignty under Challenge: How Governments Respond*. New Brunswick, NJ: Transaction Publishers, 2002.

Useful websites:

http://www.hrw.org/advocacy/corporations/index.htm
Human Rights Watch on corporations.
http://multinationalmonitor.org
An online magazine that tracks corporate activity.
http://www.oxfam.org.au/campaigns/mining/ombudsman/2002/humanrights.html
Oxfam 2002 report on human rights and TNCs.

The following debates in the Pro/Con series may also be of interest:

In this volume:
Topic 11 Has globalization increased inequality?

In *International Development*:
Part 3: Trade

In *Commerce and Trade*:
Part 3: Corporations and the law in the global economy

HAVE TRANSNATIONAL CORPORATIONS HELPED ERADICATE POVERTY?

YES: TNCs often build roads, dams, and schools to facilitate the operation of their companies in poor and remote regions

YES: TNCs train many people in new skills and offer them job opportunities they would not normally have

INFRASTRUCTURE
Have TNCs put vital funding into poor nations' infrastructure?

EMPLOYMENT
Have TNCs created significant new job opportunities?

NO: Even though TNCs may construct public works that benefit communities, the works are often essential to a TNC's operations. Communities struggle to maintain the facilities after the TNC moves or closes its operation.

NO: TNCs often employ children or make people work in unsafe conditions for long hours and low pay

HAVE TRANSNATIONAL CORPORATIONS HELPED ERADICATE POVERTY?

KEY POINTS

YES: Many TNCs have implemented corporate social responsibility programs that improve life for the local community as a whole and involve community members in decision-making

YES: It is not in the interest of TNCs to destroy the environment. Many have good, sustainable development policies in place.

ENVIRONMENT
Have allegations of environmental abuse been exaggerated?

CORPORATE RESPONSIBILITY
Do TNCs treat social responsibility as a serious issue?

NO: TNCs often seek to minimize costs by investing in countries that have little or no regulation concerning environmental protection

NO: TNCs are ultimately only interested in profit, and their gestures toward social responsibility are not serious

Topic 16
CAN MALNUTRITION BE ERADICATED?

YES
"WE CAN FEED THE WORLD"
THE HEARTLAND INSTITUTE, *POINT OF VIEW*, MARCH/APRIL 2002
JAY LEHR

NO
"MALNUTRITION AND FAMINE: GET USED
TO THEM THEY'RE HERE TO STAY"
JACOB PRIMLEY AND GEORGE LEWIS

INTRODUCTION

The term "malnutrition" literally means "bad nourishment." According to the World Health Organization (WHO), it is "characterized by inadequate intake of protein, energy, and micronutrients and by frequent infections or disease." The Food and Agriculture Organization (FAO) estimates that malnutrition affects around 800 million people in developing nations, some 200 million of whom are below the age of five. About two-thirds of all malnourished children live in Asia, and one-quarter live in Africa; by comparison, around 1 percent of children in the United States suffer chronic malnutrition. The eradication of malnutrition is considered to be a key issue in poverty and hunger reduction.

Many commentators believe it is unacceptable that people still suffer and die from malnutrition in the 21st century. They contend that advances in technology and new science, especially genetics, mean that everyone should be able to eat regularly and healthily. The General Assembly of the United Nations recognized the eradication of extreme poverty and hunger as the first of its Millennium Development Goals. By 2015 it aims to reduce by half the number of people whose income is less than $1 a day and also to halve the proportion of people who suffer from hunger. In 2003 the FAO calculated that reductions would need to increase to 12 times their current annual rate of 2.1 million people in order to meet the second target. Some observers suggest that the eradication of malnutrition is simply not possible. Others claim it is also undesirable: Malnutrition acts as a natural check on population, they say, and to eliminate it would only lead to more problems, such as the exhaustion of already stretched resources.

Many people associate malnutrition with a lack of food, but it is more than that. Lack of access to safe drinking water, sanitation and medical services, and inadequate information about child nutrition are also causal factors. Malnutrition can occur in people who are either undernourished or overnourished. Undernutrition is usually associated with poverty and social and economic deprivation. It results from consuming an inadequate amount of calories from proteins, vitamins, and minerals (protein-energy malnutrition) or from the body using or excreting nutrients more quickly than they can be replaced due to, for example, diarrhea or kidney failure. Overnutrition usually occurs in people who have a sedentary lifestyle and who live in affluent societies where food security is not a problem. It results from overeating, eating too many of the wrong things, insufficient exercise, or from taking too many vitamins or other supplements. Both types of malnutrition develop in stages over a period of time and should, many people claim, be preventable.

"If we could give every individual the right amount of nourishment and exercise … we would have found the safest way to health."

—HIPPOCRATES (ABOUT 460–377 B.C.)

Malnutrition has a significant effect on the body, particularly the immune system. Sufferers are more susceptible to infection and disease, and that can result in death in extreme cases. For example, protein-energy malnutrition is the leading cause of death among infants in developing countries. Severe forms of malnutrition also include marasmus (chronic wasting of fat, muscle, and other tissues), irreversible brain damage due to iodine deficiency,

and blindness and increased risk of infection from vitamin A deficiency.

Mothers in particular are considered to be at risk from malnutrition; a pregnant woman suffering from over- or undernutrition is likely to give birth to a malnourished child. Some experts believe that better nutritional education for pregnant women would reduce the incidence of malnutrition. Prenatal care forms part of some aid programs that target malnutrition. Other programs include school feeding and emergency feeding. Some critics, however, believe that these measures are not very effective, and they seek new solutions.

Some manufacturers in the United States add vitamins and minerals to common foods to prevent certain nutritional deficiencies, especially in pregnant women. For example, the addition of folic acid to some foods can help prevent birth defects, and added iron can help prevent anemia. Some people have suggested these nutrient-enhanced foods could be introduced on a larger scale to help eradicate malnutrition in developing nations.

Other experts believe that genetically modified (GM) foods may hold the key. Rice, which forms the staple diet of many people in poor nations, does not contain sufficient nutrients to prevent malnutrition, but a GM version with added vitamins and minerals might. Researchers have created a strain of "golden rice" containing the compound beta-carotene, which the body converts to vitamin A (see box on page 206). This vitamin is essential to a healthy immune system. Some critics counter that GM foods are unsafe, and it would therefore be unethical to test them in developing countries.

The following two articles examine issues in this debate in greater depth.

WE CAN FEED THE WORLD
Jay Lehr

Dr. Jay Lehr is science director of The Heartland Institute, a nonpartisan think tank based in Chicago. This article was published on the institute's website in 2002.

In the United States and the European Union farmers are guaranteed a minimum payment for their produce in the form of government subsidies. While advocates say that subsidies prevent many farmers living in poverty, critics argue that they drive down prices, creating surpluses that are exported cheaply to poor countries, whose farmers are unable to compete. See Volume 14, International Development, Topic 11 Have heavy agricultural subsidies damaged the economies of poorer nations?

The Stockholm International Peace Research Institute reported global military spending in 2003 as $956 billion—an increase of 18 percent since 2001.

YES

Over 160 million children today suffer the stunted growth, weakened condition, and chronic illnesses that afflict the world's malnourished populations. A report recently issued by the International Food Policy Research Institute (IFPRI) offers a very gloomy outlook for ending their suffering.

While dramatic declines in the number of malnourished children under the age of five occurred between 1960 and 1990, the rate of decline has slowed markedly. IFPRI projects that number is likely to fall by only 20 percent in the next 20 years, to about 130 million.

This is unconscionable in a world whose increasing productivity has caused the food supply in every developed country to be in such huge surplus as to make fair economic returns for most farmers a major challenge.

Little hope for the future?

Every year, malnutrition plays a role in more than half of the nearly 12 million deaths of children under five in developing countries. Due to poor diet and disease, fully one-third of the children in those countries suffer from stunting—below-normal height for their age. Undernourished children are more susceptible to severe illnesses, have difficulty learning in school, do not reach their full height, and have trouble with coordination and mobility. These problems plague them in adulthood.

Unless something drastic is done, there is little hope for the future. But drastic is a subjective word, and when defined in terms of world health it is not a big mountain to climb.

IFPRI concludes that an additional expenditure of only $10 billion worldwide would more than double the projected decline in malnutrition, from 20 percent to 42 percent. That sum represents less than one week of global military spending prior to September 11 … and it's now a whole lot less.

A bigger problem than money, however, are the roadblocks thrown up by shortsighted nations who refuse to allow the spread of advanced agricultural technology or free trade in food.

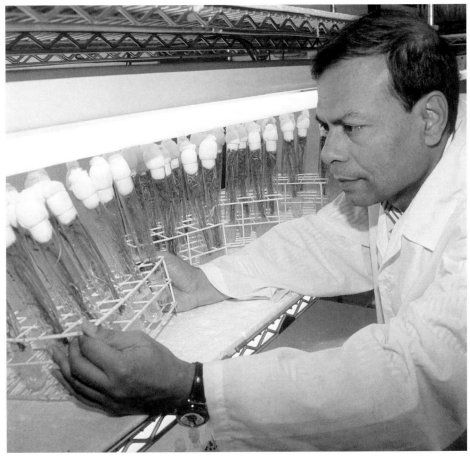

A biotechnologist at the International Rice Research Institute in the Philippines examines test tubes of genetically modified (GM) rice. Some experts claim that GM foods may have a vital role to play in eradicating malnutrition.

Most governments have been unwilling to turn food production over to the forces of the free market. They intervene in agriculture in countless ways to promote domestic food production, keep domestic food prices low, or reduce dependence on foreign suppliers.

Biotechnology is key

Far and away the largest obstacle to feeding the world's children a healthy diet has been the resistance to bio-engineered foods. Biotechnology is a science far advanced beyond the initial work of Gregor Mendel, who first crossed common, garden-variety peas to create more useful hybrid plants.

Gregor Mendel (1822–1884) was an Austrian monk who had a great interest in botany. Through his experiments with garden peas he became the first person to recognize the basic laws of heredity and to suggest the existence of genes.

COMMENTARY: "Golden rice" or not?

Vitamin A deficiency (VAD) is a major problem in developing countries, where it affects as many as two billion people, particularly children and pregnant women. VAD causes a weakening of the immune system, an increased risk of infection, and in extreme cases leads to partial or total blindness. Some estimates state that around 500,000 preschool-age children become blind and about one million die as a result of VAD-related problems each year. Since many poor nations rely on rice as their staple diet, and rice is deficient in vitamin A, scientists have genetically engineered nutrient-enhanced varieties. In 1999 Swiss and German scientists announced that they had developed a new "golden rice," so-called because it contained beta-carotene, the yellow-orange compound that gives carrots their color, and which the human body converts to vitamin A.

A miracle cure?

Golden rice was immediately heralded as a miracle cure for VAD. Among others, the Council for Biotechnology Information, an industry group, publicized the importance of this development. A series of commercials was aired on U.S. television, including one showing scenes of children in developing nations accompanied by a voiceover describing the wonder rice that could save millions from blindness. Despite this publicity, however, golden rice is still not readily available. Created by splicing three foreign genes—two from the daffodil and one from a bacterium—into japonica rice, the variety originally produced was suited to temperate climates. Scientists have since been working to breed a strain that is more suited to the often extreme conditions of developing countries. Conservative estimates predict that this research will take several years, but some experts believe this is optimistic, especially since it will be vital to test the product properly before it can be introduced anywhere.

In the meantime, some critics have queried the alleged benefits of golden rice. For example, the environmental organization Greenpeace has argued that unrealistic amounts of the rice would need to be eaten daily before it had any positive effect on health. Some people calculate that a woman would need to eat 16 pounds (7 kg) of cooked rice every day to obtain sufficient vitamin A, and a child would need 12 pounds (5 kg).

Alternatives to "golden rice"

Critics point out that alternative sources of vitamin A are available. For example, the FAO has been working in Bangladesh to help people grow vitamin A-rich crops such as pumpkins. Similarly, a campaign in Thailand has educated farmers about the benefits of growing ivy gourd, another good source of the vitamin. Advocates maintain that these programs are safer and more effective than any GM equivalents.

Today, with the surgical precision we have learned from our studies of genetics, we are able to create a variety of positive new traits in plants … with no harmful side effects. Study after study of biotech products has turned up not a single negative outcome in the face of overwhelmingly wonderful advances in human nutrition.

Improving on the staples

In the Third World, nearly 40 percent of all grains are contaminated in storage by microtoxin residues left behind by such pests as the European corn borer. Those microtoxins are responsible for 25 percent of the premature deaths of adults in the Third World. Those deaths can be eliminated with bio-engineered Bt corn and related grains that carry a natural toxin, *Bacillus thuringensis*, which kills the corn borer soon after it bites into the corn.

Rice, the major food staple throughout the developing world, has been nutritionally enhanced through bio-engineering for increased iron and beta-carotene, which can dramatically decrease childhood blindness and iron deficiency in the Third World.

Bananas can now be grown with a hepatitis C vaccine built right in, reducing from $150 to *two cents* the cost of protecting a person in the Third World from this dreaded disease.

The real answer to solving the world's malnutrition is to stop allowing shortsighted bureaucrats and fearmongers to prevent the scientific advances made in industrialized countries from spreading throughout the world.

Steps toward a future of global food security will have enormous payoffs worldwide, offering all people a higher quality of life and greater economic potential. If decision-makers fail to reform key policies or make adequate investments, the costs of human misery and wasted potential will be enormous.

We can feed the world … if only it will let us.

Many people believe that whatever the outcome of studies, it is unethical to tamper with nature. Go to http://biotech.about.com/od/ethics/ to read a collection of essays on the ethics of biotechnology. See also Volume 4, Environment, Genetic Modification, pages 160–161.

Hepatitis is a disease of the liver. Experts estimate that around 300 million people carry the hepatitis virus, and that about one-third of this number die from its effects each year. Does the possibility of saving the lives of 100 million people override any ethical concerns about biotechnology?

MALNUTRITION AND FAMINE: GET USED TO THEM THEY'RE HERE TO STAY
Jacob Primley and George Lewis

Jacob Primley and George Lewis are journalists. They wrote this text for a pamphlet published in December 2001.

Oxfam is an international relief organization dedicated to fighting poverty and injustice. Originally established in the United Kingdom in 1942 as the Oxford Committee for Famine Relief, it now operates in over 100 countries worldwide.

"Displacement" is the substitution of behavior that is appropriate for the circumstances with something unexpected. In a stressful situation, for example, an animal might start grooming in order to reassure itself.

Are the problems associated with malnutrition and famine insurmountable? Does it follow that rich nations should do nothing at all to help the poor?

NO

There is plenty of malnutrition in the West—it is the product of any bad diet, not just of insufficient food—but it is large-scale occurrences in the developing world that attract the greatest publicity and concern. According to UN statistics, 800 million people in the world today are chronically undernourished. From Africa and Asia come harrowing accounts of scurvy, rickets, osteomalacia, anaemia and beri-beri—diseases of malnutrition that are often early warning signs of famine.

Famine is an emotive issue. In the relative comfort of our Western homes we deplore the sight in the news of living children with distended bellies and truckloads of skeletal corpses being driven off for burial. We regard it as unacceptable that the other half of the world should be starving while our half has more food than it can possibly eat. We do what we can to help—individuals make donations to Oxfam, nation parachutes grain unto nation.

Nothing we can do

Such attempts to relieve the plight of the malnourished may salve our consciences but they are little more than displacement activities. We may think that we are mighty, and can influence the course of world events with love, trade and democracy, but we are shouting in the gale. If there is one thing more unpalatable than famine, it is the realisation that there is nothing we can do to end it.

Charitable donations are insufficient. Humanitarian relief may be hijacked by black marketeers. Financial aid may be syphoned off by corruption; even if it reaches its intended recipients there may be nothing for them to buy. The United States and Europe have surplus food, but most of it is perishable and practically impossible to get to where it would do most good. Like minerals that are valuable only if they can be used close to the sites on which they were extracted without incurring transportation costs, food is place specific.

COMMENTARY: Conflict and malnutrition

Throughout recorded history there has been a strong link between malnutrition and conflict. In northern Europe, for example, unusually cold and wet weather in 1315–1317 ruined three successive harvests. Countless peasants starved to death or died of malnutrition-related diseases, and law and order broke down as food prices soared. Historians often suggest that a disastrous harvest in France in 1787, followed by a sharp increase in the price of bread, contributed to the tensions that led to the French Revolution two years later. Similarly, widespread disease and malnutrition played a part in precipitating the Russian Revolution in 1917.

While malnutrition can cause conflict, it is equally true that conflict can lead to malnutrition. The deliberate destruction of crops and food supplies is a war strategy employed by both attacking and defending armies. When Napoleon's troops invaded Russia in 1812, the Russian army adopted a "scorched-earth" policy as it retreated, destroying everything that could be of value to the French. By the time Napoleon reached Moscow, his men were suffering from malnutrition and disease. Although the tactic forced the French to retreat, it also left many Russian people to starve.

Siege tactics are also used in conflict to weaken the enemy through the disrupted distribution of food. For example, some sources claim that an Allied naval blockade of Germany caused as many as 800,000 civilians to die from malnutrition during the final two years of World War I (1914–1918).

Sub-Saharan Africa

Warfare remained a major cause of food insecurity into the late 20th century and beyond. The International Food Research Institute estimated that conflict had left nearly 24 million people worldwide lacking access to food by the end of 2000, about 18.5 million of them in sub-Saharan Africa.

In the early 1980s chronic drought in Ethiopia caused a famine that reportedly led to the deaths of 500,000 people. An international relief program raised funds to ship food donations to the famine area. However, many relief supplies were hijacked and diverted to the army of dictator Mengistu Haile Mariam (1974–1991). The regime then used food aid as a means of forcibly resettling opposition populations from the drought-stricken northeastern regions of the country. A war with Eritrea in the late 1990s, coupled with severe drought, led to malnutrition affecting 51 percent of the population in some parts of Ethiopia.

A famine in southern Sudan killed an estimated 250,000 people in 1998. The United Nations (UN) launched Operation Lifeline Sudan (OLS), but the relief program was thwarted by the government militia and the rebel opposition Sudanese People's Liberation Army (SPLA). Both sides diverted or looted food from the starving or blocked supply deliveries. In 2004 the UN launched an emergency program to save the lives of refugees suffering severe malnutrition in camps in the Darfur region of the country.

Bangladesh is one of the world's most densely populated countries. Once dependent on food imports, it is now self-sufficient in rice and enjoys the second-highest rate of economic growth in South Asia. Some experts credit the work of foreign aid agencies and international research institutes, such as the International Rice Research Institute, with this achievement. See http://usinfo.state.gov/journals/ites/0502/ijee/bangla.htm for details.

Of course emergency relief is required only in times of crisis, and many great long-term schemes have been implemented to reduce the intensity and frequency of future famines. Through the development of high-yield crops and new farming techniques, farmers can now produce more food per acre than ever before. Engineering projects, such as the Aswan High Dam on the Nile River, have allowed water to be held over from periods of high rainfall for use in times of drought. Other scientific projects are aimed at finding new sources of food—one of the main hopes is that staple crops such as corn and rice can be grown in larger quantities over wider areas and genetically modified for greater nutritional value. The ultimate objective of these schemes is to bring self-sufficiency to nations that have historically depended on overseas food aid. The most conspicuous success to date is Bangladesh, which has been transformed in a generation from a state of extreme indigence into one of South Asia's most productive farm economies.

Futile efforts

Yet all these efforts are futile because they are destined to be undone by the effects of global warming. According to a report by the International Institute for Applied Systems Analysis, if the effects of damage to the ozone layer continue to increase at their present rate, by 2080 nations in tropical climates, including India, Brazil and much of sub-Saharan Africa, will produce less food, while countries in the temperate zones—which include most of the developed world—will experience large gains in crop yields as higher temperatures lengthen growing seasons. Many of the same conclusions were reached independently by a UN report entitled "Climate Change 2001: Impacts, Adaptation and Vulnerability." The 40 nations that have the greatest difficulty in feeding their people are all in the tropics: the possible effects on their 450 million inhabitants are unthinkable.

The International Institute for Applied Systems Analysis (www.iiasa.ac.at), based in Austria, is a nongovernmental research organization that studies environmental, economic, and social issues.

Sadly they are also probably unavoidable.

The United States, the world's leading producer of the greenhouse gases that cause global warming, has refused to ratify a proposed amendment—the so-called Kyoto Protocol—to the 1992 UN Framework Convention on Climate Change, which seeks to limit such emissions. Among the reasons adduced by the administration of George W. Bush to justify this policy is that the treaty is one-sided—it demands proportionally greater reductions from the West than from the developing countries.

See Volume 22, International Law, The Kyoto Protocol, pages 188–189. Do you consider the viewpoint of the U.S. government to be justified?

Yet there is no certainty that Kyoto is the answer, and no universal agreement that the prophets of climatic doom know what they are talking about. Since weather trends have been studied scientifically for only the last 200 years, our understanding of them may be imperfect. Many people—not all of whom have vested business interests—suspect that what is now widely taken to be climate change may be no more than part of a cyclic pattern that we have yet to recognise. Glenn Kelly, executive director of the Global Climate Coalition, represents American commercial and industrial interests in Washington, D.C., but he spoke for many sceptics when he cast doubt on the Austrian research, saying: "Modeling capability is so poor, it makes it impossible to do regional impacts. That right there calls the accuracy of the results into question." Meanwhile the world gets hotter…

The Global Climate Coalition was an industry group that represented oil, coal, and other energy and transportation companies. It campaigned against the Kyoto Protocol until it was disbanded in 2002.

Famines and democracy

Even if every nation that has not signed up to Kyoto were to do so tomorrow, and if there were a sudden normalisation of the weather the day after, malnutrition will remain with us until food is uniformly available throughout the world. That will not happen until it is either transportable without limit or capable of being produced wherever it is needed. Neither of those conditions will be satisfied without political will, and it is noteworthy that there are no famines under democracy. So until we have eradicated the greenhouse effect, perfected techniques of food cultivation and preservation, and brought an end to dictatorship, we must resign ourselves to occasional parades of living skeletons across our television screens. In other words, the procession will go on forever. Famine is unfortunately as much a part of life as death, and although we may regret the passing of individuals, we realise that it is what the poet Gerard Manley Hopkins called "the blight man was born for." According to legend, when Marie Antoinette, queen of France, was informed that her subjects had no bread she replied: "Let them eat cake." That may be not be the soft answer that turneth away wrath recommended by the Book of Proverbs, but it is no use pretending that we can influence occurrences that are out of our hands.

Nobel prize-winner Amartya Sen (see box on page 147) claimed in his book Development as Freedom (1999) that "No famine has ever taken place in the history of the world in a functioning democracy." He argued that this is because democratic governments "have to win elections and face public criticism, and have [a] strong incentive to undertake measures to avert famines." Do you think nondemocratic regimes therefore have a disincentive to prevent famine? How might food be used as a political weapon?

Summary

In the first article Dr. Jay Lehr argues that the fact that millions of people die from malnutrition is inexcusable in a world in which productivity in developed countries has created huge food surpluses. He maintains that there is little hope for the future unless drastic action is taken. Lehr claims that spending an extra $10 billion would more than double the decline in cases of malnutrition around the world. He points out that this is a fraction of global military expenditure. Lehr also believes that free trade in food production and advances in bioengineered foods are key to food security. He blames "shortsighted bureaucrats and fearmongers" for preventing developing nations benefiting from biotechnology. He concludes, "We can feed the world … if only it will let us."

Jacob Primley and George Lewis, however, disagree. They point out that malnutrition is a problem in the West as well as in the developing world. Despite being moved by images of malnourished children, we should, they say, accept that there is nothing we can do. They maintain that charitable donations are insufficient, and that food surpluses cannot help since the produce perishes before it reaches its destination. Primley and Lewis claim that even countries like Bangladesh that are trying to become self-sufficient will be thwarted by changes in world climate. They contend that the problem would remain intractable even if the climate were normalized because political will is required to fight famine. This and other preconditions necessary for the eradication of hunger are lacking, they say, and we should therefore accept famine as part of life.

FURTHER INFORMATION:

Books:

Foster, Phillips, and Howard D. Leathers, *The World Food Problem: Tackling the Causes of Undernutrition in the Third World* (2nd edition). Boulder, CO: Lynne Rienner Publishers, 1999.

Sen, Amartya, *Development as Freedom*. New York: Knopf, 1999.

Useful websites:

http://www.fao.org/docrep/006/j0083e/j0083e00.htm
FAO 2003 report on the state of global food insecurity.
http://kidshealth.org/parent/nutrition_fit/nutrition/hunger_p2.html
Hunger and malnutrition pages at Kids Health site.
http://www.who.int/nut/
World Health Organization information on nutrition.

The following debates in the Pro/Con series may also be of interest:

In this volume:
Part 3: International development

In *Environment*:
Topic 3 Are famine and hunger avoidable?

In *International Development*:
Water: A crisis situation?, pages 212–213

CAN MALNUTRITION BE ERADICATED?

YES: Nutritional advice for pregnant women in particular would reduce the incidence of infant malnutrition

YES: Governments can help increase awareness of this type of malnutrition and encourage people to eat a healthy diet and do regular exercise

EDUCATION
Can nutritional education help eradicate malnutrition?

OVERNUTRITION
Is overnutrition avoidable?

NO: Food security and adequate water supplies are far more important than nutritional education

NO: Governments can try to educate people about nutrition, but they cannot force them to eat the right foods in the right quantities

CAN MALNUTRITION BE ERADICATED?
KEY POINTS

YES: Genetically modified foodstuffs, such as "golden rice," could provide nutritious food for poor nations and improve food security

YES: Water security is a major problem in developing nations. Adequate clean water would help reduce disease and prevent malnutrition.

GM FOODSTUFFS
Could GM foodstuffs help prevent malnutrition?

WATER
Would access to clean drinking water prevent malnutrition?

NO: Until the possible risks associated with genetically modified foodstuffs have been thoroughly assessed, it would be unethical to supply them to poor nations

NO: This is just one factor among many. Adequate food supplies, medical supplies, and sanitation are all important for the eradication of malnutrition.

GLOSSARY

Al Qaeda literally "the base," this Islamic terrorist organization was formed in the late 1980s by Osama Bin Laden and his associates.

apartheid the official South African policy of separating the races in force from 1948 until 1990. *See also* discrimination.

Bill of Rights the first ten amendments to the Constitution, passed by Congress in 1791.

capitalism an economic system in which private individuals and firms control the production and distribution of goods and services, and make profits in return for the investment of capital, or money.

carbon sink landscape features, such as forests and oceans, that absorb carbon from the atmosphere.

civil rights rights guaranteed to the individual as a citizen, such as the right to vote. *See also* Bill of Rights.

consumerism an economic practice based on the buying and selling of goods by private individuals.

corruption a decline in moral principles, especially in politicians, which leads to abuse of power, lying, or taking bribes.

cyberspace the virtual environment created by the Internet. *See also* digital divide.

democracy a system of government based on the rule of a majority of the population. Citizens elect representatives to carry out their wishes in government.

developing countries poor nations that are undergoing economic modernization through developing an industrial and commercial base.

digital divide the gap that exists between those with access to new technology (computers, the Internet, and so on) and those who do not. *See also* Internet.

discrimination treating some people differently than others, usually unfairly, on the basis of race, gender, religion, color, or economic status.

ecological debt the idea that wealthy countries owe reparations to developing nations for their past use and exploitation of their natural resources.

ethics the system or code of morals of a particular person, group, or organization, or the study of those codes.

food security when a population has unhindered physical and economic access to enough food to meet its dietary needs. *See also* genetic engineering.

foreign aid financial or other assistance given by rich nations, international humanitarian organizations, or financial institutions to countries in need.

free trade international trade that is not subject to tariffs, quotas, or other barriers.

gender the physical, economic, social, and cultural attributes that are associated with being either male or female.

genetic engineering the technique of modifying the genes of a living thing to change its characteristics—for example, to produce vegetables with more flavor.

genocide action intended to destroy or kill an entire national or ethnic group.

globalization the worldwide expansion of private corporations and of the culture of the countries they come from.

gross national product (GNP) the total cash value of all goods produced and services provided by a country during one year.

human rights the rights people have as human beings (the right to a fair trial, say), irrespective of attributes such as race, citizenship, or abilities.

inequality a disparity in the distribution of resources, such as income. *See also* discrimination.

international debt money owed by one country's government to a government or bank in another country, or to an international financial institution such as the World Bank. *See also* World Bank.

International Monetary Fund (IMF) an international organization founded in 1945 to promote monetary cooperation and orderly exchange arrangements.

Internet the global network of computers by which users can communicate using protocols such as e-mail, file transfer protocol (ftp), or the World Wide Web.

Internet service provider (ISP) the generic name for a company that connects people to the Internet.

malnutrition a health problem caused by a lack or excess of essential nutrients.

morality standards of conduct or behavior that establish what is right or wrong in society. *See also* ethics.

national sovereignty the freedom of a country to conduct its internal affairs without external interference.

nationalization the transfer of a privately owned enterprise to state ownership.

natural monopoly an industry in which the cost of building the infrastructure prevents the efficient existence of more than one operator in a given area. An example is an electrical grid.

neocolonialism a relationship between a country and an ex-colony in which the business interests of the former continue to dominate the economy of the latter.

nongovernmental organization (NGO) a not-for-profit organization independent of government. NGOs lobby on human rights and environmental issues, and monitor governments and other organizations.

poverty the position of people who have little or no money or material possessions.

privatization the transfer of a publicly owned enterprise to private ownership. *See also* nationalization.

renewable resources materials that can be replaced by natural regeneration, for example, lumber from managed forests.

reparations the act of making amends for a wrong, usually by paying money.

social responsibility a set of behaviors and beliefs that includes a commitment to foster the well-being of everyone in society and to counter bias and prejudice.

structural adjustment programs (SAPs) economic policies that countries must follow to qualify for loans from the World Bank or the IMF. SAPs emphasize privatization and export-led growth.

sustainable development a form of economic growth that seeks to use renewable rather than finite resources and to minimize the permanent damage done to the environment by economic activity.

taxation the method by which national, regional, or local government collects money from individuals and businesses to fund society's collective costs, such as education, defense, and public health.

transnational corporation (TNC) an enterprise that operates in several countries and has production facilities outside its home country.

Universal Declaration of Human Rights a codification of basic human rights and freedoms drafted by an international committee after World War II and adopted by the United Nations in 1948.

World Bank the collective name for five international agencies founded in 1944. They finance projects that enhance the economic development of member states by providing low-interest loans and grants. *See also* foreign aid, structural adjustment programs.

World Health Organization (WHO) founded in 1948, WHO is a body of the United Nations (UN) that promotes the good health of people around the world.

World Trade Organization (WTO) an international organization founded in 1995 as a result of the final round of the General Agreement on Tariffs and Trade (GATT) negotiations. It handles trade policies and disputes between members, and promotes trade liberalization.

Acknowledgments

1. Do Wealthier Members of Society Have a Duty to Help the Poor?

Yes: From: "Sticks and Carrots: Musings about the Wealthy and Ourselves" by Ana Arias, *Conscious Choice*, July 2000. Used by permission.
No: "Coerced Charity Destroys" by Kyle Sing, *The Chicago Report: A Journal of Politics and Culture*, May 19, 2004. Used by permission.

2. Can Money Buy Happiness?

Yes: "Materialism, Poverty, and the Root of Evil" by The Mystic, www.unquietmind.com, June 17, 2000.
No: "Can Money Buy Happiness? UC Berkeley Researchers Find Surprising Answers" by Carol Hyman, *UC Berkeley News*, June 16, 2003. Used by permission.

3. Is Begging Wrong?

Yes: "Begging for a Downtown Begging Ban" by Richard Shumate, *Creative Loafing Atlanta*, September 4, 2003. Used by permission.
No: "Court Orders San Francisco to Pay Legal Fees in Begging Case" by American Civil Liberties Union, ACLU NC Press Release, July 11, 1997. Used by permission.

4. Should People Have to Look After their Elderly Relations?

Yes: "We Have Nationalized the Elderly, As We Are Too Busy to Care for Them" by Johann Hari, *The Independent*, February 21, 2003. Copyright © *The Independent*. Used by permission.
No: "In Rural Communities, Elderly Helping Themselves and Looking to Networks of Volunteers" by Curt Woodward, *Fosters Health Beat*, 2004. Reprinted by permission of The Associated Press.

5. Is Income Inequality Related to Race?

Yes: "Prosperity Can't Close Metro Area Income Gap" by Brad Heath, *The Detroit News*, September 10, 2002. Used by permission.
No: "Context, Please" by J.A. Foster-Bey, *National Review* online, May 18, 2004. Used by permission.

6. Are Women More Likely to Be Poor?

Yes: "Women in Poverty" by Marilyn Hartlauer, Iraq Journalism Project, Department of Communication, University of Washington, May 27, 2003. Used by permission.
No: From "She Works, He Doesn't" by Peg Tyre and Daniel McGinn. From *Newsweek*, May 12, 2003. Copyright © 2003 *Newsweek*, Inc. All rights reserved. Reprinted by permission.

7. Are Income Taxes an Effective Way of Redistributing Wealth?

Yes: "Tax Facts and Fair Shares" by Dave Thomer, www.notnews.org, May 2001. Used by permission.
No: "Let's Abolish the Income Tax" by Sheldon Richman, from *Your Money or Your Life*, published by The Future of Freedom Foundation. Copyright © The Future of Freedom Foundation. Used by permission.

8. Do Indirect Taxes Discriminate against the Poor?

Yes: "Taxing Habits" by Phineas Baxandall, *Regional Review*, Quarter 1, 2003. Used by permission.
No: "Fairness and Federal Tax Reform" by Americans for Fair Taxation, www.fairtax.org. Used by permission.

9. Does Welfare Perpetuate Poverty?

Yes: "Why the War on Poverty Failed" by James L. Payne. © 1999, Foundation for Economic Freedom (www.fee.org). Reprinted with permission from the January 1999 issue of *The Freeman: Ideas on Liberty*.
No: "Myth: Welfare Increases Poverty" by Steve Kangas, home.att.net.

10. Should People Have to Pay for Natural Resources?

Yes: "Water Is Not 'Different'" by Richard Tren, *Tech Central Station*, December 9, 2003 (www.techcentralstation.com). Used by permission
No: "Who Owns Water?" by Maude Barlow and Tony Clarke, *The Nation*, September 2, 2002. Used by permission.

11. Has Globalization Increased Inequality?

Yes: "Globalization Resistance Brings Down a President" by Jim Schultz, *New Internationalist,* Issue 363, December 2003. Used by permission.
No: "Globalization Should Not Be a Scapegoat for the Existence of Poverty" by Maria Livanos Cattaui. Copyright © 2001 International Chamber of Commerce. All rights reserved.

12. Should Developing Nations Take More Responsibility for Their Own Poverty?

Yes: "Now, Think Small: Poor Countries Could Help Themselves Get Richer by Fixing Their Institutions" by *The Economist*, September 13, 2001. Copyright © 2001 The Economist Newspaper Ltd. All rights reserved. Reprinted with permission. Further reproduction prohibited. www.economist.com.
No: "Can the Financing Gap Be Closed?" by Jullyette Ukabiala, Africa Recovery, United Nations. Used by permission.

13. Should Rich Nations Compensate Countries Whose Economic Resources They Have Exploited?

Yes: "What Is 'Ecological Debt'?" by Friends of the Earth (www.foei.org). Used by permission.
No: "Ecological Debt: A Response" by Marilyn Freeman. Used by permission.

14. Is Bridging the Digital Divide Essential to Lessening the Gap between Rich and Poor Communities?

Yes: "Global Digital Divide: Targeting Rural and Economically-Challenged Communities" by Mugo Macharia, Benton Foundation. Used by permission.
No: "National IT Sector Overrated" by *The Hindu,* www.thehindu.com, March 4, 2004. Used by permission.

15. Have Transnational Corporations Helped Eradicate Poverty?

Yes: "The Lifecyle of Corporation's Socially Responsible Initiative Program: Inti Raymi Goldmine" by Kellee James, Inter-American Foundation, www.iaf.gov. Used by permission.
No: From "Mapuche Lands in Patagonia Taken Over by Benetton Wool Farms" by Sebastian Hacher and Pauline Bartolone, *CorpWatch*, November 25, 2003. Used by permission.

16. Can Malnutrition Be Eradicated?

Yes: "We Can Feed the World" by Jay Lehr, *Point of View*, March/April 2002, The Heartland Institute. Used by permission.
No: "Malnutrition and Famine: Get Used to Them, They're Here to Stay" by Jacob Primley and George Lewis. Used by permission.

The Brown Reference Group plc has made every effort to contact and acknowledge the creators and copyright holders of all extracts reproduced in this volume. We apologize for any omissions. Any person who wishes to be credited in further volumes should contact The Brown Reference Group plc in writing: The Brown Reference Group plc, 8 Chapel Place, Rivington Street, London EC2A 3DQ, U.K.

Picture credits

Cover: photos.com
Corbis: Pallava Bagla 205, David Mercadol/Reuters 143, Vivian Moos 44, Jehad Nga 176/177, Joel Stettenheim 17, Underwood & Underwood 22/23, Alison Wright 6/7, 79; **Photos.com:** 122/123; **Rex Features:** AXV 48/49, BEI 53, Rob Crandall 156, Jim Pickerell 58, Karl Schoendorf 148, Sipa Press 185, Les Wilson 31; **Still Pictures:** Helga Lade 171, Jorgen Schytte 129